Everyday Life in Byzantium

1   The Emperor Constantine the Great (306–37)
From a fourth-century bronze

Everyday Life in
BYZANTIUM

TAMARA TALBOT RICE

Drawings by Helen Nixon Fairfield

DORSET PRESS
New York

First published by B.T. Batsford 1967

This edition published by Dorset Press,
a division of Marboro Books Corporation,
by arrangement with B.T. Batsford Ltd.
1987 Dorset Press

ISBN 0-88029-145-1

Printed in the United States of America
M 9 8 7 6 5 4 3 2 1

To David, with love and gratitude for his unfailing help

CONTENTS

THE ILLUSTRATIONS

Note: *The italicised numerals in parentheses in the text refer to the figure-numbers of the illustrations*

8

ACKNOWLEDGMENT

The Author and Publishers wish to thank the following for permission to reproduce the illustrations appearing in this book:

The Church of St Eusebius, Auxerre for fig. 61
The National Museum, Belgrade for fig. 1
The Trustees of the British Museum for fig. 31
Cleveland Museum of Art for figs. 62 and 64
Cortona Cathedral, Italy for fig. 95
The Marquis de Ganay for fig. 52
The Greek National Tourist Office for fig. 24
The Hermitage Museum, Leningrad for fig. 73
The Kunsthistoriches Museum, Vienna for fig. 84
The Metropolitan Museum for figs. 63 and 74
The Cathedral Treasury, Monza for fig. 85
The Pushkin Museum, Moscow for fig. 6
The Bibliothèque Nationale, Paris for figs. 30, 75 and 76
The Pierpont Morgan Library, New York for fig. 86
Miss Josephine Powell for fig. 96
The Gallerie delle Marche, Urbino for fig. 5
The Victoria and Albert Museum for fig. 87

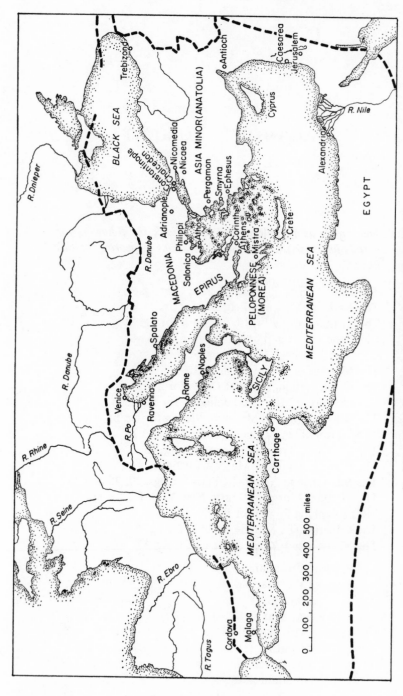

2 Map of the Byzantine Empire in the sixth century

1

CONSTANTINOPLE, JEWEL OF BYZANTIUM

The Byzantine or East Roman Empire lasted for over a thousand years—from AD 330 to 1453. During this period it often ranked as the foremost power of its day and it played a most important part in shaping European culture. Byzantium was the first of the great nations to accept Christianity as its official religion, and the first to set out both to live, and to govern others, in accordance with Christian teaching. Thus, even though the Byzantines often acted with cruelty, harshness and meanness in both their private and their public affairs, Christian principles nevertheless remained all-important to them, and the respect with which they regarded the virtues on which Christianity was based was handed down from generation to generation to form the framework of Europe's essentially Christian civilisation. But for Byzantium our own way of life would have developed along very different lines from those which it has followed. This is especially the case with regard to the Orthodox countries—Russia, Greece, Bulgaria and Yugoslavia— all of which have followed the same branch of the Christian Church as that of the Byzantines, and which, from an early date, developed independently of Rome.

Great changes always seem to occur suddenly, and this must have appeared especially true to many of those who witnessed the establishment of Christianity in the Roman Empire. It may have been as early as the year AD 323, and probably before the year 325, when Constantine I (the 'Great')(1) convened the First Council of Nicaea, that Roman citizens learnt that Christianity was to contend with paganism as their official religion, because their caesar, Constantine (306–37), had seen a vision which had convinced him that the change had become necessary. The event is believed to have taken place one October night in the year 311

13

when Constantine had encamped with his army outside the walls of Rome intending to engage Maxentius in battle on the following day. He saw—and some accounts state that his men also saw—a symbol in the sky and heard a voice telling him that his men were to paint it on their shields before engaging in battle. Constantine appears to have doubted whether he had really seen the symbol, but, according to Eusebius, shortly afterwards Christ appeared before him telling him to paint the device on the personal pennant he was to use when leading his army into battle. In his vision Constantine had seen the sun, Apollo's symbol, which had also been adopted as such by Rome's caesars, and which was thus, by right, Constantine's emblem. Silhouetted against its rays was an immense standard lavishly decorated with gold and intersected near the top by a cross-piece, from which flowed two purple streamers shot with gold and studded with jewels. It was surmounted by a coronet of gold containing a gold cross, the arms of which formed the Greek letters Chi Rho, the initial letters of Christ's name with, according to some accounts, the words *hoc vinces* also appearing. The purple streamers, like the rays of the sun, indicated that Constantine was involved because purple garments—the most expensive and rarest of all materials, since the dye could be obtained only from the relatively scarce murex shell—had, by order of Diocletian, been reserved for the exclusive use of the ruling family.

The meaning of what he had seen could not be doubted: it clearly indicated that Byzantium was to become a Christian state with Constantine ruling it as God's representative. Constantine lost no time in carrying out the dictates of his vision. His troops defeated Maxentius and Constantine gave orders that the Eagles, which had been used by the Roman legionaries as their standards, should be replaced by the emblem of his vision; at the same time he put an end to the Roman practice of using the cross as an instrument of torture: henceforth it should be regarded as the symbol of Christianity. Eusebius states that he actually saw the pennant bearing the new design which Constantine had used when fighting Maxentius. Though Constantine continued to use it as his *labarum*, that is to say, as his standard, he nevertheless remained a pagan, worshipping the sun till he lay dying, and only then did he ask to be received into the Church. Yet Constantinople, the city which he made his capital, was from the start dedicated to the Trinity and the Virgin; when, in the fifth century, Eudoxia sent the empress Pulcheria the icon which St Luke had painted of the Virgin Hodighitria(*3*), or Pointer of the Way, the panel came to be regarded as the capital's protective genius.

3 Icon of the Virgin Hodighitria

In reality changes as drastic as the rejection of one faith in favour of another are seldom introduced as the result of one man's personal experience; they tend to grow out of a changing outlook and attitude to life developed by thoughtful people during periods of trouble and unrest. Ever since the start of the Christian era Rome had gone through just such a period. As a result, on the one hand, of the Jewish belief in one god and, on the other, of the popularity of mystic faiths of eastern origins, many Romans had started to question the validity of their old pagan faith, based as it was on the irrational behaviour of a multitude of gods, many of whom suffered from the worst human foibles. Rome's increasing economic and political difficulties also helped to aggravate such doubts. Furthermore, with its vast population of slaves, whose work enriched their owners without greatly benefiting the state; with its enormous territories stretching from Northumberland in Britain, across Gaul and Spain, to North Africa and from there spreading across the whole of Italy, Greece, Turkey, Syria and Egypt; and with the immense diversity of nationalities that this implies, the Roman Empire had become too large to be manageable. Its ruling classes were too self-indulgent to be efficient, its administrators had become indolent, its intellectuals increasingly critical of the government, while Rome itself was torn by dissensions. Caesars had replaced caesars, but to no avail. The device of co-rulers was introduced in an attempt to stop the rot. Diocletian (284–305) came to believe that matters would improve if regional centres of government were formed to take the place of the administration centred in Rome. He therefore moved his court to Nicomedia, in what is now Asiatic Turkey, and set himself up there as ruler of Rome's eastern territories, surrounding himself with all the pomp and ceremony of an eastern, or rather a Persian, potentate. At the same time he appointed three co-rulers, assigning one, Maximian, to reign over Italy and Africa from Milan, another, Constantius, to rule over Gaul, Britain and Spain from Trier (in modern Germany), and lastly, Galerius, to govern Illyria (present-day Dalmatia and Transylvania), Macedonia and Greece from Salonica. However, these measures failed to improve the situation. Instead, this principle of co-rulership introduced the idea of division to peoples who had prided themselves on being part of a single entity. Despondency, corruption and indolence continued to prevail in Rome and, when civil war broke out, Diocletian turned his back on his difficulties and retired to live his own life in the magnificent palace he had built for himself on the shores of the Adriatic, in what is now Split. Fourteen hundred years later the great British eighteenth-century architect Robert Adam was to examine its ruins with wondering admiration and to adapt many of their features to the taste of his own times.

Constantius, ruler of Gaul, Britain and Spain, had been obliged by Diocletian to divorce his wife Helena—daughter, according to tradition, of the English King Cole of Colchester, and mother of his son and heir Constantine. In her loneliness Helena seems to have turned to the intellectuals of her day and to have pursued a course of religious and philosophical studies. She may even have become converted to Christianity at this early date, though there is no proof of this. On Constantius' death Constantine succeeded him as ruler of the western provinces. Helena must have remained in close touch with Constantine after her divorce and may well have been chiefly responsible for winning him over to Christianity. In 324 when, as a result of his own efforts, Constantine became sole ruler of the vast Roman Empire, he published an edict designed to protect Christians from persecution. Twelve months later, by convoking a Council of churchmen at Nicaea, he made the practice of Christianity legal within the Empire. The step was not only wise but virtually inevitable, for by then two-fifths of the Empire's population was probably Christian, seeing in Christianity the sole hope of relief from the hardships of their daily lives. To these people Helena became the embodiment of the Christian way of life. She was among the first to set out on a pilgrimage to the Holy Land, at Constantine's express wish bringing back with her a piece of the true cross. The fragment became Byzantium's most venerated relic. It was kept in the Great Palace of the Byzantine emperors in Constantinople, but, in 565, Justin II granted the request of St Radegonda, the forsaken wife of Chilperic, for a small piece of it; she had it mounted in the superb reliquary of St Croix, which is still kept at Poitiers, but from then onwards the original fragment was gradually frittered away in gifts. Although it was the Emperor Theodosius I who, in AD 381, adopted Christianity as the Empire's official religion, it was Helena and Constantine who were both given the rank of saints in the Orthodox Church as a reward for the services they had rendered to Christianity; that is why they are often represented in paintings or on other works of art standing side by side, Helena usually holding a cross between them.

In Rome Christianity had been introduced and spread by missionaries, converts and fathers of the Church, all of whom, whilst fighting to establish the new faith, had followed the directions of their leaders; as a result, when once the Church became established in Rome, the first clerics were automatically drawn from among these leaders. But this was not the case in Constantinople. There the religion had been sponsored by Constantine who held a supreme position in both the political and the religious sphere, for he was both ruler of the state and protector of the Church, a secular emperor and also God's vicar on earth. His successors on the throne continued to regard themselves as divinely inspired and, as such, took precedence over the clergy, the emperor alone among laymen being entitled to enter the most sacred parts of the church normally reserved for the ordained. It was due to the emperor's dual functions that, when the Grand Duchess Olga of Kievan Russia decided, whilst on a state visit to Constantinople, to become a Christian, her baptism in 957 was performed during a magnificent ceremony conducted jointly by the emperor of Byzantium and the patriarch of Constantinople.

Well-informed people in Rome were probably not surprised by Constantine's decision to legalise Christianity, nor astonished by his wish to re-establish his capital in some city other than Rome. They must, however, have been startled when, in 324, he made it known that he had decided to set up his headquarters in the small town of Byzantium which occupied a triangular promontory at the northern end of the Sea of Marmora, at a point where Asia and

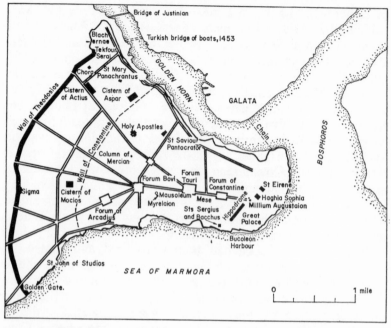

4   Plan of Constantinople at the time of Emperor Theodosius

Europe are within finger-tip distance of each other(4). Apart
from the emperor few men were at the time aware of the site's
numerous geographical advantages or of the splendid harbour
which could be made from the pocket of water lapping the
triangle's northern edge. The Byzantines were aptly to name the
inlet the Golden Horn, for such it was to prove when merchants of
all nations started to use it, quickly turning it into the world's
richest port. Not only could Byzantium keep in touch with the
western world by means of a network of roads running inland into
Europe, but, by sailing northwards up the Bosphorus, contact
could also be maintained with the many ports ranged along the
shores of the Black Sea. Thus, by way of what is now Russia, trade
could be developed with the Scandinavian countries on the one
hand and with Central Asia, India and China on the other. In
addition, by turning southwards the Aegean could be reached
through the Dardanelles and shipping could enter the Mediterranean, while merchants, merely by crossing a short expanse of the
Marmora, could reach Asia Minor and from it establish contact with
the whole area which we now refer to as the Near and Middle East.

Those who failed to appreciate these geographical advantages were not the first men to misjudge the value of the site. Centuries earlier, at a time when Greece, though a leading power, was beset by economic difficulties, many of her city states encouraged their citizens to seek their fortunes in places from which they could ship food-supplies and other essentials back to the motherland. As a result many Greeks had founded independent, self-governing coastal cities, known as colonies, along the shores of the Black Sea. During the seventh century BC a group of emigrants from Megara placed themselves under the leadership of a man called Byzas. Before departing from their native town they consulted their favourite oracle, hoping for advice as to where to found their colony. In the manner of oracles the reply took the form of a riddle: 'Go, settle opposite the city of the blind'. The Megarians embarked and in due course reached the southern entrance to the Bosphorus, where the Greek colonial town of Chalcedon stood on the Asiatic shore of the Marmora (near present-day Moda). As they gazed with delight upon the splendid landscape unfolding before them their eyes rested upon the triangle of land projecting into the sea from the opposite (i.e. the European) shore. As quick as Constantine to appreciate its possibilities, the Megarians concluded that the inhabitants of Chalcedon, who could well have chosen that site in preference to their own, must have been the blind people referred to by the oracle. They founded their townlet on the promontory. Yet in spite of its advantages the city, when Constantine saw it, was still too small to serve as a capital. In the year 324, therefore, he delineated new boundaries for its defensive walls and set workmen to build a palace, essential administrative buildings, a forum and a church which he dedicated to Haghia Sophia, the Holy (or Divine) Wisdom. These indispensable works were completed in six years, and in AD 330 Constantine proclaimed the town his capital.

To ensure that the capital of his choice should become the Empire's leading city not only in name but in fact, Constantine altered the whole structure of the Roman Empire and devised a new system of administration, replacing the customary type of official by men of a new stamp. He re-named the city Constantinople, Constantine's city, yet the town was often referred to as Nova Roma, or the New Rome, whilst Byzas' name came to be applied to the eastern part of the Roman Empire instead of to the city itself. There was good reason for referring to Constantinople as the New Rome, for virtually the entire ruling class, consisting as it did of court and government circles, was made up of Romans and, even though the local inhabitants were Greeks, Latin remained the official language until the fifth century, when the western and eastern parts of the Roman Empire separated. Within a century or so the Greek language replaced the Latin as the official tongue, whilst the eastern section of the Empire came to be known officially as Byzantium. Yet still today, in parts of Turkey, Iran and Arabia, the old link with Rome endures and the word Rum, meaning Rome, is quite often applied to the region of Constantinople or to people coming from Europe.

In contrast to Rome's caesars, who were at pains to give the people the impression that they wished to be regarded as commoners who had been raised to supreme office by the will of the people, Constantine, from the moment he became sole ruler, assumed the position, powers and dignities of an emperor. Furthermore, both as ruler of the Roman Empire and as God's vicar on earth, he insisted on taking precedence over all other kings. This conception of the emperor of Constantinople as supreme ruler on earth was upheld by Constantine's successors and remained unchallenged in 395 when, at the death of Emperor Theodosius I, it was decided to divide the Roman Empire into an eastern and a western section. The eastern was to be ruled from Constantinople, where Arcadius became emperor, whilst the western, which was governed from Rome, was regarded as subordinate. However, within five years the Goths, who were then overrunning Europe, had advanced to the very outskirts of Rome. In 402 the government was obliged hurriedly to move first to Milan and then to Ravenna for safety, though it was not till six years later that the Goths, under Alaric, actually succeeded in capturing and looting Rome. From the start the situation in Ravenna was fraught with difficulties; differences multiplied and ruler succeeded ruler at very short intervals until finally, in 476, the Germanic chieftain Odoacer deposed Romulus Augustus, the last member of the Imperial house to reign in the West. With his fall the mantle of Rome automatically passed to the ruler of the East, that is to say to the emperor of Byzantium reigning in Constantinople. At the time the throne was occupied by Zeno, and because of the glamour with which Constantine had been able to invest the office of emperor of the East, Zeno's prestige stood so high in the West that Odoacer, though victorious in Italy, felt it

5 The Emperor Constantine and his mother Helena
Gold reliquary for a fragment of the True Cross,
eleventh century

6 Christ crowning the Emperor Constantine Porphyrogenitus
From an ivory, c. A.D. 944

necessary that Zeno should recognise him officially as *Patricius* of Rome and prefect of Italy. The ties between Rome and the East remained so strong that, in the fifth century, the Gothic ruler of Ravenna, Theodoric, wholeheartedly adopted Byzantine culture. But even so, soon after his death, Emperor Justinian the Great (527–65) considered it his duty to reconquer Italy. His commanders-in-chief, first Belisarius and then Narses, managed to do so by 555, but the result was ephemeral and in the course of the next two centuries East and West fell apart and, whilst the pope lost his influence in Byzantium, the emperor of the East lost his in western Europe. In 590 Gregory, bishop of Rome, became pope. He was to go down in history as 'the Great' largely because he was the first pope since Leo the Great who asserted his right to act independently of Constantinople. From his day onwards the pope's influence steadily increased in the West at the cost of the patriarch of Constantinople. Then, in the year 800, Charlemagne challenged the supremacy of the emperor of Byzantium by reviving the office of emperor of the West and persuading Pope Leo III to crown him as such on Christmas Day. It is interesting to note that the influence of Byzantium led the pope to take his title from the Greek word *Pappas*, meaning father, the name by which the Greek Church called its first bishops, but later applied to all its priests.

Although many buildings had been erected in Constantinople in Constantine's lifetime the town remained comparatively small and unable to compete in either size or splendour with such ancient and magnificent cities as Alexandria or Antioch nor, indeed, could it compare with Rome or even Athens. Yet within 100 years of its foundation more people were living in Constantinople than in Rome. Nevertheless it was to take the best part of 200 years and the genius of the Emperor Justinian and his chief architect, Anthemius of Tralles, before the young capital could eclipse all other cities in its beauty, wealth, importance and range of amenities. Not only did it then become the leading political and economic centre of its day but, in addition, it stood out during the first few centuries of its existence as the great religious centre to which Christendom looked for direction, in much the same way as Catholics today look to Rome. Furthermore, Constantinople, like Paris since the later nineteenth century, became the capital in which art was to be seen at its best and most vital; it was there that the world's latest fashions were launched and there that luxuries were to be found in greater abundance and variety than anywhere

23

7 The Golden Gate and part of the land walls of Constantinople

else in Europe. By the time of Justinian the population must have numbered close on half a million.

Constantinople's original population had been Greek, descendants of the men of Megara who had founded the city. Most of the people whom Constantine brought to it were Romans, wearing the Roman toga and speaking Latin. Yet even when the Romans merged with the native Greeks, when their language was forgotten by all save the most ardent scholars and when their costume had evolved into something wholly national, the draperies of the Roman toga were nevertheless preserved for all time in art. Regardless of the date at which they were produced, both the exquisite illuminations in Byzantine copies of the Gospels and other holy books, and also religious paintings and mosaics, clothed the Evangelists and saints in the voluminous draperies derived from the dress of classical times. This usually consisted of a himation or cloak worn over a chiton or shirt. Few of these draperies remained white in colour; instead, as befitted those destined to spend eternity amidst the glories of Paradise, the garments were rendered in shades more splendid than the rainbow's; frequently, in the manner of an Indian sari, they are shown shot with gold and, in the case of white draperies, the folds are generally indicated by shading of deep and varied tones.

The Roman Empire was a multi-racial state and all its freemen,

24

irrespective of nationality or religion, enjoyed equal rights. So it was in Constantinople, where from the first Greek and Roman combined in evolving the Eastern Empire's new, essentially Christian, culture and way of life. Roman regard for orderliness seems to have been mainly responsible for contributing the basic structure of the state. But Greek thought and tastes, often reflecting the influence of people from farther east such as the Syrians, became increasingly dominant as more and more easterners flocked to Constantinople, drawn there by the town's growing prosperity. They (the Greeks and orientals) were particularly attracted to the mystical side of Christianity and often became deeply involved in religious experiences and discussions. It was largely due to their influence that the Byzantines developed a regard and love of symbolism which, throughout the whole of their long history, expressed itself not only in their religious writings but also in their art and literature. It was again primarily due to the Greeks that the interest the Romans had taken in Greek culture was fanned by the Byzantines into an enduring love of the Greek classics. The Byzantines became as familiar with the Greek myths as were the pagan Greeks of earlier times. In consequence they were able to use them as parables which they adapted to events of their own day in literature, comparing an idea or occurrence to some well-known text or incident or depicting it in their art by means of some appropriate mythological scene. Yet all these Greek and oriental threads were fitted into so rigid a canvas that the latter must assuredly have been supplied by the painstaking, methodical, logical Romans. Every branch of the Byzantine administration, of its Church, of its social structure and its services was carefully regulated and fully defined. Byzantium became an authoritarian but not a dictatorial state since, within prescribed limits, its people were free. It is perhaps easier for us today than for any other generation to appreciate the subtle differences which distinguish a dictatorship from a highly disciplined society. For all our love of individuality and freedom, we voluntarily submit ourselves to a great many orders. For example, let us take the most trivial, but by no means the least necessary regulations, those governing parking of motor-cars and speeding; to enable our highly complex society to function we have to accept these and numerous other rules. In times of national emergencies, too, most of us readily abandon our customary way of life in order to carry out the instructions of our governments. It was in much the same spirit that the Byzantines, tired of the years of instability and insecurity which

8 Tenth-century cross

had accompanied the decay of Greece and Rome, accepted the measures on which their constitution was based, and the tasks and duties assigned to each social class of the population. Yet within the rigid framework all retained considerable freedom of thought and action; in the intellectual sphere Byzantine life made up for what it lacked in originality by its fervour and vigour, and when the people objected to an edict or to an emperor they never hesitated to express their disapproval. Often they resorted to methods no modern dictator would tolerate. Rioting and mutinies were common occurrences in Constantinople during every period of its history and many an emperor, for all his divine rights and limitless powers, was ruthlessly deposed, often tortured and, at times, even put to death by his angry subjects.

Throughout much of their history the Byzantines were involved in warfare. Though by nature far from belligerent, their traditions as rulers of an empire obliged them to defend the far-flung territories they had inherited from Rome and to cling to distant outposts in the face of rising nationalist movements. In 572 they lost Spain; this was the first of a series of major defeats. It was followed soon after by the loss of Italy. Jerusalem, the holy of holies, the cradle of Christianity, fell to Persian infidels in 613 and in 626 the Persians advanced on Constantinople, but the Virgin, so the Byzantines firmly believed, came to the aid of her fervent adorers, enabling them to beat back the invaders. Then came the rise of Islam, and by the year 640 all of Syria, Palestine and Egypt was in the hands of the Arabs and Constantinople itself was attacked. But a decisive victory over the Arabs in 678, largely due to the use of Greek Fire, saved not only Constantinople, but most of Asia Minor. This was a timely achievement for, from the latter part of the seventh century, the Byzantines had to devote increasing attention to curbing the ambitions of their Slavic neighbours; first they had to acknowledge the Bulgars as an independent kingdom, later the Russians and last of all the Serbians. From the eleventh century onwards the Byzantines found themselves menaced by the Seljukid Turks; then western Crusaders proceeded to undermine their strength, sapping so much of their vitality that at the end they were unable to stem the advance of the Ottoman Turks. In 1453, when Byzantium consisted of little more than the city of Constantinople, the Ottomans launched their last attack. Advancing under cover of cannon fire they breached the walls of the city; Byzantium's last outpost succumbed when the greater part of its population lay with their emperor dead on the ramparts they had defended with the utmost valour. During three days, according to Ottoman traditions, the vanquished city was handed over to the conquering soldiery to loot and destroy. Many of the Greeks who had survived the siege were massacred at the time. Some of those who escaped later agreed to serve in the Turkish treasury or to accept posts as provincial governors in such conquered provinces as Armenia. Known by their fellow Greeks as Phanariotes, these men were hated by the other Constantinopolitan Christians. The Ottomans made the latter pay for their hatred by hounding and persecuting the most active among them.

The Byzantines were ruled in turn by several dynasties. The first traced its descent from Rome's caesars and was so strongly Roman in origin and habits that many scholars regard this opening phase in Byzantium's history as an early Christian rather than a purely Byzantine one. In their view Byzantium came into its own only with Justinian the Great. In art Justinian created a golden age. The standards and ideals which he established endured till the reign of Leo III (717–41). That emperor believed that the veneration which his subjects accorded to icons verged on idolatry. To save them from this, one of the greatest of all sins, Leo determined to ban all forms of figural representations in religious art. In 730 he issued an edict ordering the removal of the famous icon of Our Lady of the Copper Market, but even though he was upheld in this by the support of many men of influence the order was so violently and so passionately resisted that nothing could be done for four years. By then the iconoclasts (as those who were opposed to figural representations in religious art were called) had become so powerful that they were able to enforce the ban. In the face of intense opposition they remained in power from then onwards, with but a short gap of four years, until 843 when they were finally defeated.

A new dynasty, the Macedonian, came to the throne in 867; this dynasty was responsible for the flowering of a second golden age in art and produced rulers as diverse as Leo VI, known as the Wise, or the ruthless, pleasure-loving Zoe who murdered her husband Romanus III in order to marry Michael the Paphlagonian and crown him emperor, only to replace him in his turn in 1042 by her third and last husband, Constantine IX Monomachus. That dynasty ended with Zoe's sister after a reign of only one year after the death of her brother-in-law Constantine IX.

A palace revolution carried out by courtiers brought Isaac, the first of the Comnenes, to the throne in 1057. His heirs were obliged to fight both the Seljuks in the East and the Normans in the West whilst also having to deal with the turbulent Crusaders. Intoxicated by the wealth and beauty of Constantinople the members of the Fourth Crusade, led by Venetian commanders, forgot that they had set out to fight the infidel rulers of Jerusalem in order to free the holy places and turned instead on Constantinople. They took possession of the city in 1204; after sacking it they installed themselves as its rulers. The Latin occupation lasted till 1261. Whilst it was in force members of Byzantium's imperial families established refugee kingdoms in the Empire's outposts. Theodore Lascaris set himself up in Nicaea and claimed to be ruler of Byzantium. A branch of the Comnenes created a kingdom for themselves at Trebizond, in the south-eastern corner of the Black Sea. Others established independent despotates in Greece, notably in the Morea, at Mistra and in Epirus, where the Angelus family seized control. It was a member of that house, Theodore Angelus Ducas Comnenus, who managed to capture Salonica from the Latins in 1224 and who then attempted to lay claim to the imperial title. However, it was Michael VIII Palaeologus, a member of the aristocratic Comnene family, who became the founder of the last Greek dynasty to reign in Constantinople. Crowned co-ruler with John IV Lascaris in Nicaea in 1259, on the ejection in 1261 of the Latin usurpers from Constantinople he re-entered the city as emperor of Byzantium. A descendant of his, Constantine XI, crowned emperor in his despotate of Mistra in Sparta in 1449, was to die gallantly defending the walls of his capital against vastly unequal odds in 1453, when the Ottoman Turks launched their final attack. Only his purple slippers remained to show his subjects where he had fallen whilst fighting beside them to defend their city.

2

THE EMPEROR, HIS FAMILY
AND COURT

When Constantine became sole ruler of the Roman Empire he was still a pagan. Though Rome was now a monarchy, daily life continued to conform to customs which had become established in the days of the Republic. Constantine's assumption of supreme power was therefore not confirmed by means of a coronation service of the type which was to become usual in feudal times in Europe. Instead it was ratified by a ceremony which dated back to the days when Rome's caesar was elected to the highest office in the Empire by his fellow-citizens. In accordance with that ancient custom Constantine was placed on a shield and lifted up on it in full view of his army and the assembled people (9). Their cheers sufficed to establish him in his new position. That method of informing the nation of the elevation of a new sovereign to the Empire's throne persisted in Byzantium during the best part of 100 years, the first rulers to succeed Constantine being presented to the assembled Senate, army and people of Constantinople in the same manner as Rome's caesars. Like them, they received from the hands of an eminent official the coronet which served as the emperor's emblem of office. However, by the year 457 when Leo I came to the throne, the patriarch of Constantinople had become so important in the state that his authority almost equalled that of the emperor and it therefore fell to him in preference to a layman, however distinguished, to place the crown on Leo's head. Leo's immediate successors decided to be similarly crowned by the patriarchs of their day, with the result that from Justinian's time onwards the ceremony was always performed in the capital's principal church, the great cathedral of Haghia Sophia. The original structure begun by Constantine I had been destroyed in the Nika riots in 532, but it was rebuilt on a grander scale by Justinian.

9 Emperor raised on a shield

Over the years, coronations were celebrated in Byzantium with ever-increasing pomp and magnificence. By the tenth century the ritual had become so elaborate that Emperor Constantine VII Porphyrogenitus (913–59)(6) thought that it would prove helpful to his son and heir if he recorded it in detail in a book he was engaged in writing for the boy's use later in life. It was called *The Book of Ceremonies*; the description of the coronation occupies several pages, for the emperor listed in full the part played by all officials, senators and members of the factions (see page 35), their precise positions in the official procession, the clothes each wore and the badges of office they carried. Thus patricians were to appear in white *chlamydes* or cloaks trimmed with gold.

On entering the cathedral the sovereign was met by the patriarch, who assisted him in changing his robes for some which were believed to have been given to Constantine the Great by angels, and which were therefore carefully kept in the cathedral for use by the emperor only on certain specific occasions. Then the patriarch took the emperor by the hand to lead him into the body of the great church. On reaching the silver gates the emperor lit the special candles reserved for his use and moved to a porphyry slab set into the floor in front of the royal gates of the *iconostasis* (an altar screen designed to display icons) to pray. Only then, accompanied by the patriarch, did he penetrate beyond the *iconostasis* to enter the altar enclosure. This procedure was followed whenever the emperor attended a religious ceremony in the cathedral—it is estimated that his presence there was required on an average some 30 times a month. The patriarch always conducted the religious service which followed, in the case of a coronation reading a prayer over the crown before placing it on the emperor's head amidst the acclamations of the assembled worshippers. The emperor then moved to the throne, often one made of gold, which had been placed in the *mitatorion*. When he was seated all the assembled people, following a strict order of precedence, passed before him, paying homage by prostrating themselves before him.

By the ninth century the habit of crowning an emperor during a religious ceremony had become so firmly established that it was henceforth observed by all other Christian monarchs. However, in Byzantium it also remained necessary for the emperor to sign a profession of faith before he was crowned. From the start the crowning of an emperor by a patriarch was regarded throughout Byzantium as an act of outstanding significance, being interpreted as the visual confirmation of the belief that the emperor was God's chosen representative on earth. As such, emperors were soon being revered almost as sacred personages. In art they were sometimes represented wearing a halo; in conversation and literature they were often compared to the apostles, and a ruler was even occasionally described as the 'thirteenth apostle' and his residences as 'sacred palaces'. An emperor's semi-celestial nature was reflected in his use of an immensely wide throne. In reality it was a double throne, which enabled the pagan custom of the partially empty throne to be retained and adapted to Christian observances: henceforth, the right side of such thrones was dedicated to Christ, and to make this visibly apparent a copy of the Gospels was placed on it. It remained vacant on Sundays and during religious festivals, when the emperor occupied the left side of the throne. On working

10 Empress leading a procession to honour a holy relic

31

days, on the other hand, the emperor, acting as Christ's representative on earth, used the right half, doing the same on all state occasions as well as when granting audiences to visiting ambassadors.

When the emperor appeared in the streets of his cities, the crowds often acclaimed him as God's representative, and as he advanced hymns to that effect were sung by choirs, the members of which were drawn from the city's political guildsmen and factions. Candles, torches and incense were carried before the emperor as they were before the holy icons and prelates in religious processions(10). Even inefficient and bad rulers—of whom Byzantium had more than her fair share—were thought to have been raised to their exalted position by the Almighty, who had selected them for their high office for the purpose of testing the faithful.

The Roman conception of an elected ruler, whether acting as the head of state or as emperor, was so firmly embedded in the Roman mind that, in Byzantium, the office of emperor was not at first regarded as hereditary. When time and events permitted it was therefore considered right for a dying or ageing ruler to choose his successor. In the event of an emperor's sudden death the members of his immediate family were entitled to select the new ruler, but if the dead man had no close relatives or if, as often happened, his rule had been brought to an end as the result of a revolution, it then fell to the Senate to make the appointment. Justinian, perhaps the greatest of all the Byzantine emperors, came to the throne in that manner. No significance was attached to ancient lineage, and class distinctions were considered of so little importance that the fact that Justin (518–27) was by birth a Macedonian peasant did not prevent him from occupying the throne for nine years.

In early Byzantine times there was a good deal of confusion concerning the emperor's correct title. To begin with he used a Roman one, calling himself either *Imperator*, *Caesar* or *Augustus*. However, towards the end of the fifth century growing jealousy started to poison the relations between the Greek and Latin inhabitants of Constantinople, and soon each group wished their native culture to be chosen as the national culture of Byzantium. When in 491 Emperor Zeno died without naming a successor, with the result that it fell to his widow to appoint one, vast crowds assembled outside her windows, some shouting to her to choose a Greek for the office, others to select a Roman. Her decision conformed to the desires of the former group, for she nominated as emperor an unexciting, though experienced and reliable, elderly court official called Anastasius (491–518). Nevertheless, it was not until Emperor Heraclius (610–41) adopted Greek as the official language of the Byzantine Empire that the Greek title of *Basileus* replaced the Latin ones as the only official designation of the emperor. It was at about the same time that the emperors also adopted Jupiter's em-blem of an eagle as their

11 The double-headed eagle of Byzantium

crest. In the fourteenth century it became a double-headed eagle (*11*). The change was made to parry the German emperor's decision to use the single-headed eagle as his crest, by publicising the belief that the Byzantine rulers had made use of the double-headed eagle to symbolise the Roman Empire's eastern and western territories; as such, the latter form passed by marriage into the arms both of imperial Austria and of Russia.

By the seventh century it had become the custom for the emperors to choose one of their sons, not necessarily the elder, to succeed them. First they waited to appoint him till they were well on in life or until they thought that death was drawing near, but before long they found it wiser to ensure the survival of their dynasty and to guard against sudden death by choosing their heir early in their reigns, and for similar reasons they gradually started selecting two sons for the office, naming them in order of preference. These appointments were legalised by a religious ceremony conducted on very much the same lines as an emperor's coronation. (There were two minor differences: the coronation was held in one of the palace churches instead of in the cathedral of Haghia Sophia and, after blessing their crowns, the patriarch passed them to the emperor who, as in the case of his wife's coronation, personally placed them on the heads of his co-rulers.) The senior and favourite co-ruler gradually came to be spoken of as 'the little *basileus*' and his picture often appeared beside his father's on the country's coinage. As senior co-ruler he often instantly appointed his own co-ruler and successor. As a result there was sometimes a multiplicity of rulers living, or rather of members of the imperial family who, to distinguish them from the emperor and his immediate heir, were invested with the Roman title of caesar; in the case of a woman the title bestowed on her was that of Augusta. The mistress of Constantine IX, though allowed to use that title, was not permitted to wear the imperial diadem or to be accompanied by an imperial bodyguard. To make up for this she, and many other Augustas, wore numerous strange and costly head decorations, gold necklaces, bracelets in the form of snakes, heavy pearl earrings, and girdles of gold with chains of pearls threaded through them. Each member of the imperial house invested with the title of a minor sovereign had his appropriate rank conferred upon him by means of a modified version of the imperial coronation ceremony, yet there was never more than one ruler with, at most, two co-rulers in power. Invariably the emperor remained the supreme authority throughout the Empire; it was his duty to supervise and be responsible for everything relating to the state. It has been aptly remarked that the Byzantine conception of life was based on the belief in one religion, one God, one source of law and one government—that is to say in one emperor. When the latter's unique position was contested by Charlemagne, who persuaded the pope to crown him emperor of the Romans in Rome on Christmas Day in the year 800, the Byzantine ruler assumed the title of *Basileus Romaiōn*, meaning emperor of the Romans, so as to establish his right to rule over Rome; by doing so he in his turn challenged Charlemagne's claim to that position.

As soon as it became possible for them to do so the emperors naturally chose one of their sons to succeed them, and so the office of sovereign gradually came to be accepted as a hereditary one. But because the emperors were not obliged to appoint their eldest son to succeed them, gradually particular importance was attached to the children who were born to a reigning couple. Such children were born in the Purple Bedchamber in the Purple Palace—a residence which owed its name to the fact that the walls of the empress's bedchamber were hung with stuff, generally silk, the colour of porphyry. Though a very small number of senior court officials were allowed to wear purple cloaks, stuffs of that colour were reserved for the exclusive use of members of the imperial family. They alone could wear purple-coloured robes and shoes, and be buried in porphyry sarcophagi. Children born in the Purple Bedchamber in the Purple Palace automatically received the appellation of Porphyrogenitus, meaning 'born in the purple'—an expression which lives on in our own language and times—and, in the case of boys, this lucky occurrence increased their chances of inheriting the crown. Such princes were surrounded by every conceivable luxury. Inevitably, when it eventually became customary for the first-born of these sons to succeed his father, rivalry broke out between him and his brothers, some of them his elders. It was made all the fiercer by the fact that an emperor's sons were often no more than half-brothers, their father having married more than once. Many an heir to supreme power ended his days in prison, in solitary confinement, having first had to submit to tortures which included blinding, having his tongue or nose cut off, or even worse. A deposed brother who was allowed to withdraw for ever to a remote monastery, to become a monk and spend his days in prayer and contemplation, was to be counted fortunate.

Imperial weddings were accompanied by an extremely solemn, elaborate and magnificent ritual. All wore their finest clothes and official robes for the occasion. The imperial bridal couple appeared wearing their imperial crowns below the wedding crowns which are still used at Orthodox weddings. But whereas today the wedding crowns are held above the heads of the groom and bride, throughout the religious ceremony in Byzantium a sumptuous purple-coloured fabric was suspended above the heads of the imperial couple. The patriarch performed the marriage ceremony; after it all those who had attended the wedding, patricians and eminent officials, were expected to prostrate themselves before the bridal couple. Then they formed themselves into a procession and accompanied their newly wedded sovereigns to the Magnaura Palace where the choirs of the Blue and Green factions were waiting to welcome them by singing to the accompaniment of an organ belonging to the Green faction. The bridal couple then proceeded to their bridal chamber still wearing their crowns; there they received their guests and in their presence they removed their crowns, placing them on their bridal bed. Then all went to the Dining Hall of the Nineteen Couches where, changing into simpler garments, the emperor and empress sat down to their wedding breakfast with their guests. On such occasions women were included in the party, but they were not permitted to dress their hair in the high style known as the *propoloma*. Generally, however, the empresses, many of whom possessed large fortunes, and all of whom were waited upon by numerous courtiers and retainers, entertained the eminent women of Byzantium at sumptuous banquets held in their own apartments.

Women were not quite so free in Byzantium as they had been in Rome, where they were generally treated as the equals of men. In Byzantium, though empresses took part in many aspects of public life, they were nevertheless expected to spend much of their time in the women's quarters. Like women of lower station, many must have used much of their leisure, if not weaving like their humbler subjects, then at any rate in doing fine embroidery as adornments for their favourite churches. Time and again empresses and other women greatly influenced public events and were often the dominating members of their family circle. Many an empress became a powerful autocrat, even to the extent of ruling at times in her own right. At certain periods of Byzantine history, and more especially during the opening phase (when members both of Rome's ancient aristocracy and of Greece's nobility were establishing the standards and conventions which were to characterise Byzantium) empresses were chosen regardless of rank and origin from among the Empire's most beautiful girls. In contrast to office, birth counted for astonishingly little in Byzantium. We have already seen that Anastasius was raised to supreme power from the position of a court official and Justin from that of a Macedonian peasant. It is therefore scarcely surprising to find that when Justinian fell in love with a beautiful circus girl called Theodora he was able to marry her. She appears with him, in all the splendour of a Byzantine empress's apparel, in the magnificent, contemporary wall mosaic of San Vitale at Ravenna(*12*). High office is as likely to bring out the best in its holder as the worst. It did so in the case of Theodora.

Though Theodora's origins were humble and her conduct prior to her marriage not above criticism yet, on attaining the throne, she quickly became conscious of an empress's obligations. Soon after her marriage one of the many riots which mar Constantinople's history broke out and quickly developed into an unusually violent political rising. The imperial palace was set on fire, the cathedral of Haghia Sophia built by Constantine I perished in the flames. Justinian contemplated flight. It was then that Theodora showed

12   The Emperor Justinian, Bishop Maximian, Empress Theodora
(Ravenna mosaic)

her true greatness. Apologising for daring 'as a woman to speak
among men' she set out to show how foolish it would be to resort
to flight. She appealed to the courage of her listeners, arguing that
'it is impossible for a man, when he has come into this world, not to
die; but for one who has reigned', she said to Justinian, 'it is
intolerable to be an exile. May I never exist without this purple
robe and may I never live to see the day on which those who meet
me shall not address me as queen. If you wish, O Emperor, to save
yourself, there is no difficulty; we have ample funds. Yonder is the
sea and there are the ships. Yet reflect whether, when you have
escaped to a place of security you will not prefer death to safety. I
agree with the old saying that "an empire makes a fine winding
sheet".' Her brave words gave Justinian new courage and his
general Belisarius made a fresh, and this time successful, attempt
to dispel the crowd. The rebellion collapsed and Justinian's throne
was secured.

It is no exaggeration to say that Theodora saved the throne for
Justinian and enabled him to go down in history as perhaps the
greatest of Byzantine emperors; when rebuilding the burnt-out
cathedral of Haghia Sophia Justinian created a masterpiece which
still stands to rank as one of the world's finest buildings; he also

introduced the legal measures which are perpetuated in the Justinianic code. However, because Theodora was a woman she was never Justinian's consort, that is to say his co-ruler. Nor, years later in 641, could Heraclius, realising that his life was running out, appoint his wife Martino co-ruler with his own young son, who was but her stepson. When his intentions became known to the people they expressed violent opposition to being governed by Martino on the grounds that it would be unseemly for a woman to receive ambassadors in audience. Martino tried to defy them and, helped by her own son, endeavoured to seize power, but her stepson managed to forestall her. On coming to the throne himself he punished Martino most cruelly for her ambition, having her tongue cut out and ordering her to live in exile on the island of Rhodes. However, things became easier for women by 780 when Leo V died leaving his ten-year-old son, the future Constantine VI (780–97), as heir whilst appointing the boy's mother, the Empress Irene, as his co-ruler. In the face of strong opposition and almost continuous unrest Irene succeeded in reigning for ten years, but was then forced to hand over her powers to her son and to go into exile. It was unfortunate for Constantine that he was both foolish and unreliable, for at the end of seven years Irene was recalled to the capital and asked to resume control of the nation's affairs. She thus became the first woman to rule over the Byzantine Empire in her own right. Though she thereby automatically became the head of all the services, including the fighting forces, state and official documents continued invariably to refer to her in the masculine, calling her *Basileus* and not *Basilissa*. Having reached so exalted a position it is sad to find that Irene marred her good name by ill-treating her deposed son. Though she was his mother she had Constantine blinded in the Purple Bedchamber in which she had given birth to him. In the mid-eleventh century the two imperial sisters Zoe and Theodora reigned jointly for a few months; then Theodora, the more forceful of the two, acted as sole ruler for a year.

Yet even so, empresses rarely appeared in public and women of lesser rank hardly ever did so. However, empresses attended the official functions held in the palace, but they seldom took part in state processions or public festivities. In 481 Ariadne wearing her state robes (16) appeared in the imperial box in the Hippodrome of Constantinople to address the people, but, until the eleventh century, none accompanied her husband when he went to the Hippodrome to attend the games. Like other women, however, empresses went to church regularly, like other women attending the services from the gallery, though occupying a special imperial pew. In the cathedral of Haghai Sophia it extended over the whole of the west end of the gallery. After a service it was customary for the emperor and empress to make their way to separate halls situated in the cathedral, where each was served with refreshments. When the empress and her ladies departed, to return to the palace, the emperor was conducted by the patriarch to the Holy Well—a structure close to the cathedral which was believed to contain the well where Christ met the woman from Samaria. There the emperor distributed gold pieces among the minor clerics and choir singers who had taken part in the service and then handed back to the patriarch the golden bag he had used for the purpose; then he resumed the crown which he had worn in the procession accompanying him as he left the palace for the cathedral, but which he had removed on reaching the Holy Well.

Daughters generally counted for little in Byzantium; so little, in fact, that Romanus II (959–63) did not hesitate to relegate all five of his to a convent in order to please his new wife, the beautiful Theophanu. Princesses born in the purple, though less pampered than their brothers, were nevertheless valued, if only because they made useful brides for minor rulers whom the emperors wished to conciliate; in the tenth century one was even married off to a Mongol Khan.

The emperor and his family spent the greater part of their free time within the grounds of their palaces; indeed, the womenfolk seldom ventured beyond them, the empress herself rarely did so. Within that large and sumptuous enclosure or compound the imperial family lived a close and intimate family life, meeting in private for meals and amusements. Byzantium's royal residences did not, as in the West, consist of a large residential block situated in pleasure grounds and flanked by stables and domestic dependencies, but as in the Orient, took the form of walled enclosures containing a large number of separate buildings dispersed amidst gardens and walks. Emperor Theophilus (829–42) was so passionate an admirer of Arabian culture that he laid out much of the western quarter of the Great Palace enclosure in the eastern style; a part of it was thereafter called the Persian House.

Until the twelfth century the Great (or Sacred) Palace in Constantinople served not only as the home of the reigning family

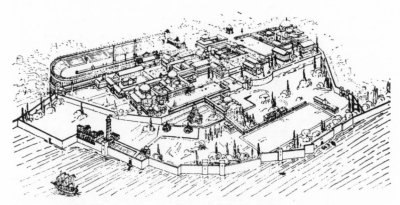

13   Vogt's reconstruction of the Great Palace district

but as the centre of the nation's government for every public function, whether civil or religious, evolved at any rate in part within it; and every official, whether civil or military, had a position in court corresponding to his rank in the administration. The palace occupied a magnificent site (*13*) extending along the sea front from the Hippodrome to the cathedral of Haghia Sophia and embracing the whole area occupied in later times by the palace of the sultans of Ottoman Turkey, the Saray. Its grounds sloped down to the sea walls and its views extended over the Sea of Marmora to the Golden Horn and, further eastward, to the opening of the Bosphorus, to embrace the coast of Asia and its hinterland. There were numerous buildings within the enclosure and Steven Runciman has aptly compared this great complex to Spain's Escurial since, in both instances, in addition to the emperor's dwelling and possessions, some of the Church's most venerated relics and the nation's most treasured antiquities were preserved within.

Apart from seven palaces, the Constantinopolitan enclosure included the emperor's official quarters, known as the Octagon. The empress's official residence, known as the Pantheon, was situated near the church of St Stephen, which was in its turn attached to the Daphne Palace. Both the latter were used by the emperors on the most solemn occasions. The state throne-room was situated in the neighbouring Chrysotriclinium which, from late in the seventh century, was roofed with a dome. The throne, somewhat in the manner of an altar, stood in the apse forming the end of the great hall. The floor there was raised above the level of that in the body of the hall and was covered with a cloth of gold; the steps leading to the platform were of porphyry; the throne, like all the others used by the emperors, resembled a couch with a double head-board surmounted by a canopy; it was provided with a footstool. The conch of the apse above it was adorned with a glass mosaic representation of Christ, inscribed 'King of Kings'. This throne-room remained the principal and most holy of all till the tenth century, and it housed the imperial regalia. It was furnished with two organs inset with jewels and it was there that the mechanical throne commissioned by Theophilus was set up, astonishing the ambassadors who saw it. Ranged behind the throne, in a semi-circle corresponding to that of the apse, stood the most distinguished members of the imperial bodyguard, grouped according to nationality; those whom the emperor wished particularly to distinguish were placed closest to him. A second circle of rather less important guardsmen stood behind them, all wearing armour; the third and last circle was made up of men of still lower rank, mostly, to use the Byzantine term, 'Barbarians', that is to say Varangians. As such, they did not wear armour but carried lances, shields, and single-edged battle-axes suspended from their shoulders.

Theophilus did not admire the Golden Triclinium and in 838 built for himself the Triconchus Palace. It derived its name from the three domes with which he roofed it; it consisted of a hall divided into three parallel sections by columns, which served also to support the three domes. The building had three entrance doors, the centre one of which was made of silver and the other two of bronze. Theophilus' throne probably stood under the central dome, with those of his wife and son on either side. The building is believed to have served as the model for the church of the Nea built within the palace enclosure in 881. In 1042, when Zoe and Theodora were joint rulers, Zoe's throne was always placed a little in front of her younger sister's. Near them, forming a semi-circle, stood Varangian guardsmen carrying the double-edged swords known as *rhomphaia*. Assembled within the semi-circle were the special favourites and courtiers of the empresses. All stood with their eyes fixed to the ground as a sign of respect.

There were a great many more halls, conference chambers and state rooms within the palace enclosure, each of which was used for a specific series of ceremonies. Among the more important of

41

these were the buildings known as the *Onopodion* (entrance hall to the Daphne Palace), the Chamber of Candidates (used by gentlemen-at-arms), the Excubitors' Hall (the Excubitors were part of the palace guard who acted as an imperial militia), the *Lychni* (a circular, domed structure near the Tribunal where emperors were received when they visited the Tribunal), and above all the *Chalke*, a palatial structure giving access to all the buildings within the enclosure. From Justinian's time the latter contained a domed chamber whose inner walls were faced with marble and whose ceiling was decorated with glass mosaic compositions. Two scenes took the form of imperial portraits: one showed Justinian alone, the other with Theodora; both must have resembled the magnificent, almost contemporary mosaic portraits of Justinian and Theodora which survive in Ravenna (*12*). On a line with the *Chalke*, but to the north of it, another gateway in the form of a pavilion connected the palace to the emperor's box in the Hippodrome. This entrance was faced on its Hippodrome side with ivory panels which must have been quite the most impressive ever made out of this scarce and lovely material.

Numerous churches and chapels were to be found within the palace enclosure. Among the most venerated were the oratory of St Theodore situated in or near to the Chrysotriclinium, the Sigma and the Baptistery. The famous lighthouse, the Pharos, which guided mariners safely into harbour and also sent signals to distant parts of the Empire by means of a relay system, stood on a promontory within the enclosure. So too did numerous essential offices and store-rooms as well as the silk looms and the imperial factories and workshops where luxury products of superb quality were made for the emperor's personal use. The emperor's personal stables, sheltering his chargers, riding horses and polo ponies, were close at hand; so too were those set aside for the racehorses used in the Hippodrome contests. These were situated close to the gates opening on to the race-track and were kept in impeccable condition, the gold trappings of each horse being displayed above its stall. The kennels sheltering the dogs and cheetahs used by the emperors when hunting deer or bears in Asia Minor, and the cages holding the falcons which he used when pursuing hares or game birds, stood close to his private zoo containing his remarkable collection of outlandish animals. Near by were his aviary, his armoury, his mint, his treasury, his archives. Some 20,000 retainers are believed to have been employed in the enclosure which also contained

14 Big game hunting

residences such as the Pearl Palace, where the imperial family resided in summertime, and others which they used only during the winter months; there were also residences which served particular purposes, such as the Purple Palace or the bridal suite in the Magnaura Palace, standing close to the waters of the Marmora. The latter was equipped with a bathroom used by the empress only during the three days following her wedding day when she was obliged to bath in it according to specially prescribed rules. Thus, on the last of the three days both factions were expected to assemble near the bathroom. To the playing of three organs clean linen, a box of perfume, caskets, ewers and basins were carried to the bathroom under the watchful eye of consuls; then the empress, walking between two of her ladies and followed by a third, each of whom carried a purple pomegranate studded with jewels, entered the bathroom. The terrace of the Magnaura Palace was decorated with statues; the last which is known to have been placed there was a bust of Emperor Phocas (602–10). The palace was abandoned in the ninth century and converted soon after into a university; the large hall in which the famous throne of Salomos had once stood served to make an excellent lecture hall. Its plan was similar to that of a three-aisled basilica terminating in a central apse. Many of the earlier emperors had preferred the Daphne Palace to the Magnaura. It was the oldest of all the buildings in the enclosure, dating back to the days of Constantine I, and could be reached from one of the main banqueting halls.

Only two ruins survive to give us some idea of the appearance of these buildings. Both are to be found in Istanbul. One, a portion

15   The Blachernae Palace

of the Blachernae Palace, stands close to the north-eastern section of the city's walls; the other, erroneously called the 'House of Justinian' rises from the edge of a cliff overlooking the Sea of Marmora; it dates from the eighth century. To judge from their appearance palace buildings must have borne quite a close resemblance to the façade of the building depicted in the early sixth-century wall mosaic in the church of San Apollinare Nuovo in Ravenna or the ruined Roman houses of Ostia. Both ruins follow rectangular plans and are built on fairly severe lines. The Blachernae building was originally three storeys high, the 'House of Justinian' two. Both possessed large, well-proportioned windows which made the rooms pleasant to live in. They also prove, what can likewise be learnt from their art, that the Byzantines were keen observers of nature and lovers of its varied aspects. This is borne out by the character of the trees, flowers and rural scenes included in the magnificent marble floor mosaic adorning a sort of cloister or peristyle discovered in what was originally part of the Great Palace enclosure. The magnificent sites which were chosen by Byzantine monks for their monasteries were also governed by their love of nature.

The main entrance to the Great Palace was through a magnificent pair of bronze gates. Within beat the heart of Byzantium in a setting of unimaginable splendour. By the sixth century, when

Justinian set up there the bronze horses which he had brought from Ephesus, so many ancient works of art had been assembled within the enclosure that the area had become a veritable museum. From the eighth century the statues of emperors and of heroes of the Empire were regularly added to the collection. Many were set up near the Hall of Tribunals situated close to the main entrance gates, whence smaller halls led to a series of dining chambers. The finest of the dining halls held 19 couches and the gold plate used in it was kept in a building called the Castresiacon, which was entered by ivory gates, and which was entrusted to a senior official of the empress's household. Another hall held 36 couches and one of the smaller ones 12; the banquet given in honour of the emperor's birthday was held in the Triclinium of Justinian, where a ballet could be conveniently performed after the roast meat course. The largest table mentioned in surviving records was designed to hold 36 couches and was entirely made of gold. In the tenth century the German ambassador Liutprand was astonished on dining at court to find that all the guests were served off gold plate, and that the three gold bowls containing fruit were so immense and so heavy that they could not be lifted; they were therefore suspended from the ceiling by ropes encased in gilt leather attached to a mechanical device which enabled them to be moved from one guest to another.

By the eighth century the emperors had begun to build new palaces. The Great Palace had become a trifle cumbersome and was beginning to fall out of favour. Already in the sixth century Justin II (565–78)—nicknamed the Noseless because his nose had been cut off as a punishment for conspiring against his sovereign— had started to use the Blachernae Palace in preference to the Great Palace. The Blachernae Palace was situated, as we have seen, at the opposite end of the town to the older palace, close to the church of the same name which had been built by Emperor Marcian (450–7) and his wife Pulcheria, but it was not until the end of the eleventh century that Alexius I Comnenus (1081–1118) decided to abandon the Great Palace in its favour. In the eleventh and twelfth centuries the Blachernae Palace was admired for its marble courtyards, its great central hall made of porphyry and for the profusion of its gold decorations. Nevertheless, Alexius and his family lived in it in comparative simplicity and it was only in the reign of Manuel I Comnenus (1143–80) that the Blachernae became the centre of a gay court life. Manuel loved it and filled it with beautiful objects. He enjoyed entertaining and was eager to devise unusual ways of doing so. His parties were amusing and stimulating, for he often surprised his guests by the novelty of the diversions he arranged for them. Thus he was fond of organising tournaments of a western type and of inviting ladies to attend them. In 1204, when the Crusaders occupied Constantinople, sacking the city instead of attempting to rescue the Holy Land from the Muslims, they stripped the Blachernae of its magnificent contents, destroying the palace in the process. The Latins remained masters of Constantinople till 1261, when the Palaeologues re-entered the town and regained the Byzantine throne. By then, however, the emperors were reduced to relative poverty. By the end of the fourteenth century even at state banquets they were obliged to use pottery vessels in place of gold or even of silver ones. Indeed, the imperial family found itself so hard-pressed that Anne of Savoy, the wife of Andronicus III (1328–41), pawned her state jewels to the Venetians for a mere 30,000 ducats. She never managed to raise this comparatively small sum to reclaim them and so they remained the property of the Republic of St Mark.

The gates of all the imperial palaces were regularly locked at three o'clock every afternoon and unlocked at dawn on the following day. The task of closing and opening them was entrusted to a head porter who was also an ordained priest. The imperial family's private life started when they closed. During the warm summer evenings the men could indulge in such sports as archery, javelin-throwing or tennis, or watch boxing or wrestling matches. Constantine VIII revived the *gymnopodia*, a form of combat recalling gladiatorial fights. In the sixth century the games of chess and draughts were introduced to Constantinople from the Orient and were often played at court, Constantine VIII being an almost compulsive player of chequers and dice. In the ninth century Theophilus introduced the game of polo from Persia. It quickly became popular in Byzantium; public matches were frequently played in the Hippodrome at Constantinople and in those of other towns. It remained so popular that in the thirteenth century, on the formation of the Trapezuntine Empire, a polo ground was especially laid out for the emperors of Trebizond. The Constantinopolitan emperors so enjoyed the game that many played it on their private polo grounds, but when the weather was bad jesters, dwarfs, mimes and acrobats were always at hand to entertain their imperial masters.

Under the Comnenes life was particularly gay and light-hearted, somewhat western and essentially up-to-date. The empresses of that dynasty were fond of giving balls and of organising concerts or mimed plays in their country villas. These were situated on the outskirts of the capital, invariably in attractive surroundings where the emperors had from early times built their hunting lodges, shooting boxes and castles. Theodora had chosen to build her favourite villa on the Asiatic shore of the Bosphorus.

Although every aspect of Byzantine life was organised in the smallest detail the poor of Constantinople were in such constant need of the essentials of daily life that they had little to lose by being unruly. They therefore never hesitated to express their discontent and were often so turbulent that even when the hereditary succession to the throne had come to be generally regarded as constitutional rioting often broke out in the capital. It frequently ended in a change of ruler. When a rising had been successful the crowd was apt to express its pleasure by dancing in the streets and composing songs about the event, as it did in 1042 when Michael V was deposed. In 1057 they expressed their gratitude to Isaac Comnenus for deposing Michael VI by lighting torches in his honour, sprinkling him with scent and dancing in the streets. Palace revolutions also often brought an unexpected sovereign to the throne and so too sometimes did misfortunes of a personal or national character. As a result nine dynasties and several usurpers succeeded each other on the Byzantine throne. Nevertheless, from the start the office of emperor, if not always his person, was deeply respected throughout the Empire. Diocletian had been the first Roman to claim for the sovereign's person a touch of divinity. In Byzantium the emperor's position as Christ's vicar on earth assured him of the veneration of the great majority of his Christian subjects, and the ceremonial which the Church had evolved for the emperor did much to encourage that attitude. Furthermore, during early Byzantine history, the influence of her most serious rival, Persia, where the Sasanian rulers ranked as virtually divine, did much to encourage the emperor's assertion that his office entitled him to respect or even adoration.

Though Persia and Byzantium were frequently at war with each other, vying for world supremacy until the rise of the Arabs in the seventh century, the reverence with which the Persians treated their sovereigns appealed to the Byzantine emperors. Nevertheless, none of them ever cut themselves off from their subjects to anything like the same degree as did the Sasanian kings, though they used every

16 The Empress Ariadne in her regalia

visible means to stress their uniqueness and importance. Diocletian had introduced the conception of the divinely clad king; Constantine endorsed it by reserving for himself and his family the use of purple-coloured stuffs and slippers. Soon all excepting the patriarch of Constantinople were expected, regardless of rank, to prostrate themselves when greeting the emperor. Every member of the cabinet or Sacred Consistorium, when assembled in the presence of the emperor, though absolved from prostrating himself, was obliged to stand throughout the entire session.

An elaborate court ceremonial grew up throughout the centuries for the purpose of enhancing the glamour surrounding the sovereign so as to increase both his personal standing and the dignity of his office. Each of his official appearances was precisely regulated and designed as carefully as any ballet, unfolding invariably in a setting of great splendour. Thus, in the early fifth century, to celebrate the baptism of Emperor Arcadius' son, the future Theodosius II (408–50), the streets of Constantinople were decorated with silk hangings adorned with gold and other costly ornaments; this was at a time when the method of producing silk was still unknown in the West, so that all available supplies had to be imported at great expense by caravan from China. All those taking part in the official procession to and from the cathedral wore white, creating, in the words of a contemporary, the impression of an eddy of snowflakes. The highest dignitaries of the realm walked at the head of the procession. They were followed by units of the imperial regiments carrying lighted candles which flickered like myriads of stars. A nobleman of high rank carried the imperial baby, whilst the child's father, dressed in purple, followed. Even the onlookers were gaily dressed.

Court ceremonial was both complicated and strict. By the tenth century it had become so involved that the learned and gifted Emperor Constantine VII Porphyrogenitus thought it necessary to record it in all its details in his *Book of Ceremonies*. The emperor was an historian and distinguished writer and he also wrote for his son's benefit *The Book of Government*. We owe much of our knowledge of Byzantine court life and administration to these two works. In the first Constantine defined ceremony as 'the outward form of inward harmony' and expressed the belief that 'ritual helps to enhance royal dignity'. The broad lines of the ceremonies he described had been laid down in Justinian's day, when the observances had been worked out that were to be followed at coronations, royal births, marriages and burials as well as at a sovereign's departure from and return to his capital, during his presence at such ceremonies as the Hippodrome games, at ambassadorial audiences and at religious and state festivals. But the final details were not established till the tenth century. Then even mechanical contrivances were resorted to to help stress the superhuman nature of the sovereign. The most intriguing of these was the mechanical throne commissioned by Theophilus. However, even less ingenious thrones were extremely impressive, for they were made of precious materials, adorned with jewels, surmounted by canopies, draped in rare and precious stuffs, set up on a dais or tribune, furnished with brocaded cushions and accompanied by ornate footstools.

Whenever an emperor departed from or returned to his capital he was either speeded on his way or welcomed home by his sons, the patriarch, the senators and the senior army and naval officers at a convenient point close to the city's boundary. If he was returning from a European campaign the welcoming ceremony was held in the Hebdomon castle standing close to the capital's western land walls; often it took place in a pavilion situated in the same neighbourhood. After the welcoming ceremony had been performed it was customary for the emperor to enter his capital by the Golden Gate, riding at the head of his bodyguard along the Mese or Central Street, past the Forum of Theodosius and that of

Constantine, skirting the Hippodrome and so back to the Great Palace.

The emperor, in his role of Christ's representative, had special duties to fulfil in the main religious festivals, each of which was celebrated in its own particular way. Many pagan customs had been incorporated in the Christian ritual. Thus the pagan custom of celebrating the grape harvest on 15 August became the occasion for the emperor and the patriarch to leave the capital at the head of a procession to hold a harvest festival in some not too distant vineyard. On such occasions the legs and tail of the emperor's horse were bound in silk ribbons and its trappings were studded with jewels. Until the end of the tenth century, when the date of Christmas was fixed, it was customary to hold a public holiday in honour of the Sun God on 25 December. In the course of the festivities the emperor, impersonating the Sun God, performed a sort of traditional pantomime, appearing wearing a halo, originally the Sun God's emblem. Christ's birth had until then been celebrated on 6 January when, in one of the audience chambers of the Great Palace before an assembly of specially invited guests, the emperor invested newly appointed or promoted officials with their diplomas, badges of rank and carved ivory plaques similar to those known to us today as consular diptychs. The officials had prepared themselves for the event by fasting throughout the previous day; they received their diplomas from the emperor, kneeling before him. On such occasions the gentlemen of the bedchamber met the emperor's guests at the palace gates and conducted them to the audience chamber to await the emperor. When he entered the hall each guest was expected to greet him in the manner prescribed for persons of his rank, senators being accorded the privilege of kissing the emperor's right breast as he bent forward to kiss their heads, whilst men of lesser rank were obliged to fling themselves down on the floor and kiss the emperor's feet, with their arms outstretched—a posture known as the *proskynesis* and one which is still today imposed by certain religious orders on monks or nuns taking their vows.

The ceremony prescribed for ambassadorial audiences was very similar, but its opening stages began when the envoy and his staff reached the frontier of Byzantium—in the case of a Persian mission, at the Euphrates. There a reception committee bearing royal gifts assembled to greet the envoy. Similar ceremonies were repeated at every regional capital situated on the ambassador's route to Constantinople, the local governor presenting him with gifts the value of which varied in accordance with the ambassador's importance. On reaching Constantinople the diplomat and his staff were conducted to a house which had been prepared for their use. Daily fresh supplies of food would be provided whilst they waited as patiently as they could to hear when the emperor would consent to receive them. On the day chosen for the audience the gifts which the envoy had brought for the emperor from his own sovereign and those which he was himself to receive from the emperor were displayed in the palace for all to see. Meanwhile the imperial guard, wearing full-dress uniforms of gold helms and breastplates over white undergarments, would ride carrying their lances to the ambassador's residence, where the envoy and his suite,

17 Emperor in full regalia

dressed in their finest clothes, awaited them. The ambassador would mount the splendidly caparisoned horse which had been specially selected for his use from the emperor's stables and the whole group would set out for the palace along streets gaily decorated with carpets and hangings suspended in the envoy's honour from the windows and balconies of the houses lining his route. The spectacle was so superb that, on public holidays, the Venetians later decorated their streets in the same manner.

At the main entrance to the palace the ambassador was met by a senior official who conducted him, together with his interpreter and retinue, to the audience hall where the throne stood on a platform concealed from view by sumptuous hangings. At a given moment these were drawn apart to reveal the emperor seated, dressed in his state robes and wearing his crown. His clothes consisted of a long, close-fitting robe made of a sumptuous brocade, decorated round the neck and waist and down the centre of the back and front with jewelled and embroidered bands(*17*). The crowns varied slightly in shape according to date, but the superb eleventh-century crown of Monomachus preserved in Budapest is made of eight beautifully enamelled gold plaques. The shimmer created by his crown and jewels probably explains why an enthralled visitor compared the costume of Emperor Manuel Comnenus (1143–80) to 'a meadow covered in flowers'.

On perceiving the emperor all were expected to fall on their knees. When the majesty of the spectacle had made its full impression on those privileged to see it the ambassador was led towards the throne, but he was made to halt three times in his advance in order to kneel to the Basileus. On reaching the throne he handed his letter of credence to the Master of Ceremonies and greeted the emperor in the name of his own sovereign. The emperor replied by inquiring after the latter's health, in the case either of the king of Persia or of the caliph of Islam referring to him as his brother, but in that of a European ruler calling him his son. He then named the day on which the ambassador was to return to the palace to discuss affairs of state.

When an ambassador had completed his mission the emperor often gave a farewell banquet in his honour. The guests were seated in strict order of precedence. Though the tables used were what we would call T-shaped, the Byzantines—their lives centred on their Christian faith—described them as half cross-shaped. The top end —or cross-piece—formed the high table and was made of gold. The emperor sat at its centre, wearing a purple robe over a white tunic, with the empress on his left; the male guests and his equerries, all wearing sashes of honour, were ranged along the right side of that end of the table, the ladies along the left. Until quite a late date (the tenth century has been suggested by some authorities) all reclined on couches in the Roman manner, though when dining in private the imperial family appear to have used chairs from rather earlier times. A court official called a *silentarius* held a rod of office and stood behind the emperor throughout the banquet, whilst a lady-in-waiting holding a wand stood behind the empress. If the visiting ambassador represented a major power his place was set at the high table; if not, or if the emperor wished to affront him, he sat at the transversal section, where his suite and his interpreter

18   Emperor Theodosius with courtiers and guardsmen in the Imperial
box at the Hippodrome

were placed. In the tenth century Liutprand of Cremona, ambassador of the emperor of Germany, was so incensed at being
assigned to the lower end whilst the Bulgarian ambassador was
seated at the upper table that he failed to enjoy the music, miming
and dancing provided as entertainment for the diners.

When in residence in Constantinople or other large towns it was
the emperor's duty to preside at the circus games and chariot races
in the Hippodrome (*18*). Though pagan in origin, diversions of
this type were held at regular intervals throughout the greater part
of Byzantine history, taking place not only in Constantinople,
where a special meeting was held annually on 11 May to commemorate the founding of the city, but also in the provincial
hippodromes. The main features of these events were chariot races,
four horses being harnessed abreast to each chariot. In Constantinople it fell to the emperor to give the signal for the Games
to begin. He did so by dropping a white handkerchief called a
mappa. Four races were run during the morning and as many
again in the afternoon. The emperor gave a lunch party between
the two series; on the occasion of the Gothic Games he held it in
the Hall of the Nineteen Couches. At the end of each day's events
he awarded prizes to the final winners; these consisted of an
aurigarion (a gold emblem), a silver helmet and a belt. During the

intervals between the races the audience was entertained by mimes, dancers, acrobats and circus turns, many of who performed to the accompaniment of music played on organs and lutes. Distinguished visitors from Kievan Russia were so impressed by these entertainers that, in the eleventh century, the grand duke of Kiev had some of the scenes which had diverted them recorded on the walls of the staircase leading to his pew in the gallery of Kiev's cathedral of Haghia Sophia; many of these paintings survive as the only known pictorial representations of these entertainments (53).

As the sole fount of law and order, the emperor was necessarily a very busy man. His day was a long one. He was woken at six o'clock every morning by three knocks on his door. He rose and dressed himself unaided, dispensing with any semblance of the ceremony evolved later by Louis XIV of France and known as the *lever du roi*. He went straight from his bedroom to the Golden Hall to pray before an icon of the Saviour placed there in a special alcove. Then he seated himself on his golden throne to breakfast. When he had eaten he received his chamberlain and discussed the day's business with him. Then he received those ministers and officials who had business matters of importance to lay before him. All came to his presence wearing the elaborately and diversely embroidered robes to which their rank and functions entitled them. With the exception of the patriarch they all remained standing in the emperor's presence. When the day's business had been concluded the ministers withdrew, but the patriarch often stayed on to lunch with the emperor. Before entering the dining-room both men removed their robes of office; they resumed them at the end of the meal, the patriarch embracing the emperor before taking his departure.

The emperor was obliged to sign virtually every state document that was drawn up. To begin with these were written on parchment, but from the eleventh century a particular kind of paper called bombazine (because it was made in Baghdad) came into use. The emperor's name and titles were written at the top of each document in very large letters of a special script, the emperor signing his name at the foot of the page in purple ink. All writing material was placed in the charge of a special high-ranking official. He was expected to provide the purple ink at his own expense, but he was doubtless able to find ample compensation for this in the influence he was able to wield. Every document signed by the emperor was recorded in the Chancery's files. A special government department was responsible for translating those communications which were sent abroad. Copies of the translations were attached to copies of the original texts and filed with them. Special charters known as bulls were often written in gold; when headed with a picture of Christ and of the emperor wearing his robes of state and his crown they were known as *chrysobulls* or golden bulls.

Although the emperors were very busy men, and although Byzantine life (and more especially court life) was rigidly controlled by carefully defined regulations, it would be wrong to think of the rulers of Byzantium as mere puppets. They were all men of temperament and of marked individuality; many had wide interests and spent their leisure hours pursuing their personal tastes. Some were sociable and made a habit of inviting guests to dine in private with them and members of their families, readily accepting in return invitations to dine in the houses of their subjects. All lived a full family life pursued in privacy. Justinian spent as much time as possible with Theodora, whom he adored, but in order to do so he generally rose at dawn and went to bed very late, often even getting up during the night in order to read and study. He never ate meat nor drank wine. Nicephorus Phocas (963–9) and Basil II (976–1025) were also abstemious. Leo VI made a habit of walking the streets of Constantinople at night, alone and incognito, in order to see for himself whether the police were carrying out his order to imprison vagrants. One night, when dressed as a tramp, he was able to persuade two patrols to let him pass, but the third paid no attention to his pleadings and imprisoned him. In the morning he rewarded the last of these and severely reprimanded the first two. Leo was also fond of visiting monasteries unannounced and, on the spur of the moment, staying on to dine there. Michael IV (1034–41) lived in terror of revolution and used to ride through the streets of Constantinople at night to see whether people were gathering into groups, perhaps to conspire against him. Constantine VII Porphyrogenitus was keener on writing and illuminating books than on governing; Theodore Lascaris was a fine calligrapher and book illuminator. Practically all were patrons of art and passionate collectors of beautiful objects.

When an emperor died his body was laid out in the Hall of the Nineteen Couches, showing him wearing his crown, *divitission*, *chlamys* and purple slippers. The clergy who were attached to the cathedral of Haghia Sophia and the senators stood round him singing dirges. After crying three times, 'Depart Emperor: the King of Kings, Lord of Lords calls you', the body was removed to the Chalke by members of his bodyguard. From there it was taken along the Mese to its final resting place. Sometimes a church was chosen for the purpose, Romanus Lecapenus and his wife Theodora being buried in the church of the Mirelaion. On reaching the late sovereign's final resting place it fell to the master of ceremonies to step forward and again proclaim, 'Enter Emperor: the King of Kings, Lord of Lords calls you'; then he would cry 'Remove your crown'. At these words the crown of state was lifted from the dead man's brow and in its place a purple circlet was laid on it. Then the coffin was closed and the burial performed. A similar ritual was observed in the case of an empress.

3

THE CHURCH AND CHURCHMEN

Emperor Justinian wrote the preface to the collection of legal codes issued under the title of *The Sixth Novel*. In it he expressed the opinion that the 'greatest gifts which God in his love of mankind has given to men from above are the Priesthood and the Empire, for the one ministers to things divine whilst the other guides and takes care of human affairs'. This belief was shared by the Byzantine people, many of whom were in the habit of comparing the Empire and Church to the human body and its soul. Such an attitude naturally led every layman to take as passionate an interest in religion and the Church as did the emperor and his clergy. It is hardly surprising that this should have been the case in early Byzantine times, for the years which witnessed the establishment of Christianity were marked by an ever-increasing dissatisfaction with such older and, until recently, popular creeds as the sun cult, Mithraism, Zoroastrianism or veneration of the gods worshipped in Greece and Rome. Christianity presented a code of ethics which raised new hope in the most disenchanted hearts. Its affirmation of a single God as the ultimate source of all life appealed to those who had lost faith in the squabbling, malicious inhabitants of Olympus. The opportunities which Christianity offered to women opened the way to developments which were ultimately to affect every aspect of daily life. Furthermore, every convert believed that the fulfilment of the promise of a better life on earth and the salvation of his soul in the hereafter depended upon his ability to conform to every canon of the new faith. This conviction in its turn led him to attach immense importance to Christian dogma. The belief that a theological error might well jeopardise a Christian's chance of entering the celestial kingdom remained firmly embedded in the Byzantine mind throughout the Empire's history and, as a result, even during the final years of its existence, every practising Christian remained as profoundly concerned with Church affairs as were the earliest converts. Furthermore, the imperial constitution itself helped to tighten the bonds between Church and state, until each played an almost equal part in making the rules which governed the life of the people.

Christianity was essentially eastern in character, and for that reason found its earliest, most fervent supporters in Egypt, Syria and Asia Minor. The spiritual elements in the new creed evoked a spontaneous response from the inhabitants of those areas, their minds being far more closely attuned to it than were those of the somewhat cynical Greeks or the cold, logical Romans, both of whose outlook was clearly reflected in the cult of the gods of the classical age. Though Constantine remained a pagan he must have been aware of the existence of these contradictory elements, for soon after legalising Christianity, as early as the year 325, he convened a council of clerics at Nicaea. They met under his chairmanship to discuss matters of dogma, and more particularly what is known as the Arian Heresy, that is to say to decide whether God and Christ were of like nature or, as the Arians maintained, whether they differed in kind, since Christ, as God's son, came into being after God the Father.

Seven major religious assemblies were held between then and the ninth century. They came to be called General Councils of the Church(*19*). The Second Council, convened in 381, gave the patriarch the second place in the state, ranking him next after the emperor. The Third, meeting at Ephesus in 431, discussed the Nestorian sect whose members agreed with the opinion expressed by Nestorius of Antioch that Christ's human nature was more important than His divine. The Fourth Council met at Chalcedon in 451 to discuss the two natures of Christ, and as a result of the conclusions reached by that assembly the Egyptian Church broke away from the main Orthodox institution and became known as the Coptic. By the ninth century all the major doctrinal issues had been dealt with by the Church's General Councils. As a result, until about the middle of the eleventh century, so few clerics attended the meetings of the assembly that these lost their former international character. The first assembly of the Church's General Council was probably the most important of all since it established the procedure to be followed at future meetings. Constantine, as chairman, had taken the initiative then and had modelled the debates on the lines of those held in Rome's senate, retaining for himself the powers of a moderator. As a result the Byzantine

19   The Gospels on the Sacred Throne, Church Council session in the
Emperor's presence, Constantinople 362

emperors were able to exercise far greater influence over Church
affairs than were the rulers of any other Christian state. If an
emperor found it impossible personally to preside over one of the
Councils he was entitled to appoint anyone he wished to act as his
representative. In early times the pope and his legate had ranked as
next in importance to the emperor at these conventions, but
although the pope was entitled to vote before the emperor, it was
essential for the final communication issued by the General Council
to be signed by the emperor, not the pope. This naturally led
people to assume that the emperor was primarily responsible for all
doctrinal decisions as well as for combating heresies.

Byzantium never lacked heresies. Many were based on genuinely
mistaken interpretations of the scriptures. In early Christian times
pagan beliefs and observances were still so widely upheld that
there was as much need to stamp out any deviation from the
established doctrine as any form of idolatry. The Quini-Sectus
Council held in Trullo in 692 passed sweeping measures to that end;
though often revised and added to, they remained in force till the
twelfth century. They banned such pagan customs as, for example,

the Bacchic feasting at the time of the grape harvest or the celebration of May Day, yet the Church never succeeded in suppressing these ancient, essentially jovial and festive customs. Realising this, it quickly set out to absorb them into the Christian ritual by giving them a Christian basis, harvest festivals replacing the Bacchic rites whilst events in Christ's life were celebrated on days which had ranked as holidays in pagan times. This proved far easier than correcting false interpretations of the Gospels.

Doctrinal problems profoundly worried the Byzantines, and the Church quickly decided that anyone whose views differed from those which it had laid down was a heretic. The Arians were ranked as ungodly because they questioned the fullness of Christ's divinity. The even larger sect of Monophysites came under similar censure because its members believed in the existence of a single divinity, regarding the Father, Son and Holy Ghost as parts of the one entity and thereby, in the opinion of the Church, denying Christ's human attributes. Of other passionately propounded heresies two proved particularly difficult to dislodge. These were spread by members of the Paulician and Bogomil sects. The first

developed in the ninth century when a man called Paul, the son of a Manichaean woman, maintained that God (representing the three in one) created only the celestial sphere comprising heaven and its inhabitants, whereas the god of evil created men and the visible world; he maintained also that Christ was an angel and the son of an ordinary woman (whom it was wrong to venerate) and had been sent by God to combat evil on earth. The Bogomils were offshoots of the Paulicians; they gained a particularly large number of converts in Bulgaria and their curious tombstones survive there and in Yugoslavia as intriguing monuments of a now forgotten past (20).

Superstitions proved as difficult to stamp out as heresies. Beliefs in demons and evil spirits led many to support the Paulicians and to worship Satan, some going as far as to assert that he was

20   A Bogomil tombstone

God's eldest son. Six types of demons were believed to be especially dangerous; they inhabited the air, the ether, fire, and earth, and also lived underground; all required constant propitiation. The evil eye was dreaded to such an extent that belief in it still persists today in remote districts of the Near East, where amulets are worn —as they used to be in early Byzantine times—to counteract it. Witches and soothsayers were both feared and consulted. Even the library of the Great Palace contained a book illustrated with portraits of emperors which purported to foretell the Empire's future. As late as the eighth century Constantine V consulted his astrologers before attacking his enemies and so did Alexius I Comnenus in the eleventh century. As a result astrology was believed to be closely associated with magic; it was therefore strongly disapproved of by the Church even in the twelfth century when, though recognised by many men of learning as a science, it continued to be widely used for purposes of divination. The stigma which had been attached to it in earlier times persisted throughout the Byzantine period. In order to assist the faithful in avoiding all major sins the Church enforced stringent rules for church attendance, excommunicating those who failed to attend a service on three consecutive Sundays. On Sundays, as well as on all days falling between Easter and Pentecost, all had to pray standing, which suggests that the early Christian custom of standing to pray was no longer in force; the Russians applied this ordinance to all church attendance, and still abide by it today.

The emperor was assigned so important a part in Church affairs that in church his throne, sometimes a gold one, was placed beside the patriarch's and he was called upon to perform a number of special functions in many religious services. Thus, from a very early date he appeared in the Easter Day service swathed in white bandages and accompanied by 12 attendants; from the tenth century he censed the High Altar during the Christmas Day services; during Lent he headed the procession round the High Altar in the church of the Magnaura and he also carried out specific duties on Palm Sunday and Holy Thursday. Nevertheless, he was never able to impose his own views on the Church if these ran counter to those held by the clergy. The Church remained independent where matters of dogma were concerned and, even though it lived under the emperor's protection, it yet enjoyed powers equal to his. Even so the emperor was able, when investing the patriarch of Constantinople in his office as head of the Orthodox Church, to proclaim that: 'This man is appointed Patriarch of Constantinople by the Grace of God and by our Imperial Authority, which stems from the grace of God'. Nor could the patriarch excommunicate an emperor. In the eleventh century Patriarch Michael Cerularius attempted to make the Church more important than the Crown. He failed, yet his efforts enhanced the Church's prestige so that when the emperor's reputation and powers declined with the steady advance westward of the Ottoman Turks, those of the Church survived intact. At the Turkish Conquest of Constantinople the Church was still so strong that the patriarch was able to persuade the sultan to recognise his jurisdiction over all Orthodox Christians living in Ottoman lands, the Balkans not excepted, and to permit him to establish a school in the patriarchate in Constantinople where Byzantine theology could be taught and the Greek tongue spoken and written. The patriarchate in Constantinople thus came to play an invaluable role in keeping Christianity and Greek culture alive in Ottoman territory, even though no printing presses could be installed there. When printing was invented the books needed in the patriarchate had to be printed in Venice and shipped to Constantinople. Partly because of this, and partly too because many senior clerics fled from vanquished Constantinople to seek safety there, Venice also became an outpost of Orthodoxy.

The constitution of the Orthodox Church was worked out, at any rate in its essentials if not in detail, during the fourth and fifth centuries, but minor adjustments continued to be made throughout the Byzantine era. The decision to adopt the Julian calendar, devised in late Roman times, and to start the religious year with the civil year on 1 September, and to number the years from the supposed date of the world's creation some 5,000 years earlier, was made by the Church and not the emperor. The Church was also responsible for dividing its territory into provinces which were placed under the jurisdiction of metropolitans. Five patriarchs were created; three were established in the Empire's ancient cities of Rome, Antioch and Alexandria, two in the new cities of Constantinople and Jerusalem. Rome as the older capital was given precedence over all the others. Constantinople, in its role of the new capital, was ranked second, but in its capacity of the New Rome it was called upon to fulfil duties which had been performed by the Old Rome; it therefore became entitled to the same privileges and honours as those enjoyed by the latter. When, in the course of the seventh century, Alexandria and Antioch were captured by the Arabs and incorporated into the Muslim empire, their loss did much to add to the stature of the patriarch of Constantinople.

His position had already been considerably strengthened by Leo III's decision in 732 to transfer southern Italy, Greece and Illyria from the see of Rome to that of Constantinople. The change was bitterly resented by the pope. Ill-feeling between the leaders of the two churches increased as a result of the iconoclast controversy. This reached its height at the end of the eighth century when Charlemagne took advantage of the breach to persuade the pope to crown him 'Emperor of the West'. This move greatly angered the emperor of Byzantium, for it not only affronted his dignity as emperor, but it challenged the claim of the Orthodox Church to be accepted as the supreme authority. Relations deteriorated still further. They were gravely impaired in 1054 when the infuriated papal legate, Cardinal Humbertus, threw down the Bull of Anathema on the silver altar of the cathedral of Haghia Sophia and swept out in a rage. Manuel II (1143–80) tried, but failed, to effect a reconciliation. This marked the final rift between Orthodox Christianity in the East and Catholicism; it remains unhealed.

In 1204, on the eve of the Latin occupation of Constantinople, the emperor wanted to improve relations with western Christendom by an act of union with the Church of Rome. The move was fiercely opposed by the patriarch of Constantinople who was warmly supported by the Byzantine clergy and nation. The Latin conquest of the capital fanned the anger of the Orthodox. Nevertheless the emperor tried to mend matters at the council convened in Florence in 1439, when he attempted to obtain military aid from the western world with which to stem the ever-more threatening advance of the Ottoman Turks. Though the council deliberated till 1443, no aid was forthcoming; Europe's failure to fight Islam is still resented by the Orthodox Church. At the time it aroused such indignation throughout Byzantium that, when the victorious sultan advised Genadios (whom he had appointed patriarch of conquered Constantinople) to unite his Church to that of Rome, the Greek prelate stubbornly refused even to consider doing so.

In Byzantine times the patriarch of Constantinople lived in great state. He had a set of apartments within the cathedral of Haghia Sophia and in an adjoining building, and in addition had his own palace. He was in the habit of breakfasting in one of the former apartments after celebrating the morning service in the cathedral.

21 Prelate in bishop's robes presenting a model church to the Almighty

He often entertained the emperor there. He also possessed a series of offices and conference halls from which he administered the Church's affairs with the aid of an assembly of churchmen known as the Holy Synod. To begin with, only the bishops of Constantinople were entitled to serve on it, but when the Church's territory was divided into provinces called *metropoliae*, headed by metropolitans who subdivided these into bishoprics placed in the charge of bishops, both the metropolitans and the autocephalous (or self-governing) bishops were called upon to attend its meetings.

Metropolitans were nominated to their office by the patriarch who selected them from a list of three names submitted to him by the Holy Synod. The metropolitans appointed their bishops in a similar manner, choosing them from a short list of three drawn up by the local Synods. However, certain bishops were appointed direct by the emperor and were therefore not subjected to the metropolitan's jurisdiction. These autocephalous bishops wielded great influence in the Holy Synod.

To be eligible for a bishopric a priest had to be aged over 35 and able to recite the Psalter by heart; it was also necessary for him to be well educated. In early times a married man was considered eligible for high office provided that his wife had left him to live as a nun in a convent, but before long only monks were regarded as fitted to serve as bishops, metropolitans or—the highest office of all—as patriarch. The distinction which was then drawn between the Black Clergy (that is to say, those who had taken their vows) and the White or parish priests (who were permitted to marry) survives to this day in Orthodox communities throughout the world.

If the Great Palace was the heart of the Empire, containing as it did within its walls the emperor, his family and some of the nation's most sacred religious relics (such as Moses's staff), then the cathedral of Haghia Sophia can be described as its arteries and life-blood. If few of the poor could use the cathedral as their regular place of worship, none could penetrate within the palace enclosure. The cathedral was scarcely less effective than the emperor and patriarch in animating the faith which, to the end, was the mainspring of Byzantium's existence. This was not entirely due to the unparalleled splendour of the building's interior, though its great dome did create a visual image of heaven, and its rich furnishings and decorations did mirror an almost celestial majesty; nor was it wholly owing to the beauty of the liturgy performed by priests dressed in their sumptuous vestments. More important were the numerous relics which had been assembled there over the years, even though the holiest of all these, the Virgin's robe and girdle had, at Justinian's order, been moved from the church of SS Peter and Paul to that of St Mary of the Blachernae. When the Latins occupied Constantinople they did not hesitate to take most of Haghia Sophia's relics as well as the Virgin's robe and girdle, even though the latter had come to be regarded as the capital's *palladium* or guardian power, serving to protect Constantinople in the same way as the wooden image of Pallas had ensured the safety of ancient Troy. As such both relics were carried round the walls of Constantinople whenever the city was threatened by invaders. The Byzantines never forgave the Latins for these thefts, which included a number of their finest reliquaries. Among the most prized of these were those in the form of tiny churches. The cathedral's other treasured relics consisted of a number of miracle-working icons; perhaps the most valued of these was the Sacred Mandelion, the 'Christ not painted by human hands' of Abgar's legend, which had been captured by Emperor Romanus Lecapenus in Edessa in 944 and brought back to the capital in triumph. A huge crowd had lined the Mese to watch its ceremonial entry into Constantinople. Many a humble worshipper poured out his heart before the icon when it had been installed in a place of honour in Haghia Sophia. But, as the mother church of Orthodoxy, the cathedral also opened its arms to the saints of younger Orthodox states, in the case of Russia displaying an icon of the saintly brothers Boris and Gleb for her pilgrims to worship.

By the year 612, 80 priests, 150 deacons, 40 deaconesses. 70

sub-deacons, 150 readers, 25 cantors or singers and 65 door keepers were attached to the cathedral of Haghia Sophia in addition to the patriarch and his deputy, the Syneculla, as well as a large number of cleaners. At the time the royal keeper of documents, the Great Chartophylax, still acted as the cathedral's librarian. Soon, however, the size of the archives made such demands on his time that he was unable to combine both duties. Relinquishing his responsibilities at court he became full-time librarian to the cathedral and secretary-in-chief to the patriarch. His new duties entitled him to stand near the royal doors of the *iconostasis* at the start of the communion service held during a pontifical mass.

Justinian installed a very ornate altar in Haghia Sophia and as a result elaborate and costly altars soon became popular. The finest to survive is the twelfth-to-fourteenth-century example known as the Pala D'Oro on account of the mass of jewelled and cloisonné

22   A detail of the Pala d'Oro

enamel decorations which adorn its gold ground; it was especially made for the cathedral of St Mark in Venice, where it is still to be seen(*22*). It was probably also Justinian who evolved the earliest form of the *iconostasis*, once again for use in Haghia Sophia. His version was very different in appearance from the *iconostasis* which we have come to associate with Orthodox churches. Prior to Justinian the *iconostasis* was little more than a barrier of carved marble, stone or wooden panels set between pillars to separate the altar from the body of the church. It is thought that Justinian placed medallions of the Saviour with St John on His left and the Virgin on His right on the cross-piece connecting the central pillars, above the royal doors, as they are called, which open on to the altar. In about the fourteenth century this idea was elaborated, almost certainly in some densely wooded region such as Mount Athos or northern Russia, the partition being transformed into a screen which separated the altar from the rest of the church, and formed a frame for icons which were to be arranged in it according to a carefully prescribed order.

Amongst Greeks the word *icon* means image in the sense of a portrait, but it has come to be used throughout the world to describe any form of pictorial rendering of either a scene or personages associated with the story of the Gospels, though more especially to describe the wooden panel paintings of a religious character made for the use of members of the Orthodox Church. These panel paintings were first produced in very early Christian times. When the faith was made legal their popularity grew and churches soon became filled with them; icons of especially venerated personages were placed in chapels dedicated to them or else set up on a sort of lectern which had first been covered by a richly embroidered textile or precious fabric. Icons of the month were always displayed in that manner, the lectern bearing them being placed close to the altar. Icons were also widely used in private houses, being set up in the corner of a room, above a bed or in a private chapel. The faithful prayed to the saint whose figure was represented on the panel—often his patron saint—in the hope that he would intercede on his behalf in heaven with the Almighty. The icon acted as a go-between, and certain icons came to be credited with miraculous powers. Like many another emperor, Romanus III (1028–34) carried a miraculous icon of the Virgin with him when campaigning, in the hope that Christ's mother would guide and protect his troops.

Though the Church had always striven to emphasise that icons were nothing more than pictorial representations of holy personages, the illiterate members of the congregation often came to confuse the painted figures with the real characters. The veneration with which they treated the pictures gave rise to fears of a revival of idolatry. No doubt influenced to some extent by both the Jewish and Muslim disapproval of all forms of figural representations in religious art, those who most feared the revival of idolatry urged the abolition of icons and the use of Christian symbols in their place. These people were known as iconoclasts. By the year 726 they formed so strong a party as to arouse fierce opposition. The country became divided on the issue—the emperor supporting the iconoclasts, many leading clerics opposing them. The ban which the emperor succeeded in imposing on all forms of figural representations in religious art was especially resented by St John of Damascus, a leading cleric of the day who lived in Muslim-occupied territory. His views were shared somewhat later by St Theodore, abbot of the Studite monastery in Constantinople. Both continued to uphold the use of icons. In the long run the iconodules, as the supporters of icons were called, proved the stronger party and in 843 Michael III (nicknamed the Drunkard) was obliged to legalise religious figural art. Icons could once again be used on condition that 'the distinction between the worship due to God and the veneration due to created things were carefully observed'. The lifting of the ban represented a distinct victory for the Church, adding considerably to its influence and prestige.

Regardless of the fears of those who supported the iconoclasts, belief in the value of relics and in miracles remained as strong in late Byzantine times as it had been during earlier periods, when these sentiments could have been attributed to the influence of pagan practices. From its foundation to its fall relics were passionately venerated in Constantinople. In many cases a church's relics were kept in a separate structure called a *martyrion*. It often adjoined the church and special services were held in it on the relevant saint's day. From the fifth century onwards it also became customary to dedicate a church to a particular martyr or group of martyrs; Justinian set the example when he built perhaps the loveliest of all Constantinople's early churches and dedicated it to the two martyred saints, Sergius and Bacchus. At much the same time Justinian introduced at Haghia Sophia the practice, which came to be widely followed, of building a baptistery as an annexe to a church.

23   Interior of the cathedral of Hagia Sophia (532–7)
From a photograph taken when it was used as a mosque

24 The monastery of St. Dionysiou on Mount Athos seen from the sea

Most of the laws which the Church had evolved were collected in a work entitled the *Nomocanon*, in 14 sections. It dealt with problems ranging from questions of a purely religious character to those concerning the administration of Church property; 85 supplementary clauses dealt with matter of dogma and a final section contained the secular laws applied by the Church. The entire code was based on a collection of laws which had been assembled in book form in the sixth century by John Scollasticus of Antioch, but which had been revised and augmented soon after by a patriarch of Constantinople.

In addition to disseminating the true faith, combating false doctrines with unflagging energy, administering its property and, on certain specific occasions, administering the Christian idea of justice, the Church's main duty, at any rate in so far as laymen were concerned, lay in its ability to justify the promise which it held out of a better way of life for all the faithful both in this world and in the next. It was this promise which entitled the Church to share in every aspect of daily life, and it was the extent to which it succeeded in improving the lot of the underprivileged, whether they were women, the old and ailing or the poor, which gave support to its assurance of celestial bliss. It was also this promise which led the Byzantines to attach more importance throughout their history to the salvation of their souls than to physical or material well-being, an outlook which coloured their attitude to life and dictated their behaviour, making them look to the Church in all things. The Church took advantage of this to participate fully in their lives, baptising them in a baptistery or a church, confirming them, often in a special hall adjoining a baptistery, marrying them in a great cathedral, parish church or private chapel, administering extreme unction to them as they lay dying and burying the departed in a public cemetery or private mausoleum. In addition, the Church blessed the houses in which the faithful lived as well as their cattle and fields; it held harvest festivals for farmers, it blessed the fishing fleets as they set sail, and performed similar ceremonies at the river heads where supplies of food and water were taken. In this way, the Church ruled over the people's thoughts and imaginations, and served throughout the centuries as the pivot of their lives.

Because of the abject poverty in the towns the dispensing of charity quickly became one of the Church's chief functions. Even so, poverty remained so acute that when, in the seventh century, Patriarch John of Alexandria was persuaded by a rich landowner to accept the gift of an expensive quilt the prelate spent a sleepless night asking himself as he lay cosily wrapped in it, 'How many are there at this minute who are grinding their teeth because of the cold?' As soon as dawn broke he rose and went to the market to sell his quilt. He had little difficulty in doing so; with the money he bought 144 blankets which he had distributed by nightfall among the city's numerous down-and-outs.

The Church founded, staffed and ran orphanages, poor houses, homes for the aged, dispensaries and hospitals. Its example was followed by the emperors, members of their family and their courtiers. Michael IV (1034–41) was not content with establishing a hospice for beggars but he also built a large, admirably appointed and furnished home for prostitutes. When it was ready, in an attempt to save their souls, he made it known that all those who wished to give up prostitution but dreaded poverty and discomfort could, by becoming nuns, reside in luxury and never suffer want in the house he had built for them. A surprisingly large number availed themselves of the offer. Early in the twelfth century—perhaps modelling himself to some extent on the example set by the Seljukid conquerors of Anatolia—John II Comnenus (1118–43) founded in Constantinople an institution which embodied all the most up-to-date ideas on state aid and medicine. It consisted of two hospitals, one reserved for men and the other for women; each contained 10 wards, each of 50 beds. In either case one ward was reserved for surgical cases and one for those in need of long-term nursing. The staff consisted of 12 male doctors and one fully qualified woman as well as a woman surgeon. Each of the male doctors was given 12 qualified assistants and eight helpers, but the woman doctors were entitled to only four qualified assistants and two helpers. Two pathologists were also attached to the medical staff and a dispensary treated out-patients. Vegetarian meals were available for those of the inmates who desired them and a school was attached to the hospital in which the sons of all members of its medical staff were trained as doctors. In addition the foundation included a home for old men, another for epileptics and one for illegitimate and orphaned children. Two churches built in its grounds cared for the spiritual welfare of staff and residents alike.

The emperors, their families, their courtiers and the people as a whole expressed their devotion to the Church by showering gifts upon it. These often took the form of icons, precious vessels, fine copies of the Gospels, church furnishings and vestments, but they were often gifts or bequests of money or land. As a result the Church soon became very rich, acquiring vast estates and objects of great value as well as of real beauty. The Church generally found it most rewarding to entrust much of the land to the care of stewards or bailiffs, but occasionally an emperor would intervene and allot a church property to a layman to farm. The latter then became entitled to retain for himself, as a reward for administering the estate, part of the income it produced. From the eleventh century the Church made it a rule for all those who cultivated land belonging to the Church to pay their bishops a special tax known as the *canonicum*, furnishing part of it in kind and part in money. Although the tax helped to increase the Church's already considerable wealth, the bulk of the country clergy failed to benefit from it; whether they were parish priests or chaplains to rich landlords, the majority remained abjectly poor; many were obliged to work in the fields beside the poorest of their parishioners for a living. Those service rich absentee landlords in the capacity of chaplains were even worse off than the village priests, for their master, or (as was more often the case) group of masters, regarded them as tied to the chapels in which they officiated and therefore expected them, not unlike serfs, to continue in office even when the chapel had become the property of a new owner following upon the sale of the estate to which it was attached.

Till the sixth century the difference between a rich and a poor parish church was clearly reflected in the clothes of the officiating priests, for there was nothing until that date to distinguish the clothes worn by laymen and clerics; every individual dressed according to his station and his means. However, in the sixth century, civilian dress started to evolve, the Roman toga ceding its place to garments of a different style. The clergy refused to follow the newest trends and as a result the clothes they wore altered very slowly, only gradually developing into the robes which came to be accepted as ecclesiastic. The evolution took several decades. Thus, in the sixth-century mosaics at Ravenna, the priests shown standing close to the Emperor Justinian are represented dressed in plain white garments not so very different from a toga. After that date the rather severe clerical robes were worn with certain distinctive features. The *omophorion*, a sort of scarf embroidered with crosses (25) became part of a bishop's costume. It was soon combined with a silk *sticharion* or main tunic, comparable to the albe of the western world, and a stole as well as with a rectangular

25 Priest wearing an *omophorion*

shaped piece of stuff, originally a handkerchief, called an *epigonation*, worn at knee height. A bishop also carried a crozier and wore a round mitre. Suspended round his neck he displayed a reliquary, known as an *encolpion*, which reached to his chest. Deacons wore a distinctive type of scarf; called an *orarion*, it took the form of a single panel falling along the wearer's left side. Bishops wore the *epitrakilion* which is best described as a stole held in at the waist by a belt, as well as long embroidered cuffs—*epimanikia*—and a chasuble. To begin with, only patriarchs were entitled to substitute the *sakkos*—a short tunic slit up the side and remarkable for its ornate sleeves—for a chasuble, but gradually metropolitans, and later still priests, were permitted to do likewise.

The splendour of Church vestments reached their height in the tenth century. Then the silk brocade or velvet robes worn by the officiating clergy were enhanced by trimmings often consisting of inset jewels and cloisonné enamels, as well as of embroidery executed in gold and silver thread, and shimmering many-coloured silks. Equally magnificent altar cloths, icon adornments and Gospel covers glowed in the light of innumerable candles, set in gold, silver, copper or bronze candlesticks. Some of these stood on altars; others, often of vast sizes, with their bases shaped like great balls or lion claws, were placed in the body of the church, whilst bronze rings of varying sizes were suspended from the ceilings by chains to serve as candelabra. Yet the altar remained the focus of all eyes for it glistened with an array of crosses, chalices, patens and spoons, all exquisitely fashioned. Metal fans used for brushing flies off the relics and for fanning the incense, and censers in a variety of shapes and sizes also contributed to the splendour of the church interiors.

But in spite of all this magnificence, and the numerous duties and tasks allotted to the clergy, the most ardent amongst them failed to find ultimate satisfaction in serving their Church as priests. In a society where both laymen and priests based their existence wholly on Christianity every action came to be judged from a religious standpoint. Every individual strove to avoid committing a heresy in order to qualify for admission to paradise, while more and more people tended to concentrate their thoughts on the fate in store for their souls in the world beyond the grave. In their eyes it became more important to ensure the salvation of their own souls, and, by their example, that of others than to improve the earthly existence of their fellow-men. People who thought along these lines often came to believe that their prime duty did not consist so much in exerting themselves on behalf of others as in ridding themselves of evil by mortifying their flesh.

This attitude was not a wholly new one. It was the logical result of the inability, following upon the legalising of Christianity, to secure salvation by dying the death of a Christian martyr. Asceticism provided the only possible alternative to martyrdom, self-inflicted pain testing the spirit no less efficiently than imposed tortures. The concept of monasticism was already widespread in the Buddhist communities of Central Asia at the time when the Christian doctrine was first preached in the Holy Land; numerous Buddhist monasteries by that time numbered thousands of inmates. Their reputation had been carried westward by the traders engaged in transporting the precious bales of highly coveted silks along the caravan routes linking China to Europe, but the early Christians added a new element of stark asceticism to the discipline evolved by the Buddhist monks.

The conception of a Christian ascetic's way of life is essentially eastern, having originated in Egypt, probably some time in the third century. The fashion spread thence to Syria; ardent Christians retreated to the Egyptian desert in ever-growing numbers to live there as hermits, mortifying their bodies and curbing their natural appetites in an effort to emulate the saints in order, like them, to save their souls from perdition. They found encouragement in such pronouncements as St Simeon's, that 'saints shine on earth and become saints in heaven' or John of Enchaita's, who taught that 'saints have the power of supplying what is lacking in life'.

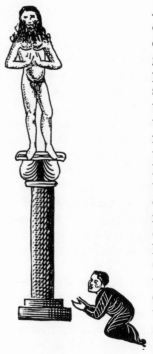

26   Stylite with disciple

Anchorites withdrawing from the world of their fellow-men to live in caves or, as dendrites, in trees, fed off berries and grasses and spent their waking hours in prayer. Many tortured their bodies by self-inflicted wounds till the hallucinations they induced put their souls to tests as severe as those which they inflicted upon their flesh. Then, in about the year 384, a fervent Christian who had already tried his spirit by spending three years living the life of a solitary, devised an even more taxing penance for himself. He decided to spend the rest of his life standing on a column which he set up on the borders of Syria and Cilicia. Simeon thus became the first of the 'Stylites', as the dwellers on columns came to be known (26). Many men of unquenchable faith followed his example, but the stylite Daniel became the best known, for he ascended a column in Constantinople, mounting it at the age of 33 and remaining on it till his death in 493 at the age of 83. He was a follower of Simeon, and had his own disciples, interrupting his devotions twice a day to counsel and comfort them.

Stylites spent their lives standing on columns some 40 cubits high and enclosed at the top by a rail to preserve them from falling when asleep. Never sitting or kneeling, they remained there never attending to their bodies, never indeed eating till a breeze, a passing bird, a traveller or disciple brought them a few berries or nuts, never cooked food. They endured the extremities of heat and cold, sometimes blinded by the sun, at other times covered by a coating of ice; in an age when cleanliness made no claim to godliness, such men as these lived in evil-smelling filth. At his death Daniel's feet were worn away by the inflammation resulting from constant standing and by the microbes which fed on his wounds; his matted hair was alive with lice which he refrained from killing in order that they might serve as food for the passing birds. In contrast to solitaries, who made no effort to clothe themselves

(St Onouphrios achieved holiness by growing a beard reaching to his ankles to cover his nakedness) some stylites wore a leather jerkin to conceal the upper part of their bodies. Daniel's column was set into a platform which was reached by three steps; according to custom a ladder was put there to enable his senior disciple to hand him each evening his only meal of the day.

In early Christian times lives spent in solitude, prayer and mortification were not exceptional. The acts of piety which ascetics performed became bywords in Byzantium and, in an effort to distinguish the true from the fabled, Emperor Justinian sent an observer called Palladius to Egypt, Palestine and Syria to examine the veracity of such accounts. Palladius conducted his inquiries with the meticulous care of a modern investigator, painstakingly reporting all he could learn about the experiences of solitaries, describing the hallucinations, temptations and sufferings which these half-starved, tormented creatures had endured, in each case noting whether the information had come to him at second hand or from the lips of a hermit whom he had himself interviewed.

The hermits and solitaries who survived their self-imposed ordeals for any length of time attracted the attention of others who, in their longing to become eligible for entry into paradise, gradually settled beside them as their disciples, little by little forming monastic communities. St Anthony, if not the first, was assuredly the most influential of the early monks. However, the foundation of the first Christian monastery is attributed to a soldier called Pachomius, who became converted to Christianity and founded a monastery at Dendereh on the Nile during the opening years of the fourth century. By the end of his life, when monks were accepted as 'the friends of God, whose lives and prayers carry special graces', his foundation consisted of 11 houses, two of which were reserved for women. He was later sanctified. Nevertheless it was the monastery which Basil of Caesarea founded in the fourth century that came to serve as the model for such famous later foundations as the Studite monastery in Constantinople, St Catherine's monastery on Mount Sinai, others in Cappadocia and many more on Mount Athos and elsewhere throughout the Orthodox world. (At Saccoudion on Mount Olympus a particularly severe penitential code was drawn up, which—as on Mount Athos—forbade females to enter the monastery.)

With the establishment of monasteries the number of hermits rapidly declined, for abbots permitted only the most holy of their monks to live the life of solitaries. Instead, from as early as the fourth century, the system of *laurae*, meaning small groups of cells attached to a larger monastery, was developed in Palestine, and spread later to the rest of the Orthodox world. The earlier monasteries had been cenobitic foundations. In these an abbot ruled over monks who were not allowed any possessions; everything within the monastery was communally owned, and clean clothes were issued to all once a week from the monastery's store. Food was communally cooked and eaten together in silence whilst one of the brethren read the Gospels aloud. A prayer was said at the start of the meal and another at the end. The senior monks were seated at the top end of the hall or *trapeza*, which was often rounded in shape to resemble the apse of a church, the others placing themselves at long tables, often built into the ground and made of stone or marble. The monks were divided into groups, according to their sanctity, the holiest fasting more stringently than the others, consuming only one meal a day, the evening one; this consisted of nothing cooked, but bread soaked for a week in water (not even oil), was their customary fare (though beans were allowed on the Church's great festivals). Cenobitic monks were permitted only three baths a year unless their health made it necessary for them to have more. Their abbots could, dependent upon the monastery's foundation charter, be appointed either by the founder of the institution, its bishop or its patriarch, or be elected by the brethren, in each case holding the appointment for life. Gradually, however, monasteries of a slightly different type came into existence, partly, it is thought, as a result of a monastery's poverty, partly too because the monks came to feel that the communal tasks allotted to them in a cenobitic foundation interfered with their devotions. These houses came to be known as 'idiorhythmic' or self-governing ones. Their inmates did not lead a communal life and were ruled by an elected committee in place of an abbot. The monks were permitted to retain some private possessions. They lived in small communities headed by a superior. As in the cenobitic foundations a junior monk was attached to a senior, the connexion lasting till severed by death. Each was allowed two cells, one to serve as a bedroom and the other as a living-room; a senior monk's attendant, whether a novice or junior monk, cooked his master's food in the outer cell. The food consisted of vegetables and oil issued from the monastery's store two or three times a week. Each monk ate his meals in solitude, except on Christmas Day, Easter Sunday or the anniversary of the monastery's saint's day when the monks assembled in the dining hall; on these feast days they also celebrated mass together, but on all other days they performed their devotions in private.

All those who wished to enter a monastery, whether they were men or women, had to undergo severe vocational tests before being admitted. Special regulations governed the acceptance of slaves, who could not be enticed away from their masters. Furthermore, runaway slaves had to be restored to their owners if traced within three years of their escape. Nor could anyone who had become engaged to marry contract out of the engagement in order to enter a religious order. Girls could enter a convent at the age of 10, but they were not allowed finally to renounce the world till they were 16 years old. Monks required only six months' novitiate before taking their final vows, yet it was almost impossible for them to transfer from one monastery to another. Until the sixth century they could be employed as civil servants on condition that they returned to their respective monasteries at the end of each day. Monasteries had only one gate, the sole key being entrusted to an elder who acted as porter.

Those living in monasteries had certain specific duties allotted to them either within the monastery's buildings or its grounds. Nevertheless, their time was largely devoted to prayer and meditation, with a minimum of sleep or food. Their lives were regulated

27   Abbess and nuns of the Convent of the Virgin in the Protovestiary, Constantinople

by lengthy services which all the monks were obliged to attend. These were held in the monastery's cathedral church. The first started at midnight to mark the approach of a new day, and ended at dawn, when the celebration which followed coincided with the unlocking of the entrance gate, to enable the local population to attend. A meal, often the only one, followed. Sometimes services were also held at prime, tierce and nones, but it was more usual to dispense with these in favour of an afternoon one starting at four o'clock and lasting till seven, while on the eve of a festival prayers began at dusk and continued until midday. The discipline or rule which came to be accepted as the basis of monastic life had been imposed verbally in the fourth century by St Basil the Great, bishop of Caesarea. Though he prescribed poverty and the dispensing of charity, the rapid spread of monasticism and the acquisition by many monasteries of vast estates brought great wealth to many foundations. From the seventh century imperial and private gifts of land were often of immense value; by the eighth century, half the population of Byzantium is believed to have taken vows— a development which served in its turn to increase the size of the Church's landed and monetary holdings.

Though some monasteries were founded by emperors and many more by patriarchal decree, private individuals could establish monasteries with the consent of their local bishop. Many in fact did so, withdrawing late in life to the monastery they had founded in order to end their days in it as monks. Though monks were buried at death their bodies were exhumed after three years; by then, except in the case of saints, their bones would be bare of flesh. Wine was poured over the clean bones and a funeral service held after which all the bones with the exception of the skull were re-buried in the monastery's communal grave. The dead man's name, together with the dates of his birth and death, would be inscribed on the skull which would then be placed on a shelf in the monastery's mortuary, to remain there for all time beside the skulls of his brethren.

Many abuses inevitably accompanied the rapid growth of monasticism. Though far from universal these were sufficiently serious in the ninth century to arouse the concern of St Theodore of Studion. This energetic cleric and ardent reformer attempted to end the laxity which reigned in certain monasteries by reviving St Basil's rule and adding to it new regulations of his own. Under his direction the monastery of Studios in Constantinople became a leading centre of learning and reform, and young monks were trained there in a school of high academic standards run on strict religious lines. Nevertheless, monasteries continued to acquire ever more land and to attract so many inmates as to endanger the existence of the state. In an attempt to check their growth Emperor Nicephorus Phocas passed a law in 963 limiting the size of monastic land-holdings and forbidding the acceptance of further monetary gifts and the creation of new monasteries. This law proved impossible to enforce, more especially since the government itself encouraged monks to settle along the Empire's frontiers, to act there as outposts both of Christianity and of defence. As a result the old abuses persisted uncurbed. Yet even when at their worst the monasteries proved to be valuable centres of enlightenment; at best they became strongholds of the Christian virtues and centres of learning and the arts.

The overthrow of the iconoclasts greatly stimulated the literary and artistic creativeness of the monks. A revived interest in Plato, though strongly disapproved of by the senior clergy, encouraged the development of a mystical philosophy which may well have had an effect upon the thought of such twelfth-century western mystics and reformers as Bernard of Clairvaux. The most far-reaching influence on Orthodox thought, learning and monasticism was, however, established by the cleric Alexius when, in the year 963, he founded the first monastery on Mount Athos, the Lavra. Alexius was a friend of Emperor Nicephorus Phocas and took this step with his full approval.

The founding of the Lavra was to bring prosperity and undying fame to the peninsula. Furthermore, because of the friendship of Alexius and the emperor the entire peninsula was placed under imperial patronage, and the appointment of the *protos* or head of Mount Athos rested with the emperor till the year 1312, when, by means of a chrysobull, Andronicus II transferred the peninsula from the Crown's jurisdiction

28   The dish of Paternus AD 518

to that of the patriarchate. Although its earlier link with the Crown had given Athos's religious community autonomy, its transfer to the Church was probably responsible for ensuring its independence under the Turks, enabling the monks to continue to live, as they do today, according to the exact rule imposed upon them by the founder of the Lavra 1,000 years ago. The close relationship which existed between the monks of Mount Athos and the Constantinopolitan court during the first 400 years of the community's existence was not at all unusual at the time. Another notable example is afforded by the monastery of St John on the island of Patmos. It too was founded under royal patronage in the twelfth century by the monk Christodoulos, its first abbot and a close friend of Emperor Alexius Comnenus. The charters which confirmed the privileges to which an imperial foundation was entitled took the form of chrysobulls. Written on a large sheet of parchment by a skilled calligrapher, they were generally embellished with illuminated headings and capital letters and carried the seal as well as the signature of the monastery's imperial founder.

Mount Athos was at the height of its prosperity from the ninth to the thirteenth century. Inspired by the example set by the Lavra, by the beauty of the peninsula and by their faith in the monastic way of life, the monks had by then built there complexes of astonishing loveliness. These were perched on 123 of the mountain's precarious ledges. In addition to these monastic enclaves groups of hermits, living under a superior in lavras and hermitages established on its wooden slopes, raised the population to some 8,000. Under the direction of its abbot each monastery flourished as an independent, highly complex community with its individual economy; thus each was responsible for its own finances, each cultivated its own land, each provided all the food and drink needed by its inmates even to the extent of furnishing travellers, pilgrims or those taking a retreat on the Holy Mountain with at least three day's free hospitality. In addition, each monastery had its own library and librarians; its treasury and *scriptorium*, where the liturgical books it needed were written, illuminated and bound; its artistic workshops and studios; craftsmen, builders, herdsmen, gardeners and farmers. Each monastery ran its own dispensary and orphanage together with its school, and also provided its own choir. Clothing was communally owned, a weekly change of garments being issued to each man. But, from the twelfth century, the religious community as a whole was governed by an assembly, a

Holy Synod; later a community or *kinotis* evolved, with an *epistasia* forming the smallest, inner governing body.

The Holy Mountain was dedicate by its monastic inhabitants to the Virgin. In her honour, the Lavra's founder decided to forbid any female creature, whether human or animal, from setting foot on the peninsula. Since that day time has stood still on Athos; life there has continued to evolve along the lines prescribed by the Lavra's founder and although the number of monks has fallen today to a mere handful they continue closely to adhere to the routine prescribed by Alexius. The Holy Trinity are still worshipped and the Virgin venerated there exactly as they were over 1,000 years ago.

Until the Fourth Crusade inflicted an irreparable blow to the greatness of the Empire the Byzantine Church was not intolerant in its attitude to people of different faiths. Jews were able to practise their religion and, though obliged to reside in a special district of Constantinople, they enjoyed full civil rights. Muslims were permitted similar freedom. The first mosque to be built in Constantinople was completed in 717. The second was constructed by John II Comnenus (1183–43) to mark his alliance with Mesud, sultan of Seljukid Anatolia. At Saladin's request another mosque was built for the Sunnite Muslims in 1189 by Emperor Isaac II Angelus, at the very time when Byzantine missionaries in Islamic territories were trying to convert Muslims to Christianity.

4

THE ADMINISTRATION
AND ITS OFFICIALS

The emperor was, as we have seen, the ultimate authority, source and essence of all law, the fountain-head of the administration, the leader and protector of his people. This explains why so many emperors, notably Theodosius, Heraclius and Maurice in earlier times, and certain later ones such as Alexius I Comnenus, disregarded the wishes of their ministers and insisted on leading their armies into battle. None of the emperors was a mere figurehead, for each played a vital part in the day-to-day running of the country, and it was precisely for this reason that the Byzantine administration remained a highly centralised one, certainly until the Latin conquest of Constantinople. Even during the final phase of the Empire's history most government departments and the senior officials working in them received their orders direct from the emperor.

During the first three centuries of the Empire, whilst the administrative machine was still in the process of formation, the emperor had to devote much of his time to government, employing to assist him men who were courtiers rather than administrators. Titles were not hereditary in Byzantium, but every courtier and official was invested with the one which corresponded to his class or office. In each case his title carried a specific rank and position in the order of precedence. Courtiers, known as *comes*, who had no administrative duties to perform, formed a class of patricians which was divided into three sections. Those belonging to the first of these ranked next in importance to the consuls. Top-ranking officials were known as *magistri*. By the ninth century there were 18 ranks, but the three highest, carrying the titles of *caesar*, *nobilissimus* and *curopalate* were reserved for members of the imperial family, and another, the *zoste patricia*, for court ladies entitled to wear the girdle as an insignia.

To begin with the senior court officials acted also as chief administrators. Thus, the lord chancellor or *praepositus sacri cubiculi*, as he was first called, though when his office became less important he became known as the *parakoimomenos* ('he who sleeps near his sovereign'), was not only responsible for the smooth functioning of the court, but also wielded considerable influence in the administrative sphere. In later times his position, like that of the *protovestiarius*, or master of the wardrobe, was generally filled by a eunuch. On the other hand, the *papias*, or administrative head of each palace, seldom wielded political power.

29   The High Admiral Apocauchus

The *magister officiorum* or master of offices, as the head of the Imperial Chanceries was called, was, at any rate till the Arabs conquered large areas of Byzantine territory, the most powerful man both at court and in the administration. It fell to him to select the men who were to administer the Empire's affairs by serving in the capital's government departments. As head of the nation's establishment he was responsible for the efficient working of the administrative machine. Since he also fulfilled the duties of master of ceremonies and was answerable for the emperor's safety he was given authority over the imperial bodyguard. He was accountable for his actions only to the sovereign and took orders from no one but the emperor. It was inevitable that his great independence often laid him open to temptations. Many a holder of that exalted office succumbed at times to bribery. More serious was the creation for his use of a corps of informers or spies. The need for them was to some extent justified. It made itself felt only gradually, arising from the master of ceremonies' duties as foreign secretary. As such it fell to him to negotiate with foreign envoys on the emperor's behalf and to carry out certain tasks in outlying districts, such as making arrangements for embassies to be met at the Empire's frontiers. To do so he used couriers. From the fifth century this gave him responsibility for the postal service, and to help him run that efficiently he had to have his own corps of messengers. As his duties multiplied he took to using the more trustworthy among them to report to him about officials who, regardless of rank, served as administrators of the Empire's far-flung territories. Inevitably these messengers came to form the nucleus of a body of informers which, by the end of the fifth century, already numbered some 1,200 experienced men, the number of officials employed in the Eastern regions being something like 10,000. The master of offices also found his informers indispensable in helping him to ensure the emperor's safety. When the occupant of the throne was popular and respected the task was not unduly difficult, but in unsettled times such as the eighth century when no fewer than eight emperors were deposed in the space of 21 years, the duty of guarding the sovereign often demanded the utmost vigilance. By the ninth century a new, very high-ranking courtier bearing the title of rector shared responsibility for many court functions. Almost equal in importance to both these senior courtiers was the emperor's master of the horse.

The emperors were naturally attended by their company of bodyguards. These possessed their own officers who took their orders from the lord chamberlain. Though the latter was answerable to the master of offices his position became increasingly important with the passing years till eventually, like many other key appointments, it came to be held by a eunuch. By the tenth century, as much to impress as for security reasons, the size of the sovereign's bodyguard was considerably increased. The difficulty of finding sufficient recruits was solved by dividing the guards into two corps. One of these, the Varangian, was made up of mercenaries of Norse origin enrolled in Kievan Russia, who were often referred to as Barbarians; the other was manned by Normans raised for the most part in Britain. Harald Hardrada of England and Norway was one of the many distinguished men who served in it. When the Emperor held court, armed guardsmen (the Varangians carrying their battle-axes) were ranged according to nationality behind the imperial throne, lining the apsidal section of the throne room. By then an office of Barbarians had been established as an adjunct to the intelligence service for the purpose of supplying the foreign secretary with information about the new

30 Diptych of Consul Flavius Anastasius; scenes from the
Hippodrome Games appear at the bottom
Ivory consular diptych, AD 517

31   Emperor Justinian on
horseback
*Gold solidus struck to
commemorate the defeat
of the Vandals
in* AD 535

32   St Michael dressed as a
contemporary foot soldier
From a twelfth-century steatite

kingdoms arising in what the Byzantines regarded as the Barbarian world.

As his name implies, the lord chamberlain as master of ceremonies was obliged to make all the arrangements for both the private and official functions held at court, as well as for all public celebrations and state ceremonies. He had to ensure that the route taken by the sovereign in a procession had been cleaned and the streets covered with sawdust, and that the houses bordering them were displaying decorations in ivy, laurel, myrtle and rosemary. He himself took part in such processions carrying the gold wand studded with jewels which was his badge of office. He was accompanied by guardsmen, armed with swords and battle-axes, carrying olive branches. Such ceremonies took place not only at royal baptisms, coronations and burials but also at military triumphs, ambassadorial receptions and religious festivals such as those associated with Easter Sunday or the day of the Virgin's birth. At the last of these the emperor had a particularly impressive part to play in the religious service held in the cathedral of Haghia Sophia. Among other specially important functions were the rites associated with the issue of free bread.

Wheat was treated as a Crown monopoly. At Constantinople's foundation the feeding of the young capital's rapidly growing population had presented many difficulties. It had finally been decided that corn grown in Egypt was to be earmarked for the inhabitants of Constantinople. A special group of officials were assigned the task of ensuring the town's corn supplies and of distributing flour to the bakers; some of the latter were responsible for making the bread for those inhabitants who were entitled to receive free supplies, whilst others were permitted to sell their bread in the open market at the price fixed for it by the government. Sometimes the price set on the bread was lower than that which the bakers had been charged for the corn, but the government would then provide a subsidy to cover the difference. To maintain corn supplies required careful organisation. To ensure the timely arrival of the winter supplies the necessary corn had to reach Antinoe by 9 August each year, so that it would be delivered in Alexandria by 10 December. There it was loaded into ships which sailed to Tenedos in large convoys to be unloaded and stored in vast granaries built by Justinian until needed in Constantinople. It was re-shipped in stages from Tenedos, and was carried to the capital by vessels of the Bosphoran merchant navy.

When Egypt's harvests failed to produce the required stocks, extra supplies were forcibly acquired from the farmers of Thrace and Macedonia. In later times the latter had to provide all the corn needed by Constantinople.

Yearly, on 11 May, the anniversary of the foundation of Constantinople, the free distribution of bread, cakes, vegetables and fish to the needy people of Constantinople was carried out with much pomp at a ceremony held in the Hippodrome in the presence of the emperor and his court. Even when in 642 Egypt's fall to the Arabs put an end to supplies of Egyptian corn, and when economic difficulties, such as Constantine VII Porphyrogenitus experienced in the tenth century, made it necessary drastically to reduce the number of those entitled to receive issues of free bread, the May distribution and the celebrations associated with that anniversary were maintained. Exceptional gifts of free bread were issued until the end; the monks of the monastery of Nea Moni at Chios continued to receive them whenever they visited Constantinople, though they were in turn expected (at any rate till the year 1119) on certain occasions to furnish the monks of the monastery of St John at Patmos with free supplies.

Constantine the Great had established the basic principles of Byzantium's constitution. In accordance with Roman practice he provided Constantinople with a senate. Though he did not give it power to govern the Empire he invested it with many of the same privileges as those enjoyed by that at Rome. However, by the fourth century, in neither case did these amount to very much, for the senates in both capitals had by then been reduced to little more than advisory bodies whose main duties consisted in drafting regulations which they could only hope that the emperor would prove willing to adopt. It was reasonable for Constantine to grant the Constantinopolitan senate as much authority as the Roman one since, during the opening phase of the new era, the Byzantine senate was staffed by men drawn from the same old Roman aristocracy as were the senators of Rome. Indeed, many of them had had to be persuaded by Constantine to abandon Rome in order to settle in the new city, to serve there as senators. However, within a generation or so Constantinople's senators were being chosen from members belonging to the three senior grades of the court officials, some of whom were by that time local Greeks. By then too, if requested to do so by the emperor, the senate could act as a high court of justice.

There were times when Constantinople's senate was more powerful than at others. It was probably at its weakest under Leo V (813–20), but it acquired considerable authority in the eleventh century when Michael Psellus, the great scholar, statesman and friend of the emperor became its president. Even so the senate only became all-important on the death of an emperor, when, in conjunction with senior service commanders, it had to ratify the succession of the next holder of the throne. If an emperor died before nominating his successor and if, as a result of death or revolution, there remained no member of his family to act on his behalf, it fell to the senate to elect the next ruler. In the eighth century, however, the army exercised so much influence over the senate that in 776, when Leo IV wished to crown his young son Constantine as his co-ruler rather than the five other 'caesars' in the imperial family at the time, he thought it advisable to obtain first not only the senate's written consent, but also that of the entire army, including regiments stationed in the provinces. In addition he sought the support of the Church and people, and called upon the nation to be loyal to the boy and to regard him as heir to the throne.

The cabinet, or *sacrum consistorium* as it was called, was from the start far more influential than the senate. It derived its name from the verb *consistere*, meaning 'to stand'. Since the emperor presided at its meetings it was necessary for all those attending to remain standing throughout the proceedings—the fact that they were not expected to remain prostrated in his presence was regarded as a gracious act of favour. The *sacrum consistorium* consisted of a chairman, the *quaestor sacri palatii*, and only a small number of regular members. Each was chosen personally by the emperor from among his top-ranking officials and his praetorian prefects, but if he so wished he could call upon any senator to attend a special session in order to give information or advice on a particular issue. To judge from a passage in Anna Comnena's life of her father it would seem that, as in ancient Athens, speeches were timed in the Byzantine cabinet. She asserts that the leading Crusaders, whom her father appears to have received standing when they called on him on official business, were so long-winded that the emperor often had no time for his meals. Furthermore, his legs began to swell with the effort of standing so that, on more than one occasion, he was obliged to drive instead of ride into battle.

The cabinet had lost some of its importance by the middle of the tenth century, when the country was being administered by about 60 men drawn from the senior grades of courtiers, administrators and service personnel. These 'ministers', as they might well be described, continued to work under the emperor's direct orders. The office of prime minister did not exist, but the emperor charged the official of his choice with the duty of carrying out whatever task he wished to allot to him. By the twelfth century the number of these administrators had grown, especially those in the military grades; the army at the time had become indispensable to the state.

Constantine divided the Empire into provinces which he subdivided into 13 dioceses; these were then split into 116 districts. By the end of the fourth century these were consolidated into four prefectures, of which the two eastern ones were by far the largest, for they included Egypt, the Orient, the Pontus and Thrace. Each prefecture was governed by a praetorian prefect invested with almost vice-regal powers, though he was not given control over the armed forces in his district. Nevertheless it was the praetorian prefect and not the emperor who paid the troops stationed in his district and provided their food, and who also appointed and dismissed the provincial governors. The praetorian prefect of the eastern region resided in Constantinople and, to begin with, ranked together with the praetorian prefect of Italy as the highest among the Empire's numerous senior officials. In times of national danger each of these posts was occasionally shared by two men of equal rank.

Constantine's successors followed his lead and continued to divide the Empire into regions. Maurice turned Ravenna and Carthage into exarchates, giving each of the exarchs full control over both military and civil affairs. Somewhat later the Byzantine countryside was divided into militarised districts known as *themes* instead of provinces. By the seventh century Asia Minor had become so heavily populated that, to facilitate its defence, it alone was divided into several *themes*. By the tenth century the system had been applied to other districts and the total number of *themes* was raised to 25, the praetorian prefects losing their importance with the abolition, or rather the substitution, of militarised *themes* for civilian prefectures. The government of each *theme* was carried out by an official assisted by three men, one of whom handled the *theme*'s guilds and commercial affairs, another its legal matters, including the administration of its prisons and labour force and who was, in consequence, also responsible for the well-being of travellers visiting his district; whilst the third administered the *theme*'s finances, industries, customs and excise dues, aqueducts, external relations and postal services, as well as all petitions addressed to the emperor. Till the Latin occupation of Constantinople these officials were directly responsible to the emperor; after that date the central government became so weak that, like many a local landowner, the governors started to behave like practically independent authorities. However, by 1354, when much of Byzantium's territory was in Ottoman hands, the *themes* system had broken down. Instead despotates were established, that is to say the few major districts remaining to the Empire, more especially those of Mistra, Janina, Epirus, the Morea, Vallachia and Rumania, were divided among the younger branches of the imperial house to rule over as princelings or despots. Though these petty rulers swore allegiance to the emperor, they in fact acted and lived as autonomous kinglets.

When Byzantium was first established two consuls were appointed annually to carry out duties akin to those of lord mayors today. One was in Rome(*33*), the other in Constantinople(*36*). Just as British lord mayors and lord provosts have to spend considerable sums of their own to pay for the pageants and entertainments associated with their office, consuls too found themselves obliged from the start to spend the equivalent of several thousand pounds on festivities. By the sixth century their expenses are estimated to have

33   A Roman consul

93

amounted to some £30,000 a year and it is thought that this is why Justinian abolished the office in the year 541. Whilst it lasted the consuls, acting rather in the manner of kings presenting their portraits to those whom they wished to honour, arranged for ivory diptychs to be sent to their friends to inform the latter of their elevation to the consulship (30). The diptychs consisted of rectangular pieces of ivory held together by a hinge and opening out like a Christmas or birthday card, elaborately carved on one face with designs which generally included their portraits, as well as decorative, symbolic or *genre* scenes and inscriptions. The decorations of the earlier diptychs that survive are essentially Roman in character, those of the later ones show features which are clearly Byzantine.

When the consulship was abolished both Rome and Constantinople were given their own city prefects. Though of lower standing than the praetorian prefects, the Constantinopolitan prefect or 'eparch', as he was called, ranked eighteenth among the first 60 court officials yet, within Constantinople, his importance was almost as great as the emperor's, for he was regarded as first among the civil officials and as father of the city (34). This gave him precedence over all the court officials and entitled him to become a senator. He was also the only official permitted to wear the

34   An eparch dispensing justice

toga instead of military uniform. In return, it fell to him to maintain order and the smooth running of life in Constantinople, to see that the factions were at peace with each other, to control the city's industrial guilds, to ensure that it possessed adequate supplies of corn, and to see that the weights and measures used by the shopkeepers were checked. To help him in all this, the eparch was assisted by two senior officials, one of whom—the Logothete of the Praetorium—was responsible for the law courts whilst the other —the Symponus—was charged with maintaining law and order. His junior assistants were very numerous.

The eparch's control of the judiciary gave him great powers, but also made him one of the busiest of the country's administrative officers. It obliged him to countersign all the decrees issued by the emperor, to draft the texts of all laws submitted to the emperor, and to ensure the correct application of all regulations. At all times new laws were issued in the name of Jesus Christ, Our Lord Master. Byzantium had taken over Rome's legal system to use it as the basis of its own, but from quite an early date a commission was set up in Constantinople to examine the old laws with a view to either amending or discarding them; when it was in session the eparch became directly concerned and the volume of work he had to deal with greatly increased. The initiative for reforming the legal code rested with individual emperors. Each, in his capacity of sovereign, stood at the head of the judiciary, but some emperors were more interested in modernising the system than others. Theodosius was the first emperor to attempt to streamline the code. In 438 he edited a collection of all the edicts issued by Constantine I and the latter's successors on the Byzantine throne, giving them the form of a *Codex* bearing his own name as its title. By assembling these laws in a single volume, Theodosius made it far simpler for them to be referred to and checked; this improvement in its turn helped lawyers to avoid errors resulting from confused or mistaken interpretations of regulations. Furthermore the *Codex* was quickly accepted in Byzantium, though not in Rome, as the basis of the country's legal system. As a result, even though the original text had been written in Latin, the book's appearance marked the first separation of the constitutions applied in the western and eastern sections of the Empire, and, as such, it had the effect of encouraging the use of the Greek language in Byzantium at the expense of the Latin. Inevitably Latin gradually fell into disuse even among members of the governing class. By the sixth century Greek was being so widely spoken that Emperor Heraclius (610–41) proclaimed it the country's official language and within the space of a generation Latin was known only to a handful of scholars.

The most far-reaching and enduring measures taken to classify, co-ordinate and rationalise the country's laws were undertaken at the wish of Emperor Justinian. As a start all the Roman laws which had been passed since the time of Hadrian (117–38) were collected and published in the year 529 under the title of *Codex Justinianus*. These laws remained in force throughout the whole of

Byzantium's existence, coming into use in western Europe in the twelfth century. Even today students of jurisprudence are obliged to study Justinian's *Codex* because some principles laid down in it remain valid in certain European countries at the present time. Four years after its appearance, once again at Justinian's order, a digest of the pronouncements made by Roman jurists of the classical period was issued. Together with the *Codex* this volume came to serve as the basis for all Byzantine law, and copies of both works were distributed to all members of the legal profession to ensure the uniform application of the law throughout the Empire. In addition, once again at Justinian's wish, a text-book on law was produced for use in all schools of jurisprudence. The head of the legal faculty at the university of Constantinople was given the title of *nomophylax* (guardian of the laws). As no form of printing or of reproducing texts mechanically, such as by block-printing, was known to the Byzantines, all books were in manuscript form, that is to say they were transcribed by hand. Many men earned their living as scribes. The original Justinianic law books were written in Latin, but they were quickly translated into Greek which had by then established itself as the language of the people. Each copy, whatever its language, stressed the supreme authority and powers of the emperor in all legal matters.

Byzantine law did not remain unchanged after Justinian's death. Throughout succeeding centuries it was often amended to conform to changes in outlook. Leo III, the Isaurian (717–41) was one of the first of Justinian's successors to find it necessary to introduce minor changes. His amendments appeared in 739 in a volume entitled the *Ecloga*; the changes incorporated in it had been rendered desirable by the more enlightened and humanistic outlook brought by Christianity. Though many of Leo's reforms strike us as barbarous today, in the eighth century they were considered far more merciful than the laws which they replaced. In many instances where the Justinianic Code prescribed death or a ruinous fine as the only permissible punishments, Leo substituted such penalties as the cutting off of noses or hands and the tearing out of tongues—measures which today fill us with disgust. A thousand years ago, however, even the kindest and most cultivated Christians lived in a society where mutilations were not only normal but also figured prominently in paintings illustrating the tortures inflicted on saints and martyrs of the

35   Torture on the wheel, from an illumination

faith (*35*), and the blunting of sensibilities which resulted may help to explain why such punishments were considered more humane and vastly preferable to death or destitution.

Basil I (867–86) also found it necessary to revise some of the older laws in force at the time of his accession. In 879 he issued his amendments to the legal code in a volume entitled the *Epanagoge*. In it an attempt was made for the first time in Byzantine history to define the parts to be played in the country's legal system respectively by the emperor, the patriarch, and the state, and to outline the duties of each. Basil's successors Leo VI, 'the Wise', and Alexander I (886–913) applied themselves to completing the revision of the Justinianic Code undertaken by Basil, but the task was left unfinished at their deaths and never again seriously attempted.

Throughout Byzantine history a pronouncement of the supreme, that is to say of the imperial, court or of the senate when acting at the emperor's request as a high court, was regarded as final. But those issued by ordinary courts of law, whether civil or ecclesiastic, could on appeal be heard anew in another local court. After the emperor's return to Constantinople in 1261 the old distinctions between the civil and religious courts became blurred and eventually they were replaced by regional courts in which both clerics and laymen were represented. Unfortunately, by 1296, the entire legal profession had become so corrupt that Andronicus II found it necessary to create a new high court. He appointed 12 judges and eight prominent officials to serve on it. However, the measure proved ineffective; corruption persisted and, in 1329, Andronicus III appointed four men with the title of 'supreme justices of the Romans' and invested them with even greater powers than those enjoyed by members of the high court. He hoped thereby to ensure fair judgments. Yet within eight years charges of corruption were being levied against these men. By then, however, Byzantium was on a decline which no one could arrest and the supreme justices remained in office, dispensing their duties each according to his lights during the last years before the onslaught of the Ottoman Turks.

From the start the inhabitants of Constantinople as well as of all other towns of any size and pretensions were grouped in factions not unlike the political parties of today. These never numbered more than four in any one city and it has been suggested that originally each group represented a geographical rather than a political division, corresponding to that section of the town situated at a major point of the compass. Each faction in due course acquired a distinguishing colour worn by its members on their shoulders. Constantinople's four factions were known as the Blues, Greens, Whites, and Reds, but by Justinian's day the Whites and the Reds had merged respectively into the Blues and Greens. It has been established that each did live in a separate part of the town—which tends to support the suggestion that originally the divisions were drawn on geographical lines. It seems probable that, rather like present-day Mods and Rockers, the factions quickly acquired social and ideological characteristics in addition to regional distinctions. According to Procopius, the Blues (at any rate in Constantinople) included many wild young aristocrats who trimmed their beards in the Persian style and partially shaved their heads in imitation of the Huns. They wore narrow tunics with puffed-out shoulders but with the sleeves gathered into long tight cuffs at the wrist, close-fitting hose and shoes similar in style to those worn by the men referred to by the Byzantines as 'barbarians'. When in battle dress they wore a cuirass. The Greens were not as interested in their appearance as were the Blues.

So long as four factions existed the Blues and Whites often

sided together; in 602 in Constantinople they numbered some 900 men as compared to 1,500 Greens and Reds. Rivalry between the Blues and Greens persisted until the end perhaps because, even though membership was in each case open to all freemen, the Blues included many landowners and senators of Romano-Greek origin, whilst the Greens were largely made up of businessmen, industrialists and civil servants. Each worshipped in its own church: the Blues, who belonged to the established Church, in the Dagisteus, and the Greens, who sympathised with the Eastern heretical sects, in the Diaconissa. Each had its own organs, choirs and other essential musical instruments, yet all the factions had to perform similar duties. They had a specially important part to play in the Hippodrome games; they also had the honour of lining the routes followed by royal processions, and certain functions to perform during specific imperial ceremonies. Among the most important was their task of maintaining the town's defensive walls in good repair and of acting as a militia or police force. In times of national danger they also had the right to enrol and arm supporters. It was this privilege which made them so dangerous an element in Constantinople during periods of political unrest.

Established originally to serve as a police force, it was only gradually that the factions came to be linked with the Circus, to rank there as athletes competing in the Hippodrome games. Like the Agora in Athens or the Forum in Rome, Byzantine hippo-dromes were used for political meetings. When these occurred, the athletic teams drawn from and backed by each faction came to represent the nation's leading political parties, so that, just as players in present-day international football matches stand for their respective countries, so did the athletes of Byzantium represent particular political parties. By Justinian's reign only the Blues and the Greens remained, and both were extremely powerful. They had a great many followers made up of people who shared their political opinions. Since these supporters did not hesitate to make their political views known, and to fight for their side if need be, the political importance of the factions cannot be exaggerated. When the people felt that they had been too sorely tried the fac-tions joined forces with them in overthrowing the emperor, the government, or both.

Justinian had unwisely increased the importance of the factions during his uncle's reign by making use of them to further his own ends. Instead of maintaining discipline the factions became unruly, but Justinian did nothing to curb them till he came to the throne. In January 532 he decided to punish them for their lawlessness. The orders he issued led to rioting which seemed little worse than outbreaks of a similar kind to which the Constantinopolitans had become accustomed. Some mutineers were arrested and tried; seven were found guilty of murder and were therefore condemned to death by the eparch, four of them by execution, three by hanging. Two of the latter, one a Blue, the other a Green, fell from the noose twice without being killed. Monks from a neighbouring monastery could not endure the painful spectacle or countenance a third attempt; seizing the men they rowed them across the Golden Horn to sanctuary in the church of the monastery of St Laurentius. The eparch sent some soldiers to surround the church. The factions petitioned the emperor for mercy, but received no reply. Three days later a large race-meeting was held in the Hippodrome. On the third day, at the end of the twenty-second race, a great cry of 'Long live the humane Greens and Blues!' showed the public that the factions had joined forces on the issue. At the end of the last race a great cry of '*Nika!*' meaning 'Victory!' went up—it was the watchword of the factions and the signal for the worst rising in Byzantine history. The mob supporting the factions broke into the prisons, releasing the inmates, killing the guards and firing the buildings; it then moved on to set fire to the great gate of the Chalke, to the Great Palace itself, to the senate house and even to Constantine's cathedral of Haghia Sophia. On the next day, the races having been cancelled, the mob moved to the north of the Hippodrome, to the great baths of Zeuxippus, demanding the dismissal of three officials. Alarmed by the scale of the disturbances Justinian agreed. The factions were now ready for peace, but peace could not be restored, for the vast crowd of countrymen who had come to Constantinople for the Christmas festivities, angered by the heavy taxes which had been imposed on them, took advantage of the disorders to try to depose Justinian. The rebellion raged all week and but for Theodora's intervention it would probably have succeeded.

During the opening phase of Byzantine history, before the Empire possessed a separate department of finance, its monetary affairs were controlled by the praetorian prefect's finance officers. It fell to them, acting on his behalf, to collect the nation's most important tax, the *annona*. Levied in rural districts, it was a combination of a poll and land tax, being based on a piece of land of definite value and of a size to be worked by one man. In the eighth century, when the praetorian prefect ceased to be responsible for country districts he automatically stopped collecting the *annona*. Local treasury officials were appointed to do so and at the same time the post of *sacellarius* was created, its holder acting as the nation's senior finance officer. By the seventh century, however, the nation's monetary affairs had become so complicated that the finance department which had grown up during the preceding centuries was split into two; *logothetes* or accountants worked in one section and *chartularii* or actuaries in the other. The chief *logothete*'s office became increasingly important from the eighth century onwards and, in the twelfth, when the post of *sacellarius* was abolished in favour of that of 'great' *logothete*, the holder of the latter came to rank as equal in importance to the lord chancellor. However, since their duties brought them into close daily contact with the emperor, the head of the imperial chancery, the official who dealt with all petitions, and the imperial secretary continued to wield great influence.

It seems probable that the post of *sacellarius* was abolished because the *themes* and their respective governors had become so numerous and so powerful that by the twelfth century they often succeeded in forestalling the central government's treasury officials; the latter often stepped in first to collect the taxes imposed on the peasants and then retained these for themselves. These taxes, certainly until the thirteenth century, must have been exceedingly valuable. Though we have no means of estimating their exact worth or the purchasing power of money at the time it is thought that in the ninth century, when the Empire was at the height of its prosperity, the nation's annual budget, assessed both in money and kind, must far have exceeded in value 100 million pre-war French gold francs. Basil I (867–86) left his heir a personal fortune thought to represent 24 million pre-war gold francs, though its purchasing value must have been far higher. Nevertheless, in the eleventh century, the country was in economic difficulties, though it was still drawing vast revenues from both urban and rural Crown lands, from the taxes imposed on imports, exports and consumer goods, from the duties levied on wines and stone quarries as well as on cultivated land and grazing, and on urban dwellings no less than from the sums raised from licences imposed on private industries. The economic crisis was partly, perhaps even largely, caused by the outrageous extravagance of

Constantine VIII, Empress Zoe and Constantine IX, all of whom were so engrossed in their personal affairs that they permitted the civilian aristocracy to gain control of the government machine; having done so, the latter created an excessive number of civil service posts. Some of these were genuinely needed, for, throughout its history, Byzantine life with all its intricate ramifications continued to be as elaborately controlled as it is now in countries where the state is accepted as the sole authority. Every aspect of daily existence was regulated by the state, the government fixing prices and wages, issuing trading licences, travel permits and so on. With the years an ever-increasing number of government departments and officials were needed to deal with these tasks. Their growth, between the foundation of Byzantium in the fourth century and the tenth century when the administrative machine had fully evolved, is startling. A government department such as that responsible for the army's equipment had by then been so expanded as to enable it to assume control of the factories which produced it; the department which provided the army with horses was in charge of the Anatolian farms where many of the animals were bred; and the one which dealt with foreign visitors had

grown into a sort of Ministry of Housing to enable it to provide the new arrivals with dwellings. Examples such as these could be multiplied many times over. The growth of the civil service increased the cost of the administrative organisation. To make matters worse, the rise in expenditure corresponded with a fall in the country's revenue, caused mainly by the country-dwellers' refusal to pay their taxes, partly too because the government had started to employ private contractors as tax collectors, many of whom proved to be dishonest. That the government was able to continue to function so long

36 Areobindus, Consul of
Constantinople in 506

is a matter of wonder. The achievement must to a large extent be attributed to the efficiency and devotion of the bulk of the officials: although many key appointments were held by corrupt and selfish men, less concerned with the state's well-being than their own, who added to their personal fortunes by trafficking in state appointments and by evading payment of their taxes, yet the majority remained above reproach. This is all the more remarkable since junior officials were never well paid. As late as the eighth century a notary's average earnings seldom exceeded two *nomismata* a month, though this was supplemented by goods in kind.

Senior officials were not appointed for life. Whilst employed by the state they were expected to reside in Constantinople. Since they all owned land this regulation made it impossible for them to live on their estates whilst they held office and, as a result, banishment to their estates eventually came to rank as a punishment for courtiers who had displeased their sovereigns. Whilst in office these senior civil servants took their orders direct from the emperor, who personally paid them their salaries each year on Passion Sunday. They were well rewarded but, like teachers and officers serving in the army and navy, certainly until the seventh century, they were largely paid in kind, though after that date the proportion taking the form of money steadily increased. On Easter Sunday a special ceremony took place in the Great Palace when, in addition to receiving their emblems of office on their appointment or re-appointment to their posts, they were presented with the ceremonial robe to which their position entitled them. Thus a *magister*—a high court official—received a gold embroidered cloak, a tunic made of a white fabric shot with gold, a cloak trimmed with gold and a jewelled belt; he was expected to wear these on all official occasions. In his *Book of Ceremonies* Constantine Porphyrogenitus discusses in detail the duties and state costumes of 13 grades of senior administrators and the exact position close to the emperor's throne where each was entitled to stand during state ceremonies. *Spatharii* were entitled to a sword with a gold hilt, others to collars of different types.

All officials, regardless of whether they belonged to the old Roman aristocracy or to the new Byzantine nobility, owned land. By the end of the fourth century they already numbered more than 2,000. In a short space of time the majority had acquired so much land, and as a result, so much wealth, that they were able to

103

live lives of great magnificence. By Justinian's day many had become so spoilt and corrupt that Justinian felt obliged to curb their ambitions. He attempted to break up the large estates by forbidding the eldest son to inherit the whole of his father's property at the expense of the younger sons, attempting also to prevent a father from bequeathing all he possessed to a favourite son. He did not succeed in this, nor was he able to end such abuses as tax evasions or the sale of government appointments. As a result the aristocracy and landed gentry continued to add to their wealth at the cost of that of the state and of the peasantry. By the eighth century they had grown as powerful as they were rich. Within yet another century Leo VI found himself obliged to set many of the more important posts aside for them to fill and, in order to curry more favour with them, he raised the ban which had prevented officials purchasing goods or accepting gifts of money or land without the emperor's permission. Leo also made it easier for the nobility to acquire land. As the disparity in wealth increased, still further distinguishing the rich from the poor, class differences and titles multiplied in a society which set little store on birth and ancient lineage. Even in the eleventh century the aristocracy remained the most powerful element both at court and in the administration. Its position changed for the worse after the twelfth century, when the growing threat to the Empire's security served steadily to increase the influence and importance of the fighting services. The Latin conquest of Constantinople undermined the aristocracy and weakened the bureaucracy. Though many noblemen emerged from the experience with their fortunes intact and their way of life unaffected, the administrative machine had been weakened beyond repair. Even the efforts of the numerous efficient and upright men who continued to serve it with real devotion were unable to restore confidence either in the administration or in the country's future. And, indeed, in the realm of politics Byzantium had by then ceased to be a power to be reckoned with by the West.

5

THE ARMY AND NAVY

From the start the Byzantine emperors were in complete accord
with the rulers of Rome concerning the importance of ensuring
the Empire's security and preserving its boundaries intact but, in
contrast to the Romans, who were strongly militarist in outlook,
the Byzantines attached particular attention to methods of
defence, preferring them to more aggressive action. As a result
they built castles, bastions and fortifications which, though lacking
in originality, nevertheless withstood numerous assaults before
succumbing to the fierce attacks of the Ottoman Turks. Even when
captured, these buildings often continued in use, serving as
foundations for Turkish superstructures. Many survive to our day
as romantic ruins in areas which once formed Byzantium's border
lands. They are often to be found poised high on the summit of
the mountain peaks whence they originally kept watch over
vulnerable defiles or mounting guard over some ancient harbour,
whilst the foundations of their citadels still occupy the centres of
not a few Turkish towns. Some of the most spectacular and
enduring defences were built to protect Constantinople, for the
town's position on the coast, on the fringe of two continents, laid
it open to attacks by both sea and land.

Constantine I realised the city's danger and as early as May 324
he took steps to protect Constantinople from an inland enemy by
building a land wall round its northern, western and southern
sides. Within a century the enclosed area had become too small
to contain the capital's growing population, nor did Theodosius
II (408–50) consider the defences adequate. He decided to fortify
the city with a new line of defences(4) and entrusted the work
to Anthemius, prefect of the East, perhaps because the most
advanced defences known at the time were those which had been
erected in Antioch during the preceding century. Theodosius'
walls survive today to form, with Justinian's cathedral of Haghia

Sophia, one of the greatest glories of ancient Istanbul. They stood originally 27 feet high and were strengthened by 96 towers built at intervals of 200 feet. Alternately round and square in shape, the towers projected from the walls to a depth of 16 feet and topped them by eight feet. On the inner side they were provided with a walk along the top of the battlements which was supported by arches. As an additional security a 60-foot moat was added; it was defended by a masonry scarp and counterscarp. At a time when four gates, each set at a major point of the compass, were considered adequate for the needs even of large towns, Theodosius provided Constantinople with ten. His walls were so solidly built that 1,000 years later, when pounded by one of the first cannons to be used in battle, though breached, they did not crumble.

The scale and efficiency of Byzantium's defence works may have owed something to the pacifist outlook of her people no less than to the skill of her engineers. Their pacifism may well have been innate, yet it must undoubtedly have been encouraged in them by their Christian faith. St Basil had advised all soldiers who had killed in battle to seek forgiveness for the act by performing a three-year penance. People's dislike of warfare had led Justinian to create an army made up of a sort of territorial force which could come to the assistance of the regular, mobile army, which was largely made up of mercenaries of various nationalities. Even during the four centuries which witnessed the peak of Byzantium's political greatness—that is, from the reign of Heraclius (610–41) to that of Basil II (976–1025)—Byzantium owed her military reputation chiefly to these foreign mercenaries and even during that period the emperors preferred to use diplomacy rather than force to secure peace. Whenever possible they kept war at bay by propitiating their neighbours with costly presents or high-sounding titles, obtaining military alliances in return for monetary subsidies or annual allowances, even by conferring Byzantine princesses in marriage to barbarian chieftains. For similar reasons they also always welcomed political refugees but at the same time they lost no opportunity of parading as a highly developed military power, for although Byzantium remained a leading maritime power throughout much of her history, the army always ranked as the senior service.

The Roman army had consisted of a large frontier force which was always used to guard the Empire's boundaries, and of the praetorian guard stationed in Rome; but by the fourth century the

37　Infantrymen, showing equipment of the time

army as a whole had become outdated and inefficient, and the praetorian guard had often shown itself far from loyal to the government. Constantine therefore determined to create a new army, which he however established according to the old Roman principle. Even though he and his immediate successors built the new force round a strong mobile corps of cavalrymen, sustained by a large infantry, yet they continued to regard the imperial body-guards, the *scholae palatinae*, like Rome's praetorian guard of an earlier date, as the pivot of the army.

It was their arch-enemies the Persians who taught the emperors the advantages of mobile warfare. Until the rise of the Arabs in the seventh century Sasanian Persia was the most powerful militarised state of the day, yet on many occasions during the past millennium the Persians had found themselves obliged to fight major engage-ments against the turbulent Central Asian nomads. Those wild and fearless horsemen had exposed the Persians to many new ways of waging war, by subjecting them to the rapid onslaughts of highly mobile cavalrymen. The Persians learnt from experience and hastened to include cavalry units in their army. They used them with signal success against the Romans. The Byzantines also learnt from experience, and although the infantry remained their most important force in Europe they realised from an early date that cavalry was essential for waging war in the East, where mounted archers were particularly effective in fighting the Persians. To begin with cavalrymen (*38*) drew the same pay as infantrymen, but within a matter of decades the *cataphracti* or heavy cavalry units were being more generously rewarded than any other branch of the army including the light cavalry, the *trapezitae*. From the sixth century the safety of Asia Minor was largely ensured by mounted bowmen. The total strength of the cavalry, the *caballaria themata* is estimated at some 120,000 men.

Emperors Tiberius (578–82) and Maurice (582–602) thought it necessary to reorganise the army. Both continued to make it wholly dependent on the emperor. It was to consist of crack regiments comparable to guards regiments called *palatini* and less good ones known as *comitatenses*. Tiberius decided to divide the army into three forces to correspond to the country's three main geographical divisions, basing one in the East, one in Illyria and one in Thrace. Each consisted of from six to eight regiments each numbering 3,000–4,000 men. Each army was commanded by a *dux* or *magister militum* and each regiment by a *strategus* (general or tribune), though the title was also awarded to governors of provinces; the cavalry *strategus* took precedence over that of the infantry. In contrast to the civilian governor of a district a *dux* was given control over an area often consisting of several districts or provinces. He was responsible for the overall military organisation within his region but the *strategus* was entrusted with the actual conduct of military operations. Each general was expected to raise and main-

tain his own regiment, equipping the men with bows and swords; in return the regiment bore his name; none exceeded 7,000 men in strength and proved constant and efficient. Like the *dux*, the field commanders and generals were directly answerable to the emperor. With other commissioned ranks they were appointed

38 Bronze figurine of a horseman

and paid by the emperors, but they were given the right to select their own non-commissioned officers.

Although Maurice was murdered by his own soldiers when campaigning with them against the Slavs in the Balkans, yet he had the army's welfare and efficiency at heart. He was responsible for the appearance in 590 of Byzantium's first military manual. In accordance with the theories expressed in that work he adopted a number of reforms. The most important of these was to introduce compulsory military service for men aged under 40 and to place three divisions, each commanded by its own general, under the charge of an overall commander. Each division was to consist of three brigades subdivided into seven regiments, each of 400 men. In addition Maurice also attempted to establish a reserve force of archers, the recruits serving on somewhat similar lines to members of Britain's territorial army; in peacetime they were therefore expected to practise archery only once a week.

Almost from the start the shortage of man-power made it difficult to carry out the measures laid down by the emperors. There were never enough regular soldiers to keep the regiments at full strength and the authorities were often obliged to rely largely on mercenaries. No one was debarred from enrolling merely on grounds of nationality, even Huns and Langobardians being admitted, though most mercenaries were of German or Illyrian origin. All were highly paid and many, even from as early as the fourth century, rose to top positions in the service.

In the seventh century the army was so short of men that Emperor Heraclius devised an ingenious scheme for attracting recruits. The process was known as that of the *themes* and was applied to begin with in the eastern frontier districts. Though the most vulnerable, these were also the worst defended because they were the least popular with the army. To render posting to those remote areas more attractive Heraclius promised each soldier serving in what were to be known as the *Anatolikon* (Anatolian), *Armeniakon* (Armenian) or *Opsikion* forces a strip of agricultural land which he was to regard as his own and to cultivate for his personal benefit. He could marry and live on this plot in the capacity of a sort of military smallholder, but in return he was to present himself fully armed and mounted when summoned to defend the frontier from an invader. Picked men were expected to combine the duties of a passport officer with those of a sentry, checking the documents of travellers and mounting guard on a rota system on turrets placed 3,000–4,000 feet apart, but within sight of each other so that the men could signal the neighbouring look-out post. A *theme*-holder was entitled to bequeath his strip of land to his eldest son on condition that the latter undertook to carry out the same military duties as his father had done. Younger sons were to become peasant freemen but they were expected to fend for themselves and to obtain uncultivated land in the sparsely inhabited border regions. By doing so they were supposed to increase the peasant population in remote districts and to contribute to the nation's food supplies by working their land. Hereditary *theme*-holders were entitled to employ servants and to own slaves to help in their heavier tasks.

The introduction of the *theme* system led to a sharp division in the army, the border force becoming wholly distinct from the regiments centred in the capital. The latter consisted of an infantry regiment and an advance defensive force commanded by *domestici* together with the four most important regiments forming the *scholae*; each of these was commanded by a *drungarius* instead of a *domesticus*; the *scholae* as a whole was commanded by an officer who was often the commander-in-chief of the whole army, but from the end of the tenth century a separate *domesticus* was put in charge of the eastern army or *schola*, and another of the western. The *themes* on the other hand had been placed by Heraclius under the command of *strategi* who were to act both as military commanders of the local force and as governors of the district. Heraclius therefore withdrew the *themes* from the jurisdiction of the praetorian prefect, but he did not permit the *strategi* to collect the taxes levied on the countrymen; instead he transferred that duty of the earlier prefects to finance officers who were stationed in the *themes* for the purpose. The *strategi* were paid a higher salary than were the civilians who had governed the districts in earlier times.

Succeeding emperors were quick to appreciate the merits of Heraclius' idea and all warmly sponsored the creation of *themes*. But it took the best part of 200 years before the scheme was generally applied. To begin with, each of the militarised districts was called after the regiment stationed in it, but from the eighth century, when the number of *themes* increased as a result of their division into sections which were in their turn split up, the *themes* were called after the geographical areas in which they were situated. The *themes* rapidly acquired a high degree of autonomy and became so popular that many men volunteered for service in them.

Digenis Akritas, the semi-legendary hero of a splendid epic, was typical of the men who fostered the independent spirit of the *theme*-holders. Like many of them Digenis was of mixed origin, for his mother was a Christian and his father a Muslim petty chieftain.

Although many men volunteered for service in the *themes* in the eighth century the growing strength of the Arabs made it necessary to settle ever more men in the eastern zones, but once again the shortage of man-power made it difficult to do so. In order to fill the gap Slavs were accepted as *theme*-holders and, in addition, one *solidus* in cash was offered for each year of service in a *theme* to the total of 12. In 930 Constantine VII passed a law making it necessary for each plot granted to a member of a *theme* to be worth the same value as four pounds of gold, but by the end of the century the value of each plot had been raised to that of 12.

The shortage of men even made itself felt in the imperial body-guard, more especially during the ninth century when it was decided to expand the force to include four regiments of cavalry as well as two of infantry. As a result many more mercenaries than formerly had to be admitted into this select corps. The vast majority were recruited either among Russo-Varangians or Anglo-Saxons. Men in these picked units were called *hetairii* and with the other *scholarii* they generally accompanied the emperors on their campaigns in Thrace and Bithynia. Their arms consisted of spears, swords and shields; many wore chain mail during a battle (*37*). However, in the tenth century many Byzantines evaded military service, which had been made compulsory, by paying a tax exempting them from doing so, and the size of the army fell to 140,000 men. Whenever an emperor more interested in intellectual matters, such as Psellus' pupil and friend Michael VII (1071–8), came to the throne recruitment fell off and the army tended to be neglected. Great military achievements induced a sense of false security which encouraged the spread of pacifism and led civilians to scorn the army. When that happened the nation invariably paid heavily for its carelessness, for Byzantium's existence depended upon the efficiency of her army. During the four centuries when the Empire was at its most powerful the army was well cared for. In the eleventh century Constantine VIII set aside the equivalent of £1½ million to pay the 14,459 men stationed in Crete. At the time a corporal was paid the equivalent of £360 a year, a lieutenant £720, a captain £1,080 and a general could earn as much as £14,500. The

39 David, armed for battle in contemporary equipment

army was then at its most efficient, its sense of duty at its keenest, and its devotion to the nation fully to be relied on.

The men who contended against such formidable enemies as the Persians, Franks, Saracens and Turks were, like the Romans before them, very well equipped (*39*). This may well help to explain why their uniforms and weapons did not greatly change during the 1,000 years of Byzantium's existence. In his book on tactics Leo VI remarked with justifiable pride that each of his cavalrymen was provided with a pointed steel helm and that both he and his mount were protected either by scale armour, coat of mail, or by leather surcoats lined with metal disks. The armour was of a different type from that used in western Europe late in the Middle Ages, for whereas the latter was made of sheet metal and covered the whole of the knight's body, Byzantine protective wear was generally made of metal particles which were either sewn one to another or stitched on to a garment made of fabric or leather. Yet the use of sheet armour was not unknown to Byzantium, for from quite an early date soldiers wore plated corselets and greaves reaching to their knees. The men who attempted in the eleventh century to depose Constantine IX Monomachus are described as wearing solid metal breastplates. In addition the Byzantines wore mail gauntlets, steel shoes and metal spurs. However, when going into battle the earlier emperors had worn Roman military dress, together with stockings and high boots studded with pearls in the oriental manner.

Officers going into battle wore woollen surcoats beneath their mail shirts and steel frontlets. These shirts were dyed in the colours of their regiment, for each regiment possessed its own specific colour and distinctive uniform—refinements which were unknown in western Europe till the sixteenth century. In summer the surcoat was made of a lighter material than the winter garment, and in wet weather a linen coat replaced the surcoats. Men in the ranks were armed with bows and arrows, daggers, spears, lances and javelins. They carried their arrows in holders suspended from the right sides of their waist and swords, often double-edged, from the left. Since their helms were not fitted with visors they also carried small metal shields to protect their faces. The regiments of javelin throwers, the heavy cavalry units used primarily in the East, as well as the light mounted archers, all wore chain mail and were armed with spears, battle-axes (40), swords and shields. Their horses were also protected by chain mail. The archers, whether mounted or on foot, made use of a windsock kite to help them in assessing the force and direction of the wind, enabling them to regulate the speed and angle of their shots according to prevailing conditions. The windsock was often shaped as or decorated with the figure of a fierce dragon and was generally made of silk, features of eastern origin, which confirm the view that the Romans acquired the device from the Sarmatian nomads who had themselves adopted it from the Parthians.

The Byzantines attacked advancing shield to shield, howling as they did so. Their shouts included the slogan given to them as their war-cry by their army chaplains; it consisted of the words, 'The Cross has conquered!' The men were accompanied in their assault both by their chaplains and also by a special body of exhorters; men of both groups encouraged the soldiers by their words, songs, recitations and appeals. The advance was led by the regimental standard-bearers holding aloft the Roman *vexillum* or standard and banners of good fortune; the soldiers followed using their battle-axes, iron

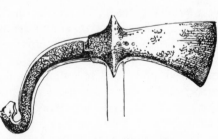

40   Romano-Byzantine battle-axe

41   A light cavalry unit assaults a town

broadswords, bows, lances, spears, javelins, daggers and stone-throwers; the latter were worked by a complicated system of ropes. When assaulting a fortress they made use of movable scaling towers. These were mounted on wheels or rollers and are believed to have been used first at the siege of Jerusalem. Bridging material and ramming devices were used in conjunction witj the scaling towers; the rammers were mounted into wooden frames, and a force of 60 men wearing protective leather clothing was needed to work each one. When necessary, engineers were called in to mine the besieged citadel. It was largely in order to contain the repeated and increasingly dangerous series of attacks launched by the Arabs in the seventh century that the Byzantines contrived their most potent weapon. Known to the contemporary world as 'Greek fire' it may be regarded as the forerunner to the grenade; it was made up of several ingredients which included sulphur and saltpetre and was evolved in the year 717 by Callinicus of Heliopolis. The final product, encased in a pottery grenade, was hurled at the enemy from a catapult. It proved signally effective, and in the navy's hands put an end to the Arab offensive. Again in the ninth century, when Russian Varangians started threatening Byzantium's security, Greek scientists improved upon the invention so that it was once more used successfully against the invaders. Greek fire was manufactured in Constantinople, and the method of its production was a closely guarded secret. Unfortunately for the Byzantines it was superseded in the fourteenth century by the invention of gunpowder and the cannon. It is a pitiful measure of Byzantium's decline that, when mortally threatened by the Ottoman Turks, the emperor and his advisers failed to appreciate the importance of the new weapon, which is thought to have been successfully used as early as 1356 at the battle of Crécy. When offered for sale to the Byzantines it was refused on the grounds that the price asked for it was too high. They would have been wiser to have paid it, for the angry munition-maker took his patent to the Ottoman sultan, enabling the Turks to pound the walls of Constantinople with cannon balls throughout the fateful siege in the spring of 1453, when the beleaguered city finally fell to Sultan Mehmet.

Though most of the country's munition factories were established in Constantinople and Salonica, some were concentrated in the provinces. The most important of these were situated in regions rich in mineral deposits. Thus Nicomedia, which could conveniently draw on the minerals to be found on Mount Olympus, became noted for its shields and swords. Caesarea, which could obtain the necessary metals from the Anti-Tauris, became, together with such minor places as Sardis, the main centre for the production of armour. Excellent lances and spears were made in Ieropolis in Cilicia, where most of the workshops producing uniforms were also situated; others were established along the north-western coast of Asia Minor.

When setting out on a major campaign the army moved off accompanied by baggage trains carrying its food supplies, spare clothing and equipment, as well as by its medical units and corps of engineers. A regiment's baggage train was made up of 350 waggons each carrying, in addition to its load, an axe, a sword and cooking utensils. Every sixteenth man in it rode a pack horse so that each baggage train consisted of 175 mounted men as well as 2,800 unmounted ones, who either rode on the waggons or walked beside them. At night the pack horses were driven into a circle and the waggons were drawn up around them. Then the engineers took over, protecting the encampment by digging a ditch round it. The medical units which accompanied the army were split into small groups; each consisted of a surgeon, eight stretcher-bearers and numerous orderlies. Horses provided with special saddles were used to transport the wounded and field baths were always available to minister to the wants both of the ailing and the fit. Priests were attached to all regiments and had many duties to perform. It fell to them to mark the start and end of each day by holding a service which was attended by everybody in the unit; it was also their duty to give spiritual comfort to the men, whom they often advised to address their prayers to military saints, such as St Michael or St Theodore Stratelites.

Scouts and spies were used to obtain advance information on enemy troop movements. A rare instance of carelessness in 1071 proved extremely costly to Emperor Romanus Lecapenus: when leading a large army against the Seljukid Turks, he omitted to send scouts ahead of his men, with the result that his entire force was trapped and defeated by the Seljuks at Manzikert and he himself was taken prisoner. Generally, however, the Byzantine intelligence service was both well run and fully used. Until the tenth century many emperors personally led their armies into battle, the sight of their personal standards encouraging the men. When on campaign the emperors were accompanied by heralds and large retinues of retainers; they travelled with a great deal of baggage, taking an enormous number of objects of great value with them. An emperor's tent was always of exceptional size and magnificence; it was furnished with costly rugs and precious vessels, and presented as valuable a prize as it was impressive to behold. Yet on numerous occasions the army and the imperial bodyguard failed to prevent its capture by an enemy eager for booty. When Romanus II (1028–34) was defeated by the Arabs he fled, leaving behind him, according to Psellus, 'a tent filled with necklaces, bracelets, diadems, pearls and precious stones'. Some two centuries earlier the Bulgar Khan, Krum, found £4½ million of army pay abandoned in the camp which he captured. Prisoners were seldom put to death; men in the ranks were used as slaves whilst those of distinction were released on payment of a ransom; when negotiations were in progress it was customary to give and to hold hostages as a guarantee of good faith.

Messengers were used to carry news from the battlefield to the capital, but their number was not great and soldiers returning from the front were expected to inform the people of the situation there. Had the army been in better heart in the fourteenth and fifteenth centuries the Turks might never have reached the Asiatic shore of the Marmora, whence they were able to pound Constantinople's defences; but the army's vitality had steadily declined from the eleventh century onwards. This had to some extent resulted from the falling off of Armenian and Isaurian recruits, a decline which was in its turn caused by the gradual break-up of *themes* following the loss of much valuable land, first to the Seljukid and then to the Ottoman Turks, and also by its sale to great landowners anxious to increase the size of their already huge estates. In 1096, after the arrival and departure of the First Crusade, Alexius I Comnenus attempted to stem the rot in the army and to restore its strength by calling on the population as a whole to provide material and labour for building bridges and ships, and also demanding them to furnish troops on the move with free board, lodging and transport. These measures made the army exceedingly unpopular among civilians, at the very time when recruiting was becoming increasingly difficult. Once again, as in earlier times, mercenaries had to be employed in great numbers and at ever-increasing cost to the state. In the twelfth century a desperate step was taken by the government; in order to attract officers into the service it was decided to make soldiering lucrative by granting them estates on conditional grants. The system, known as the *pronoia*, had been used as a reward for civilians. The holder of a *pronoia* estate generally held it for life. Even though he could not bequeath it at death, so long as he held it both the land and the peasants living on it and working it were inalienably his; his peasants paid all their dues and taxes to him, yet he paid none to the state; his right both to the sums he levied from his peasants and to the income he derived from his estate made him a rich man. In exchange, however, the holder of a military *pronoia* was expected to serve in the army, to appear in it fully equipped and mounted, and accompanied as well by a number of soldiers. The concession did not have the desired effect and, under Michael VIII (1259–82), as an additional inducement, the military *pronoia* was made heritable, a decision which had the unexpected, yet surely foreseeable effect of keeping landowners in their estates since the concession made it unnecessary for them to strive to increase their incomes. As a result, by the thirteenth century virtually the entire aristocracy was exempted from paying the land tax and a military career had come to be considered unattractive. Soldiers became so unpopular among civilians, that from then until about 1354, even though both private and Church-owned estates were subject to compulsory recruitment, the army was largely made up of mercenaries, *pronoia*-holders purchasing exemption from serving in it. The salaries of the mercenaries drained the state coffers. In desperation Andronicus II (1282–1328) imposed even heavier taxes on the civilian population while reducing the size of the army to that of a token force; he limited the cavalry to 3,000 men, 2,000 of whom were stationed in Europe and a mere 1,000 left to confront the Turks in Asia. No wonder then that the Ottomans found much to encourage them to maintain their pressure on the Byzantines and that the latter were in no position to stem their advance.

The Byzantine navy was always small in size, yet it played a vital part in defending the country, more than once saving it from enemy invasions whilst also helping to make the merchant fleet master of the Mediterranean, at least until the expansion of the Venetian and Genoese mercantile navies altered the balance of power there. The role of the Byzantine navy became especially important with the rise of the Arabs; by 698 it was therefore not only a powerful arm of the fighting services, but its political strength was such that it could depose Emperor Leontius and, with the help of the Greens, replace him by an admiral of the fleet. Yet when the Arabian navy declined, the Byzantine was permitted to deteriorate, and when it had done so its weakness was used as an excuse to reduce the sailors' pay, bringing it to a lower level than that in force in the army. In the ninth century a *drungarius*, or admiral of the fleet, occupied a lower position in the order of precedence than all the military *strategi*, but in the tenth century, as a result of the growing threat of the Kievan Varangians, he ranked next in importance to the *domesticus* of the military *scholae* and thus took precedence over all other military and naval commanders. The commander-in-chief of the navy was the *strategus* of the *carabisiani*.

Little detailed information is as yet available concerning the ships used by the Byzantines, but sub-marine archaeology may well in time supplement our knowledge. They called their warships *dromonds*; of these the *direma* appears to have been the vessel most widely used. It varied in size, needing 100–300 men to man it. The faster *birema* closely resembled a galleon. Smaller and faster ships were used in support of the larger ones, signalling by flags or lights which were the usual means of communication between ships passing at sea or sailing in convoy.

It had from the start proved more difficult to raise the recruits needed by the navy than it was for the army. In 690, under Justinian II, sailors were in such short supply that the emperor decided to transfer the Christian tribe of the Mardaites from their homes in northern Syria to the shores of the Peloponnese,

42 Boat builders at work

Cephalonia and Epirus, so as to enrol its menfolk into the navy. In return the conscripts were granted the same benefits as those offered to soldiers serving in the frontier zones, that is to say they were able to become *theme*-holders, but once again, as in the case of the army's frontier force and the regular troops, a distinction was drawn between the imperial fleet and the naval *themes*. Thus the imperial fleet remained based on Constantinople, but the naval *themes* which were eventually extended to Asia Minor, the south-western coastal zones, southern Asia Minor and most of Greece were nevertheless often called upon to provide men for the imperial fleet. In the eleventh century, after peace had been concluded with Kievan Russia, the navy was allowed to decline. It was never to recover from the setback it suffered then and was therefore never able to compete successfully against the Genoese and Venetian fleets. On regaining his throne in 1261 Michael VIII gave the Genoese the district of Galata to live in in Constantinople, together with the right to use the Straits; this proved an invaluable concession since it delivered the Black Sea trade into Genoese hands. His successor, Andronicus II, believed that he could rely on Genoese promises; he therefore decided to reduce the navy to 20 triremes, the role of which was to be largely ceremonial. Byzantium's naval vessels were dismantled and hundreds of sailors found themselves obliged to choose between forsaking their calling in favour of some other means of livelihood, seeking employment in the Turkish navy or joining a pirate vessel. Many preferred the last two of these alternatives to giving up the sea, even though it meant that they would be called upon to take up arms against their fellow-countrymen and Christians. Pirates had always menaced shipping in the Mediterranean; when the Byzantines were able to capture them they sent them to a special security prison situated on an island; escape from it was so difficult that Michael V (1041–2) banished his uncle John to it, fearing that that intriguing courtier might escape from any other place of exile to conspire against him.

6

TRADERS AND ARTISANS

The Byzantine attitude to trade and industry is perhaps easier to understand today, when state control is once again accepted as inevitable if not wholly desirable, than would have been the case during any intervening period in history. In Byzantium both were considered to be as much the state's concern as were the country's foreign relations. As in Rome, the state in the person of the eparch set out rigorously to regulate these two primary branches of the nation's economy; it also assumed responsibility for the building and control of factories and workshops; it established monopolies, handled imports and exports, fixed wages, the purchase and selling prices of all goods, customs dues and other similar charges. The state also acted as overseer of private firms, verifying the quality of the wares which they produced or handled, no less than the price at which they were sold. In addition the state made itself responsible for provisioning Constantinople, ensuring that the imports did not greatly exceed the estimated needs of the inhabitants, while avoiding rationing. Supplies were kept at a fairly uniform level proportionate to the size of the population at various periods in the capital's history. The system worked well so long as the Empire remained powerful and prosperous, and the government stable and efficient, but whenever the government's control of the economy slackened, private enterprise became buoyant and when, with the shrinking of the Empire's territory and resources, the nation's economy declined, foreign—that is to say Italian—merchants appeared as contending purchasers, the system broke down.

No one in Byzantium questioned the assumption that industry's purpose lay in providing the emperor, Church and nobility with the luxuries they desired and the state with a surplus of such goods for export. By the ninth century, when Byzantium's foreign trade (mainly of luxury wares) was at its most prosperous, the capital's industries were strictly organised under corporations subdivided into guilds. The system had been adapted from the Roman *collegia*, and had developed over the years along different lines. There were at least 23 guilds in the capital alone and the frequent references to them in Constantine VII's works and in the *Book of the Eparch* testify to their importance. Their purpose was not so much to ensure the welfare of its members or of the local inhabitants, but rather to make it easier for the state to control the city's economy and for these reasons the guilds dealing with essential foods, such as bread, fish or meat, were organised with special care. Pork butchers belonged to a different guild from butchers dealing with other meats; shoe makers were likewise split into two, to cover cobblers making special types of footwear. Of the industries formed into single guilds that of the perfume distillers was one of the largest. In each industry the guild drew up conditions of work and fixed wages, selling prices and profits. No man could belong to more than one guild and, in contrast to Rome, none was obliged to belong even to one; admittance to a guild was based on certain conditions which included skilled craftsmanship, and payment of an entrance fee. Nor was it absolutely essential, though it remained usual, for a child to follow his father's calling; even then his admittance to a guild was not automatic.

Each guild selected its own president, but his election had to be approved by the local prefect. Each guild bought all the raw materials needed by its members and distributed them to each one. The finished goods were put on sale in clearly established sections of the town or, in the manner of oriental bazaars, in the section set aside for goods of that type in the local markets. Only grocers could open a shop in whatever street they wished because they sold such essential foodstuffs as cheese, oil, butter, meal, honey, meat, salt fish and vegetables. Countrymen were also sometimes allowed to sell their produce direct to customers, and pedlars carried on a lively trade in secondhand clothes. Traders handled the sale of all other goods, including dead and live cattle and poultry, selling them in the markets at the price which the prefect had fixed. There was thus no room in the country's economy for the middle man and the prefects were able to keep prices of essential foodstuffs steady. To avoid underselling no one was allowed to buy freshly caught fish from fishermen, though the latter were permitted to set up stalls on piers and other authorised points for the sale of cooked fish. Constantinople's butchers were not allowed to buy meat from suburban farmers, but had to go beyond Nicomedia to do so; local supplies were reserved for emergencies. Bakers could be fined for not abiding by the fixed price even when, in order to increase the country's revenues, the set figure was so high that it led to rioting. The price of bread, like that of wine, varied with each fluctuation in the cost of the raw material, but it was always designed to furnish the state with a profit. In times of scarcity bakers were able to buy bread from special government stores.

Wages were regulated through the guilds. They were kept extremely low. At any rate until the end of the sixth century members were only partly paid in money and, like teachers, civil servants and soldiers, received a considerable portion of what was due to them in kind. Many guildsmen worked at home where they were helped by their wives, employees and apprentices. The latter started their training when very young. They did so under contract, their masters guaranteeing, in return for a payment in kind, to train them for two years. Breach of contract by either party was punishable by a fine. If the apprentice was paid a small wage he was expected to serve his master as a servant. The average craftsman's workshop was generally very small; excavations at Corinth have shown that a master craftsman can seldom have had more than two assistants, and this practice was doubtless generally applied.

Any breach of a guild's law was punishable by a fine, by mutilation or by expulsion. However, exclusion from a guild did not necessarily reduce the culprit to permanent unemployment. He was permitted to try to earn his living by practising his trade as a free lance, working for anyone who would employ him. Many doubtless succeeded in finding work in monasteries such as that of the Studius in Constantinople, which, at any rate in the ninth century, employed metal-workers, linen-weavers and shoe-makers, and sold the wares which they produced; others were probably able to enter the workshops owned by the nobility, where, as in the imperial workshops, a high proportion of the workers were slaves. Slave labour was so widely used in Byzantium that it became an important factor in increasing the output of luxury goods and in keeping down the prices of essential commodities.

During the opening phase of Byzantine history the rarest luxuries were imported chiefly from the East, jewels from India and Persia, silks from China. Trade with the East was so highly developed that about the year 522 Cosmas Indicopleustes was able to write a detailed account of a journey he had made to the Malabar coast. Luxury wares were treated from the start as state monopolies. The more important workshops, which made the costliest goods, especially silk and metal-work, were established in the precincts of the Great Palace in Constantinople. The guilds in charge of them ranked as imperial and took precedence over all the others. Their members were expected, like the members of the factions, in case of need to defend particular sections of the capital's walls and were entitled to take part in ceremonial processions. It was their privilege to decorate the tribunes used by the emperors when visiting a guild with purple silk hangings and gold and silver ornaments. The guild of the Purple Dyers was the oldest of the imperial guilds. It had been established during the reign of Heraclius (610–41), when it was given workshops close to the Hippodrome, in the fashionable baths of Zeuxippus, where its members worked for the exclusive use of the sovereign and his

43   Quadriga design on an eighth-century silk textile

family. Goods not needed by them were sold by the emperor for the benefit of the exchequer.

Until the introduction of the silk-worm to Byzantium silk was so scarce that it was coveted by westerners even more than spices or jewels. For that very reason Cleopatra had refused to wear anything other than silk, even insisting that her underclothes be made of it. In Rome, under Julius Caesar its cost was so high that only the richest people could afford to buy it. The method of making silk no less than the material itself had been jealously guarded by China throughout the centuries. However, in the second century AD the Han emperor Wu-ti agreed to export limited amounts of the material to the western world in return for such western specialities as glass, enamels and high-quality wool and cotton stuffs. The men bringing the coveted bales to the Byzantine capital had to undergo long, arduous and, at times, dangerous journeys. An average of 230 days' actual travel, excluding those spent in caravanserais as a result of bad weather or other mishaps, were needed to convey the silk bales back from the re-loading point in far-distant central Asia to Constantinople.

Till the secret of its manufacture had been learnt only members of the imperial family were entitled to import and wear silk. If they happened to have more silk than they needed they sometimes sold it, but only to certain merchants, and then chiefly for export. It was no more demeaning in Byzantium for a prince or nobleman to be involved in commercial affairs than it was in sixteenth- and seventeenth-century England or Florence. Even when she became empress, Zoe (1042–55) continued to spend much of her day making perfume. According to Psellus she turned her bedroom into a factory by installing braziers in it. Each of her servants was allotted a particular task, some bottling the scent, others blending it, others distilling it. In winter these duties were pleasant enough, but in summer her room became a furnace. As both she and her sister and co-ruler Theodora disliked fresh air, 'fine houses, meadows and gardens', they did not mind. Many an emperor was able to add to his income by going into business; in the thirteenth century John III Vatatzes (1222–54) was able to make sufficient profit from the sale of his poultry to buy his wife a new crown. Byzantine noblemen often engaged in trade; some were highly successful at it, especially in running carpet factories. In the tenth century the most important of these were situated in Sparta and the Peloponnese, and it is tantalising that no examples of their output survive to give us an idea of what Byzantine carpets were like.

During the early period of Byzantine silk manufacture the bulk of the silk-worms were raised near the southern shores of the Caspian and Black Seas. The cocoons were then transported to Egypt, Syria and Constantinople for spinning and weaving into lengths. At the same time, much Chinese silk continued to be imported. At first Tyre and Alexandria ranked as the foremost Byzantine centres of silk production, but as soon as looms were set up in the Great Palace's workshops very fine silks were produced there. These workshops were run as a crown monopoly, and both men and women were employed in them. Soon smaller workshops became established in the provinces, but the growing aggressiveness of the militant Arabs and the desire of the emperors to concentrate production in the capital led them to close the provincial workshops in the seventh century. Some were then transferred to Constantinople where the eparch was in a better position to regulate and control their output. Henceforth all lengths produced in the imperial workshops had to be marked by having either the emperor's name or monogram or else that of the eparch responsible for the country's two main luxury trades (silk and metal-work) woven into the selvage. None of these stuffs could be exported and the silk produced was so carefully controlled that, as in Justinian's day, the court ladies who were entitled to wear silk could do so only if they purchased it in the House of Lamps, as the Crown sale room situated in the Great Palace was called. It owed its name to the lights which were kept burning in it throughout the night, and which could be seen shining through its windows.

Apart from being confined to the imperial workshops, the silk industry was controlled by no less than five guilds. One was reserved for the merchants who handled the imported silk in its raw state and another for those who brought it in woven into lengths or made up into robes; a third included the spinners and weavers (44); a fourth was reserved for those who dyed the silk any colour other than purple; these dyers were extremely skilled and even though they were obliged to import many of their colours from the East they were also able to produce an immense variety of shades, offering by the tenth century many tones of a single colour. In exceptional cases certain weavers were, however, permitted to dye their own stuffs. The fifth guild was reserved for the men who sold the silk. As supplies increased it became easier for them to do

44   A weaver at work

so, for the government found that the sale of silk, which had to be paid for in gold, helped to keep the country's valuable gold coinage within the Empire's borders—a side effect of the industry which proved particularly valuable after Syria and Egypt had been lost to the Arabs.

The first silks woven in Byzantium were probably plain, but within a very few years patterned lengths were being made in Constantinople and by the ninth century, when the textile industry was at its most productive, silks that remain remarkable for the magnificence and elaboration of their designs were being made at any rate in the imperial workshops. They included brocades and cloth of gold and silver of great splendour. Silks of so high a quality were avidly desired by western rulers and notables, but even at that late date they were never exported. Though the emperors were reluctant for foreigners to obtain even small pieces of these fabrics, they nevertheless occasionally sent a length as a present to a person whom they wished particularly to distinguish. Even the somewhat simpler silks which were released for sale were so rigorously controlled that Liutprand, Otto I's ambassador to Byzantium, was not permitted, when leaving Constantinople at the end of his mission, to take home the lengths he had been allowed to purchase from a merchant.

The deep-rooted Byzantine determination not to let their luxury wares leave the country is reflected in the tenth century in the dues imposed on Venetian merchants: they had to pay only two *nomismata* for every ship entering Constantinople, but 15 on it leaving laden. The dues were intended to encourage foreign merchants to sell their goods in Constantinople whilst discouraging exports. A 10 per cent tax was imposed on all goods entering or leaving the country, a higher duty being charged on the few silk exports which were permitted. As a further measure to retain their luxury wares at home Greek merchants who, until the eighth century, had been allowed to go to Italy to trade were no longer permitted to do so, but in the tenth century a colony of Greek traders succeeded in establishing itself in Cairo and a Muslim one had by then taken root in Athens. In the eleventh century Greek merchants obtained permission to travel in Persia. Lest they should

45   A weaver and an embroidress

cheapen silk, Byzantine merchants were not allowed to import it for themselves from the East, but they could buy it from the Syrian merchants who came to Constantinople to sell silk made in Sidon for church hangings or noblemen's cloaks from Baghdad.

Even during the tenth century many of the Syrian importers would stay on in Constantinople for as long as ten years to act as middlemen there. By then Constantinople had ceased to be the only centre of silk production in Byzantium and both the government and private workshops were carrying on a profitable trade in many a provincial town. Thebes was among the first of these to acquire an international reputation, but Trebizond was soon competing with it and by the twelfth century Andros and Salonica had surpassed it. At the time Salonica was at the height of its prosperity, deriving much of its wealth from exporting its own products as well as those it had imported from Constantinople, sending them westward along Rome's Via Ignatia, through present-day Nis and Belgrade to countries beyond. Merchants from Egypt and Spain, Greeks from Monemvasia and traders from Sicily, as well as the local peasants, all made a point of attending its great annual fair. When at its peak the yearly tax levied on the shops, markets and imports is estimated to have reached the astonishing total of some £37 million.

The production of fine woollen fabrics and linen formed an important branch of Byzantium's textile industry. Many lengths were woven by women working at home (45). Much of the linen was of top quality. Sometimes its weavers made it up into garments, but generally clothes were made by tailors using stuffs purchased for the purpose. They sewed with bronze needles, using pottery cotton reels. Embroideries were also sought-after exports. Originally a Syrian speciality, the art of embroidery soon became a Constantinopolitan one. In Justinian's day work of such high artistry was being produced in the capital that he turned to local needlewomen for the curtains for the *ciborium* of his cathedral of Haghia Sophia. The designs they embroidered on them took the form of silver columns linked by three gold arches; in the centre one they worked a figure of Christ wearing garments of gold.

Important though the textile industry was, those of the metal-workers and jewellers were equally so. During early Byzantine history Antioch ranked as the centre where the finest jewels and the most exquisite and valuable metal objects were produced, but once again Constantinople quickly outpaced the older city. At first silver was in such

46 Silver dish showing Meleager and Atalanta

47 Bejewelled gold earrings

short supply in the capital that it carried a 10 per cent tax (from which gold was exempt). Silver vessels of that date were made in the imperial workshops for the emperor's use. Though some may have been exported, most were retained in the palace, sometimes to be used to bribe barbarian chieftains, sometimes to be exchanged or sent abroad as imperial gifts. Like the imperial silks these vessels were stamped with the name or monogram either of the reigning emperor or of the eparch concerned with their production. The craftsmen who made these magnificent pieces were also entrusted with the responsible task of testing and stamping the silver coins and iron bars which, from the year 375 onwards, were handed in to the exchequer in payment of taxes.

Though usury was strongly disapproved of it was found to be necessary and could not therefore be forbidden. Goldsmiths acted as money-lenders, but the government tried to control the rates of interest on loans. Though the average rate varied from 4 to 8 per cent, Justinian forbade more than 12 to be charged. Gradually the rate came to depend upon the borrower's rank and occupation, noblemen being charged $4\frac{1}{2}$ per cent, merchants $8\frac{1}{3}$, and others $6\frac{1}{4}$. When the Italians gained a foothold in Byzantium they proceeded to replace the Greeks as money-lenders. A highly efficient clearance system between towns existed in Byzantium several centuries before anything of the sort was known to western Europe. The goldsmiths may have been responsible for evolving it, though the credit may well lie with the state bank of Byzantium: created probably at much the same time as Byzantium's coins, the bank became the only institution in which people could buy or sell money. If they were found doing so elsewhere the sum involved was confiscated. In addition to handling currency the bank also collected the dues levied on ships using the Straits, and all customs charges.

From the start sharp distinctions were drawn between jewellers of different types. Thus not only did silversmiths and goldsmiths work in separate workshops, but in addition the men engaged in making the gold granules and wires so much used in jewellery, and the men who later made the gold partitions which the enamellers filled with coloured pastes, were all given separate places of work. There were men both among the silver- and the goldsmiths who did nothing but make regalia, insignia and badges of office, and the ceremonial vessels and dishes needed by the court and Church. Some metal-workers specialised in bronze, others in copper or lead. The majestic bronze doors which were made for the cathedral of Haghia Sophia in 838 were not in their day unique. Both bronze and silver doors were fitted to several halls in the Great Palace, but those in Haghia Sophia are the only ones to survive to testify to the skill of their makers. Between them, the metal-workers and jewellers furnished the court, Church and state with all the ceremonial vessels they required, with their jewellery, decorations, table-ware and kitchen utensils (48), as well as with the reliquaries, crosses and gospel covers needed by the faithful, and horse trappings varying from ornate, bejewelled examples to the strictly utilitarian.

In addition metal-workers, whether living in the capital, in provincial towns or in the countryside, made the innumerable articles required in everyday life, especially knives and tools such as mattocks, hatchets and spades. Iron railings were constantly

48   Table-ware: *A* Silver chalice; *B* Bronze goblet; *C* Bronze ewer; *D* Pottery cup; *E* Bronze vessel; *F* Silver strainer

needed for windows or balconies, and iron bars for strengthening doors and chests. Bolts, keys, locks and vast quantities of nails were always being sold, but the more skilled workmen also produced chandeliers, called *polycandeli*, formed of bronze or iron hoops. These were of various sizes and were suspended from the ceilings of churches, and doubtless also of palaces and mansions; oil lamps fitted with wicks were fixed to the top of the hoop and ornaments hung from them—in the case of churches, symbols such as crosses, fish or birds.

Metal-workers also made the chains and anchors required by the country's extensive shipping. The most highly skilled craftsmen fashioned the clockwork devices which became fashionable in the ninth century. It has been suggested that the demand for these was created by the works of Arab mathematicians at the time when Emperor Theophilus was strongly attracted to everything Arabic. (His admiration for the Arabs in fact led him to build himself a room in the Persian style and to adorn it with niches worked in the Eastern stalactite manner.) During his reign the jewellers employed in the imperial workshops made the ingenious mechanical devices of which the imperial throne was the most elaborate creation. The designs for these stemmed at any rate sometimes from the Byzantine and not the Arab world: for instance, a director of the imperial metal-workers' workshop, a relative of Patriarch Anthony, invented the silver tree bearing on its branches metal singing birds. This creation was melted down by Michael III (842–67) when he was in need of silver. The throne was a later work, dating from the tenth century. It was being used in the throne room in the Magnaura Palace in 968 when Liutprand was astonished to see, at a given signal, the lions which formed part of its supports start to roar, and the birds on it to sing, whilst other metal animals rose to their feet. Constantine VII Porphyrogenitus mentions some cast gold cocks, goats and sheep which, aping a fountain, sprayed out jets of rose water. Like the marble and stone needed by sculptors and builders, many of the metals used by the metal-workers were provided by convicts who worked in the quarries and mines (all of which were state-owned).

Byzantium's economic prosperity was directly related to the stability and high value of its currency. It owed much of its reputation to Constantine I's decision to replace the country's rather unstable silver coinage by a gold coin, the value of which was related to its weight. He took as his standard the gold coin which was known first as the Latin *solidus*; later it was called by the Greek word of *nomisma,* and later still, under Italian influence, it became the *besant.* Constantine stipulated that the *solidus* was to weigh 1/72 of a pound, that is to say 4·48 grammes. To begin with, large-scale transactions were calculated either on the basis of 100 *nomismata* or by weight, but when it be-

49 Gold coins showing Justinian II and John I Zimisces

came the habit to clip the gold coins as part payments for a transaction, it was usual to weigh the coins instead of counting them—a practice which established the habit of clipping the gold pieces to obtain an exact payment in preference to giving change. In the fourth and early fifth centuries the emperors were anxious to retain the gold coins within their borders. First Valentinian II (371–92), then Theodosius II (408–50) forbade barbarians trading with Byzantium to pay for their purchases in copper, and only used the *solidus* to pay for the spices they imported from India and silks from China. In the year 498 Anastasius decided to issue a large bronze coin stamped with the letter 'M' to be valued at 40 *nummia* or units as well as some smaller ones stamped with a 'K' for 20 units, an 'I' for ten and an 'E' for five. All these coins, whether of gold, silver or bronze, retained their full value both within Byzantium and abroad until the eighth century, when the Ommayad Caliphs were able to threaten the *solidus* by seizing control of the bulk of the Arab trade. As a result the Byzantines found that they could only import Eastern goods across Anatolia, whilst the Arabs were able to sell them direct to the Western world. However, the Byzantines succeeded in counteracting this move by using their navy to blockade Egypt and Syria, employing bases such as Malta, Lampedusa, Sicily and Tunis for the purpose. Thus the Ommayad threat to the *solidus* remained an empty one. The coin retained its full value till the ninth century, though under Basil II (976–1025) its value fell to 18 carats and both a light and a heavy *nomisma* were in circulation. As a result its value fell abroad until, under Constantine IX Monomachus (1042–55), it came to be worth no more than 12 carats. Alexius I (1081–1118) found it necessary to re-value it. He minted several different issues and succeeded in stabilising its value, though at a low rating. The Latins continued to use the *nomisma* during their occupation of Constantinople and its stability was therefore not greatly impaired. On re-entering Constantinople Michael Palaeologus found himself in such need of funds, especially gold, that he recalled all gold coins from circulation and melted them down. He did this ostensibly in order to mint a new issue stamped with a picture of the Virgin protecting the walls of Constantinople, but in reality, in order to debase its value. Andronicus II (1282–1328) was to link the *solidus* to the *grosso* and, as Italian traders gained an ever firmer footing in Byzantium, the Greek coin lost its international role to the Italian. Even so, few other nations, whether in ancient or modern times, can boast of a currency which retained its original value throughout close on 1,000 years.

Until about the year 490, Byzantine coins resembled those of Rome (*49*), showing one one side the bust of the reigning emperor rendered in a markedly Roman style, and on the other a Latin inscription. Somewhat later the inscriptions were partly in Latin, partly in Greek, whilst the reverse side was stamped either with the emblem of a particular city, a figure of the archangel Michael or a cross. Justinian was the first to express his deeply religious outlook by stamping one side of his gold coins with the crucifixion scene. By that time the portraits stamped on the coins had acquired a markedly Greek character. Justinian II (685–95) stamped one side of his coins with the picture of the head of Christ set against a cross—a choice which may well have been intended to commemorate the rescue by Heraclius (610–41) of a portion of the True Cross from the Persians. All such figural representations disappeared during the iconoclast period (723 to 843) though on some a cross continued to appear till about the middle of the eighth century. After iconoclasm Basil I (867–86) was the first to use religious designs on his coins; those produced during the tenth century, when the members of the gifted Macedonian dynasty ruled, are artistically the finest. They generally display an inscription on the reverse, giving the emperor's imperial titles; after some years the inscription was omitted and, instead, a rendering either of Christ or the Virgin appeared on one side and the emperor's portrait on the other. Christ and the emperor were sometimes represented enthroned, sometimes standing, whilst the Virgin was often shown accompanied by saints. Throughout the years, whenever rulers reigned jointly or an emperor had crowned his co-ruler, their portraits appeared side by side on the same face of the coin (*49*). Under the Palaeologi the designs on the coins had a narrative character, depicting either a coronation or a city.

Almost from the start the mint became an imperial monopoly with the result that gold coins were, with few exceptions, issued in Constantinople. However, during the Latin occupation of the capital, Salonica, Nicaea and Trebizond all issued coins of their own. Until the eighth century silver coins had not only been issued in Constantinople, but also in Rome, Carthage, Salonica, Nicomedia, Antioch, Alexandria, Chersonesus and Sicily, but the Macedonians put an end to the practice.

Apart from the imperial monopolies, until the sixth century the Eastern trade was by far the most profitable of all, for it dealt with such desirable luxuries as spices, ivory and jewels and such essentials as corn and cotton. Though spices were very expensive all aspired to use them, as they made it possible for food which had lost its first freshness to be consumed with pleasure. They were so much sought-after that it is not surprising to find Alaric demanding, in 408, 3,000 pounds of pepper as part of the ransom for raising the siege of Constantinople. India provided Byzantium with these condiments, yet never enough to meet the growing demands of a prosperous society. India likewise furnished the supplies of ivory needed by the master craftsmen who carved them into panels for caskets, book covers, triptychs, diptychs, even furniture and doors. As the source of these articles, no less than for political reasons, India was highly esteemed in Byzantium. One emperor even built himself a room in the Indian style in the Great Palace and many

50 Masons raising a
pillar

Greek artists found inspiration in Indian themes. One of the finest pieces of early Byzantine silver to have come down to us is the magnificent sixth-century dish adorned with a figure personifying India.

Many Persians and Arabs were among the skilled artisans working in Constantinople. Though some earned their living as quack doctors, the majority were craftsmen. They may have been responsible for teaching the Constantinopolitans how to make paper, having themselves learnt to do so from the Chinese, even though the special paper used in the imperial chancery continued to be imported from Baghdad. It was also doubtless due to Eastern influence that, from late in the thirteenth century, Byzantine architects started inserting glazed vessels produced by Byzantine potters in the façades of their buildings, and more especially in their churches.

The building trade absorbed many men and much material. Workers in stone, marble and bone also made luxury articles—beads, crosses and other ornaments—whilst carpenters and other workers in wood produced many household articles, such as bowls, spoons, and furniture. They relied on such tools as axes, adzes, gimlets and saws, with which they achieved quite remarkable results. The making of string nets and baskets provided much employment, but the soap, and more particularly the candle, industries were especially important. Candles were not only needed in the home, but also for processional purposes and above all in the churches, where they were used not only for illumination but were lit before icons and on altars as tokens of reverence. Nevertheless, the potters' and leather-workers' guilds were the largest in the country. Like the woollen clothing of the working classes, much of the pottery was produced in the country by the villagers, but many potters brought their wares to sell in the markets which were held regularly in all towns. In later times, probably as a result of Eastern influence, much pottery of really high quality was also made. Though no kiln sites have so far been discovered, the bulk of the finer wares are so beautiful that there can be little doubt that these were made in the major cities, such as Constantinople and Salonica. Nicomedia was also an important centre of production and perhaps too Nicaea which was later, under the name of Isnik, to become the main centre of the Turkish pottery industry. Especially characteristic of Byzantium are the revetment plaques which were made in the manner of a tile, both to serve as icons or to be used as mouldings, to cover joins or other structural features of a building, or perhaps to frame mosaics or paintings on walls.

Pottery was used to produce every sort of domestic article from a sieve or great wine or oil jar to cups, plates, dishes and bowls. Even chafing dishes on high perforated stands, into which some sort of heater was put, have been found. Some of the vessels were crude, but others were made and decorated with great artistry.

In early times Alexandria and Antioch handled most Byzantine imports and exports, but Constantinople's outstanding geographical advantages quickly made themselves felt, and the loss of the older ports to the Arabs did no more than confirm the role which the capital had by then assumed as the Empire's foremost industrial and commercial city. From the end of the seventh century all Europe's Eastern trade passed through Constantinople, the capital serving both as a great transit port and a terminal. All ships carrying Europe's trade with the Orient, whether imports or exports, had to be unloaded in Constantinople, even if they were only in transit, in order to undergo a rigorous customs examination. High dues were charged on all articles and intelligence officers were employed there and in such major ports as Abydos to track down smugglers. Until the seventh century much of the transit trade was handled by Syrians, but with the loss of the eastern provinces to the Arabs it passed into Jewish hands. The latter lived with their families outside the capital's main walls, and the majority settled in the Blachernae district where their quarter was enclosed by a defensive wall. Within it the Jews enjoyed considerable political independence and religious freedom. They were therefore able to build as many synagogues there as they wished. Some of these were of such obvious architectural merit that they aroused universal admiration. However, the Jews were not destined to remain prosperous for long. Their trade suffered in the tenth century when the Arabs tried to break the blockade which the Byzantines had imposed on them. As a first move towards that end the Emir of Kairouan in North Africa captured Sicily and Carthage. This made the Straits of Messina especially valuable to the Byzantines since they now afforded the only means of communication with Naples, Genoa and Pisa. Italy's maritime cities were by this time contributing to the prosperity of Hadanid Syria and Fatimid Egypt—both of which had eclipsed Baghdad—by entering into direct trade with them, bypassing Byzantium. In return for luxuries Venice in particular showed no hesitation in supplying the Muslims with wood for the manufacture of men-of-war and munitions, though both these were to be used against fellow-Christians—albeit

Orthodox Christians. The Byzantines were obliged to close their eyes to these distressing developments in order to maintain their own trade with Venice. When the Arabs gained control of the Straits of Messina (to retain it till the eleventh century), the Byzantines started to use the port of Bari in southern Italy and retained their monopoly over silks, purple dye and ivory. However, Italy was rapidly becoming an important centre of textile production and soon started exporting cheap silks to Byzantium, selling them freely there and undercutting the sale of the vastly superior Byzantine stuffs.

During the mid-Byzantine period Salonica came to rank second to Constantinople from both a commercial and an industrial point of view. Corinth which, with Sparta, lay on the route taken by Italian ships sailing from Venice, Bari, Amalfi and Sicily to Greece also became prosperous, whilst Trebizond on the south-eastern shores of the Black Sea gained control of the overland Eastern trade and exported its own silks and silver articles. Its annual fair was attended not only by Greek merchants, but also by Muslims and Armenians. Overland travel was not unduly arduous. Though the roads were not so well maintained as in Roman times they were kept in reasonably good condition; the cost of the repairs was met by tolls, paid by all except high officials.

The merchant navy contributed very considerably to Byzantium's trade. The Rhodian Maritime Law which laid down conditions for the employment of fishermen also did so for crews manning the merchant ships (51) and for the passengers sailing on them. Wages on these ships were low; in 709 a steward earned two *nomismata* a month. Space on a vessel was divided equally between the passengers and crew, though a man was entitled to three times as much room as a woman. For reasons of safety no passenger was allowed either to fry fish or chop wood on board ship, but each passenger was entitled to a daily measure of water and to purchase food from the ship's cook. A captain had the right to abandon a passenger on land or to jettison his cargo if it seemed to him essential to do so either to escape capture by pirates or to avoid running into a sudden storm or some similar disaster; a system of insurance appears to have existed for compensating those who encountered such misfortunes. Arab pirates were a constant menace to shipping, though a system of convoying did much to control them. A ship which foundered near the shore was in almost as much danger of being looted by its fellow-countrymen as it was by pirates, for the poverty-stricken villagers would descend upon a

51 Typical ninth-century coastal and fishing craft

wreck like locusts, rapidly stripping it to its hull. Ships were not always owned by merchants, as was generally the case in medieval Europe; many belonged to the merchant seamen who manned them. In the ninth and tenth centuries there were many splendid vessels, equipped with improvements unknown in other merchant fleets. The most important of these were a square stern and the rig known as the lateen sail. However, by then the bulk of the trade was being carried in foreign bottoms. Each nation had begun to transport its own goods and the Italians had acquired their own landing grounds in Constantinople, which enabled them to gain a foothold in the capital. Venetian galleys usually needed 24 days to reach Constantinople, sailing past Corfu and Patras. From the eighth century many merchants used to travel with their goods in order to be able personally to purchase from the Byzantines such essential imports as bread, wine and meat; but they were never allowed to buy fish, which was considered the basic food of the very poor. In the tenth and eleventh centuries, when England was trading with Byzantium, she used Italian merchantmen to carry the goods, at any rate as far as the mainland of western Europe.

Russian trade with Byzantium began on a large scale in the tenth century. Russian merchants converged on Constantinople, travelling either across Transcaucasia, from an eastern Black Sea port or, more usually, via Chersonesus, down the Dnieper river and across the Black Sea to the Byzantine capital. They came with fish, leather goods, honey, wax, and caviar from the Sea of Azov; they took back with them horses, pepper, silk (some of which they re-exported), wine, fine glass, metal-work and, after the country's conversion to Christianity in 988, church furnishings. Though the movements and number of all foreign merchants entering the Byzantine capital were carefully controlled by a *quaestor*, exceptionally strict rules were imposed on the Russians, probably because from about 860 they had started launching heavy attacks on Constantinople. At least two of these had carried the Russians to the very walls of the Byzantine capital. It was in fact due to their military victories that, in 907, the Kievans were able to obtain from the Byzantines trading concessions of an unusually favourable nature. The treaty exempted them from paying either entry or exit dues—a privilege which they forfeited in 944—and entitled them to receive free issues of bread, wine, meat, fish and vegetables throughout their stay in Constantinople. In addition a special bath house was provided for their use and, on departure, they were equipped with whatever sails and ropes they needed for their return journey, and an anchor. Nevertheless, like all foreigners, the Russians had to report their presence to the Prefect of Law on arriving in the capital. Their stay there was limited to three months each year; any goods unsold at the end of that period could, however, be left with the Prefect to dispose of, the sums realised by him being handed to them on their return to Constantinople a year later. In addition to these restrictions the Russians were not permitted to live within the walls of Constantinople, but had to reside in special quarters prepared for them in the Magnaura district; they could only enter Constantinople by one gate and had to be always unarmed and accompanied by a Greek official. If they came in a group their number was not permitted to exceed 50. Similar restrictions on living in the city were not imposed on others and, in the eleventh century, some 60,000 foreigners, mostly Italian merchants, resided in the capital. The Muslims amongst them were free to perform their religious practices in mosques of their own. But the Italians obtained more concessions than the others: the Genoese enjoyed particular privileges, for it was they who, in 1261, in return for helping the emperor to re-enter Constantinople and regain his throne, were given the district of Galata to live in and, what was far more valuable, the right to use the Straits at will, concessions which were to ruin the Byzantine economy within a couple of centuries.

7

TOWN LIFE

With the exception of Constantinople, all major Byzantine towns were ancient foundations. They had grown up in antiquity, expanding in a haphazard manner. In the process each acquired its own characteristic features. Thus, by Byzantine times, Alexandria had become an essentially industrial and commercial city, where the working class was always on the verge of rioting. Antioch, with its famous summer resort of Daphne about two hours' drive distant, was of a quieter temperament; its handsome stone houses were adorned with elaborate floor mosaics reflecting the stability and wealth of its theatre-loving middle class, most of them prosperous traders. Old cities such as these were essentially international in outlook, but the Byzantine government ensured that, from the very start, all became strongholds of Orthodoxy. The change probably helped the Greek inhabitants, whilst still a minority, to impose their own language and culture upon these ancient cities. They did so during the opening phase of Byzantine history, at the very time when Egypt and Syria were contributing much both to the culture and the economy of the Byzantine state. With the loss to the Arabs of these prosperous regions town life declined and Asia Minor became all-important to Byzantium. Asia Minor was valuable not only for essential supplies of basic food and of minerals, but also for its own cultural heritage dating back to Phrygian and Hittite times. It made its impact felt in intellectual circles in Constantinople, but its effect was to some extent counteracted by the increasing strength of the Slavs living on Byzantium's northern and western borders. However, Slavic influence proved scarcely more significant than that of Asia Minor, for the appearance on Byzantium's eastern borders from the tenth century onwards of the Seljukid Turks and their gradual conquest of Anatolia, coinciding as it did with the advance of Saladin's Saracens, again turned Byzantine eyes eastward; at the same time it encouraged the growth of towns at the expense of that of the countryside. The arrival of the Mongols at the start of the thirteenth century kept attention firmly fixed on the East, notwithstanding the Latin occupation of Constantinople and the growing importance of Italy's merchant states. Because of these political developments Constantinople became even more strongly international in character than any of Byzantium's older cities, her population numbering more foreign residents of more diverse nationalities than were to be found in any other Byzantine town.

As a newly created town Constantinople was laid out along new lines from the outset; these combined to some extent ideas that had been developed in Rome with those prevalent in the East, for example at Palmyra. For that reason, rather than because of its role as the capital of Byzantium, a description of Constantinople provides us with a clearer idea of Byzantine views on town-planning than would one dealing with any of the Empire's other famous cities. It is all the more unfortunate, therefore, that so much of ancient Constantinople lies buried some seven metres deep beneath the average street-level of present-day Istanbul. Travellers and pilgrims to the Holy Land have left us a vivid account of the city's beauty and magnificence, but these are worded in such general terms that they are of little help to archaeologists trying to reconstruct the town's original plan. Excavations were started in Constantinople after the First World War. Though they have disclosed many valuable facts, work has in the main been confined to small areas of open ground near the Hippodrome and the Great Palace, and the sites of most of the major buildings mentioned in early records still await discovery. Today it is possible to form only a very general idea of what this once world-renowned capital looked like.

The area enclosed by Constantinople's walls contained seven hills. This resemblance to Rome was increased by the town's lay-out for, though the main streets conformed to the triangular shape of the peninsula, they followed, in so far as the lie of the land permitted, the rectilinear plan admired in the Old Rome. To begin with, as at Ostia near Rome, the richer houses were generally two storeys high, but already the names of their owners were cut on the walls fronting onto the streets. Many entrance doors were made of iron studded with stout nails, yet the street sides of such houses can hardly be called their 'fronts' for, in contrast to Ostia, in the earlier phase these were left blank, the windows all being placed on the opposite wall, where they overlooked an enclosed courtyard. The owner's stables, cattle sheds, poultry houses and essential store rooms gave out onto the courtyard, which was generally large enough for exercising his horses and, most important of all, to include the cistern or well on which the household depended for its water supplies. However, in the fifth century, taller houses appeared in Constantinople and, although the lower sections of the walls fronting onto the street remained blank, it became customary to insert rows of windows in the upper floors. These were either rectangular or rounded at the top; stucco frames were fitted into them which were in their turn set with small panes of glass. These glass sections were either octagonal or rectangular; they were made from slabs of glass beaten flat and cut into sections measuring 8–12 inches in length, though those used in the finest houses were as much as 2 feet long. It seems probable that iron bars were fitted outside the lower windows and that some of these already bulged outward at the bottom to form a sort of window seat, as was to become general in Ottoman Turkey. Many of the upper windows were fitted with balconies; indeed, balconies became so popular and so numerous that when Emperor Zeno (474–91) came to the throne he passed a law forbidding streets to be less than 12 feet wide and balconies less than 15 feet from the ground or under 10 feet away from the front of the opposite house. Strict regulations were also in force to ensure that no house encroached on a neighbour's light or his view of the sea and that each was fitted with drainpipes and gutters. Though palaces were generally constructed of marble blocks erected on brick foundations, most houses were built of brick; the few that were of stone were generally faced with stucco. Many of the richer houses had flat roofs which were used as terraces during the summer months; others had sloping roofs made of tiles with a cross set proudly at their summit.

The houses were generally built round a central hall. These halls were used as reception rooms by the men of the household. Stone or wooden columns, though placed in the hall to act as supports for the upper storeys where the family's rooms were situated, served also as adornments. A staircase, in most cases built of wood, though stone was used in the more prosperous houses and marble in the very richest, led to the principal rooms disposed on the first floor. The windows of these opened onto galleries overlooking the courtyard. Houses such as these generally contained more than one sitting-room; like most of the others these had plastered walls which were often decorated with crosses and religious texts, but, at any rate in later times, mural paintings of a secular character were quite common. The sitting-rooms were used more by the men of the household than by the women; the latter spent most of their time in the company of their children and serving maids in the rooms situated in the top storey of the house. Like monasteries, houses such as these contained a hot room for use on the bitterly cold days that are typical of Constantinople's winter climate; many of the richer houses were also centrally heated by means of the hypocaust system used by the Romans, though most people relied on charcoal braziers. The kitchens contained a low hearth with square pipes forming a chimney above them to carry away the smoke of the wood fires, which were often used in preference to open charcoal stoves. All the houses were provided with lavatories, the drains of which eventually emptied into the sea. It was also customary for each household to have its own bath house, usually situated in the garden. Rich people also often had a private chapel, or at any rate a shrine in their grounds. In contrast, the very poor were deplorably housed, only the most fortunate among them living in small houses roofed with rushes and with beaten earth floors. However, from the fifth century, skyscraper blocks of flats, containing anything from five to nine storeys, were built to serve as tenements. They were divided into flatlets which were let off to working people, who generally lived in them in poverty and near-slum conditions. Hovels of abysmal wretchedness were to be seen everywhere, many springing up almost overnight to house squatters who, having once erected a roof over their heads, were able to stay on as permanent inhabitants. Some of the worst slums grew up in the neighbourhood of the Great Palace; in these sinister districts murders and thefts were common, and the riots which so often disrupted the capital's life frequently started here.

The authorities were never able to solve the problem presented by these slums, which owed their existence to the magnetic attraction which Constantinople exercised from the start, drawing people to itself from all parts of the Empire. By the fifth century Constantinople possessed 323 streets containing 4,383 houses, 20 state bakeries for dealing with those who were entitled to issues of free bread, and 120 additional bakeries. The population is believed to have been in the region of 500,000; by the ninth century the figure had risen to a million, but it dropped sharply during the Latin occupation of the city, and never rose again to anything like the same number.

Constantinople's founder had had a far smaller city in mind when he planned his new capital: he gave it its rectangular plan, and divided it roughly into two equal parts by means of its main street, the Mese. The Mese grew to be two miles long. It led from the main city gate at the south-western corner of the land walls to the cathedral of Haghia Sophia. Following the general line of the coast, though some distance from it, it passed such notable landmarks as the Forum of Theodosius (rediscovered by British archaeologists in 1928), the Forum Tauri and those named after Arcadius, Anastasius and Constantine. The latter was distinguished by a great porphyry column surmounted by a statue of the emperor; though the statue has disappeared, Constantine's column still survives in its original position, but the shaft is battered and the base has been repaired; it is known by the Turks as the Burnt Column. To the east of Constantine's Forum the Mese led past the Hippodrome and ended at the main entrance of the cathedral of Haghia Sophia—the mother church of the Orthodox world. The area in front of the cathedral had been laid out by Constantine as the town's main square. He had called it the Augustaion in memory of his mother, the Augusta Helena, enclosing it with columns and placing a statue of Helena at its centre. The Millium—a column which marked the start of the Mese and which, like a similar column in Rome, had the distances to various parts of the Empire inscribed on it—stood close to the Augustaion and on a line with the main entrance to the Great Palace situated farther to the east. The houses lining the Mese had low arcades with shops at street level. Some of the arcades were adorned with statues; as in other parts of the town the shops beneath them were grouped according to the wares sold in them; their entrance doors generally opened into a public hall which often contained a table with goods laid out on it.

Of all Constantinople's many entrance gates the one at the far end of the Mese ranked as the most important, for it was this gate which the emperors used whenever they set out for Europe, either to campaign against the turbulent Slavs or to inspect their western borderlands. It was at that point too that they made their official entry when they returned in triumph or presented themselves for coronation; and, with few exceptions, it was there that they were welcomed or bidden farewell by their sons and the highest dignitaries of the realm and all the senators. From as early as the reign of Theodosius this gate became associated in people's minds with ceremonial occasions. The gate was an impressive structure of white marble, and was fitted with great doors of burnished brass whose brilliance gave rise to the name, the 'Golden Gate'(7). Today, battered and bereft of these shimmering doors, the tarnished white marble structure does not at first sight seem to live up to its evocative name, but when the first feeling of disappointment has worn off the splendour of the gate's severe lines and the harmony of its superb proportions quickly kindle the visitor's admiration.

The Hippodrome was the centre of the townspeople's lives in a way which neither the Palace to the east, nor the cathedral of Haghia Sophia to the north could ever hope to be. Entrance to the Hippodrome was obtained on presentation of a token, but without charge, and the tiers of marble seats were open to the town's male inhabitants regardless of class or occupation. The first hippodrome in the city was built under Septimius Severus, but it was remodelled by Constantine I. In the Byzantine world the Hippodrome quickly came to combine the theatrical functions of Rome's Circus or Colosseum with those of a racecourse for charioteers. In addition, as was the case of the Agora at Athens and the Forum in Rome, it was also used for religious processions such as the important one on Palm Sunday, for state ceremonies and for political meetings. Political opinions were also expressed by means of athletic contests. On more than one occasion prisoners were publicly tortured in the Hippodrome.

The arena itself was primarily designed for chariot-racing and was wide enough to hold four chariots abreast; each was drawn by four horses and was therefore called a *quadriga*. The Hippodrome could hold 40,000 spectators; it was modelled on the Circus Maximus of Rome, but the games held in it were never quite so cruel as those organised in Rome. A row of monuments erected along the centre of the arena to form a *spina* marked the division between the downward and upward course. These monuments included the famous serpent column brought from Delphi on which the names of the states involved in the battle of Plataea were inscribed, and an Egyptian obelisk which Theodosius I set up on a sculptured base. Both survive in their original positions, though the racecourse lies buried under some three metres of earth and is now laid out as a garden. The base of the obelisk was decorated on all four sides with sculptures; one scene shows Theodosius accompanied by his courtiers seated in his box in the Hippodrome,

52   Children playing with hoops (mosaic detail)

presumably watching a race (*18*). The charioteers raced round the
spina in much the same way as the children shown bowling their
hoops on the mosaic scene from the floor of the Great Palace race
round two terminal structures shaped like turrets. To obtain an
idea of what an advancing *quadriga* must have looked like as it
thundered down the course we must turn to the sumptuous textiles
on which Byzantine weavers represented them (*43*) skilfully capturing the excitement of the race. Wide though the course was (about
60 metres by 480 metres long) great skill was required to race the
chariots on it at top speed. The people's excitement often reached
fever point and must have resembled that of a Spanish crowd
attending a bullfight today.

Two days of careful preparation preceded each race meeting. First
the emperor's permission had to be formally obtained, which took
the best part of a day. On the following day a notice was hung up
at the entrances to the Hippodrome announcing the meeting. There-
upon the factions assembled at the Palace's Hippodrome Gate to
acclaim the emperor and to wish themselves victory in the contests,
which were to take place next day; then they moved off to inspect the
horses in their stalls within the palace precincts, in order to make sure
that all was well with them. Many of the emperors, notably Constantine VIII (1025–8), took a keen personal interest in the horses,
some even commissioning bronze statues of them from the leading
sculptors of the day, though others preferred busts of their favourite
charioteers. It is unfortunate that none of these has survived.

On the day of the races vast crowds assembled at dawn at the Hippodrome's gates. Meanwhile the emperor, dressed in his state robes, wearing the imperial regalia and carrying the lighted candle which he had used that morning when performing his prayers in his private chapel, would be making his way to

53 Incident from a circus in the Hippodrome

the audience chamber attached to his box in the Hippodrome to receive the greetings of the city's leading dignitaries. Whilst he was occupied in this manner his Master of the Horse was checking final arrangements for the races, that is to say, making certain that the charioteers, the leaders of the factions, the imperial guards, with their standards flying, those members of the factions engaged in ceremonial duties and the crowd of spectators were in their places. On notifying the emperor that the games could begin a signal was given and the doors of the royal box slowly opened. The emperor advanced onto the tribune and mounted the throne prepared for him in the imperial box. Standing on its step he raised a fold of his robe to bless the audience by performing the sign of the cross three times, first facing towards the centre block of seats, then to the right, and lastly to the left. Then he dropped a white kerchief as a signal for the games to begin: the stable doors flew open and the first four chariots drove onto the course. They had been chosen by lot to run the first of the day's eight races. Each competitor had to complete seven rounds of the course; seven ostrich eggs were set out on a stand in full view of all the spectators, and as each round of the course was completed an egg was removed from the stand. The prefect, dressed in a toga, awarded a crown or palm to the winner of each race.

The charioteers were passionately admired and acclaimed by their supporters. Constantine VIII even had the portraits of those he admired most executed in mosaic. To begin with charioteers were chosen from the upper ranks of the working class. But, just

as in nineteenth-century England pugilists were in such favour
that young noblemen took to the ring, so in tenth-century Byzantium did young men of high birth, even certain emperors, compete
in the Hippodrome. Constantine VIII not only watched the
contests but took part in them on equal terms with other com-
petitors. The charioteers wore short sleeveless tunics held in place
by crossed leather belts and leather puttees round their calves. By
the eleventh century empresses could not be restrained from
seeing the races, but they had to watch from the roof of one of the
palace churches, St Stephen, instead of from the imperial box. The
Latin occupation put an end to the games and none was held in
the capital after 1204, though they remained popular in many
other towns.

The intervals between each of the day's eight races were whiled
away by the antics of mimers, acrobats, actors and dancers, each
performing individual turns. On state occasions, similar theatrical
entertainments and team games were held in the Hippodrome
instead of the races. In the eleventh century Constantine VIII,
Michael V and Constantine IX all adored these entertainments,
though Constantine IX disliked organ music as much as he loved
that of flutes. Individual artists were treated as stars: the juggler
Philaraius was so lavishly rewarded by his admirers that he ended
his days as a very wealthy man. Many of the dances were performed by children, but acrobatic turns, mimes, songs, fooleries
and drolleries of various sorts were more popular with the crowd
than were dances or even tragedies; some of the productions
appear to have included singing, perhaps foreshadowing western
Europe's far later operatic works. The range of available diversions far exceeded anything else in contemporary Europe, and in
later times even came to include what can only be described as
cabaret shows. Foreigners visiting the city were amazed and
delighted by these entertainments. Certain book illuminations and
gold cloisonné enamel plaques survive which give an idea of how
the adult dancers looked. The finest of these plaques form part
of the crown of Constantine IX Monomachus (1042–55) (54).
They are now preserved in Budapest. Several of them show girls
dancing in a somewhat oriental, swaying manner, holding a
drapery above their heads. Even more evocative is the illumination
of Miriam dancing, in the famous Chludov manuscript preserved
in the USSR. Both groups of illustrations show that the Byzantine
taste in dancing was strongly oriental in character, the swaying,

54 The crown of the Emperor Constantine IX Monomachus

elegant girls moving in a manner evoking the arts of Syria, Persia and India rather than those of Greece or southern Europe. From the start the Church had disapproved so strongly of theatrical diversions that it had tried to abolish them; on failing to do so it concentrated on prohibiting them on Saturdays and Sundays.

The industrial and religious communities were for the most part concentrated in the suburbs of Constantinople, but even there the principal streets were at least five metres wide and paved with stone. Much of the central area was given over to public squares where markets were held and men gathered to hear the news and discuss the burning problems of the day. According to Anna Comnena, a distinguished officer who managed to escape from the Turks and return to Constantinople made his way immediately to the Forum of Constantine to give the men who were there an account of the battle in which he had been captured. In Justinian's day the Augustaion was the favourite public meeting place in the capital, perhaps because the town's bookshops were situated close by, whilst the public scribes waited near the entrance of Haghia Sophia. Towards the end of the sixth century a large food market was also held there. Precious gems and metals were sold in the

Agora or market place between the Great Palace and Constantine's Forum, and so the metal-workers, jewellers and money-lenders were also to be found there.

Though there were a great many shops in Constantinople, street sellers were numerous; they peddled such costly wares as embroideries worked in gold thread or such everyday items as *kumis* (mare's milk), shoes and textiles. Their numbers were swelled by many travelling astrologers, magicians and fortune-tellers. Carriages, sometimes mounted on solid gold wheels, yet lacking all forms of springing, thronged the streets. The finest were often exquisitely painted and gilt, and the trappings of the mules to which they were harnessed were of gilt leather. Ladies, whether travelling in a carriage or being carried in a litter, were accompanied by eunuchs who walked beside them clearing a passage through the crowd. Noblemen generally rode white horses, probably thoroughbred Arabs, using saddles embroidered in gold thread. In town they were accompanied by servants carrying sticks, who walked beside them helping to clear the road for their masters.

There were many public gardens in the town where the male population could find peace from the congestion and turmoil of the crowded streets. The interest which the Byzantines took in gardens is reflected in the profusion of floral motifs in their art, but it was also touchingly demonstrated during the excavations of the mosaic floor of the Great Palace, when the archaeologists uncovering the mosaic discovered that the empty area forming the centre of the floor had been made up with a layer of specially good earth which had obviously been brought there for the purpose of making a garden. Theophilus' love of gardening may have owed something to Eastern influence. He made a wonderful garden beside his polo ground, laying it out between the pitch and the pavilion known as the Tsykanisterion or polo palace. In the eleventh century Constantine IX took delight in making a pond in the centre of a park of fruit trees; he had its sides sunk below the level of the ground so that it could not be seen from a distance; as a result unsuspecting trespassers who entered the park in order to steal its fruit were apt to fall into it and had to swim ashore. The pond was fed by channels of water. Constantine also built himself a pleasure house of great charm near the pond; he was fond of sitting in it whenever he visited the park. On another occasion he decided to transform a field into a garden; at his orders large fruit trees were transplanted into it and much turfing

55 Theodore Metochites giving a model of his church to Christ

was carried out. Unfortunately no picture survives showing us what Byzantine gardens looked like. The herbals which exist list and illustrate a great many individual plants, but these are mainly medicinal or edible ones and little space is devoted to flowers of a purely decorative quality.

At least until the time of Leo VI (886–912) burial within the city walls was only permitted in the case of an emperor and his relations. Only they were entitled to lie in porphyry sarcophagi placed in mausolea or in tombs within a church; the latter habit arose in later times, when emperors were often buried in a favourite church. Andronicus I, for example, was laid to rest in the church of Mary Panachrantus (Fenari-issa Camii). After the Latin occupation of Constantinople the reinstated emperors could no longer afford to build churches or even chapels to serve as their mausolea, yet some of their courtiers included men who were in a position to do so. Early in the fourteenth century the Great Logothete Theodore Metochites devoted a considerable part of his large fortune to building in the neighbourhood of the Blachernae Palace a church dedicated to the 'Saviour in Chora', from the designation of Christ Chora or Heart of the Living (55). It was to serve as his mausoleum and was attached to a monastery; the church is now one of Istanbul's finest monuments and is known there under the name of Karieh Camii. Metochites adorned the lower sections of its walls with intricately veined marble panels and their upper sections with wall mosaics and paintings which are one of the glories of later Byzantine art. Having completed the church Metochites fell into disgrace and ended his days as a monk in the monastery which formed part of his endowment. Though by that time burial in tombs had become customary, in the early Byzantine period the rich, like their forebears of classical times, were buried in sarcophagi; these were generally made of marble and richly adorned with sculptures executed by leading artists of the day. Ordinary people were expected to use cemeteries situated outside the walls, yet graveyards nevertheless became established in many urban churchyards. In both cases graves were marked by tombstones simply inscribed with the dead person's name and occupation, followed by the good wishes of their relatives, and sometimes by their portraits. At a death, as in pagan times, professional mourners were employed. Though an emperor wore white when in mourning, all others wore black; this even applied to empresses, for Anna Comnena mentions that, at the death of her father, the empress removed her imperial veils, cut her hair and replaced her purple dress and shoes with black ones. On the third, ninth and fortieth days after burial (the intervals prescribed by Babylonian astrologers who based their calculations on the lunar cycle), the family would gather round the tomb to intone laments. The metaphors coined by friends in memory of the dead were not inscribed on the tombs, but were recited verbally and written down to be handed round and read over the tomb. The majority abounded in mythological allusions and were often based on mythological themes.

The attempts to limit burials in towns were probably as much for reasons of health as of lack of space. We know that plague and leprosy were widespread. Other diseases had by then been correctly diagnosed; more than one emperor had been found to suffer from arthritis, gout, dropsy, heart disease or consumption, whilst Michael IV was an epileptic. To treat these, and probably many other ailments which are not mentioned in surviving records, the Byzantines had an efficient and well-developed medical service. Each town had what was thought to be sufficient doctors for the size of its population, and contained hospitals, almshouses and orphanages. Each of these was in the charge of a trained professional who was answerable to a special eparch, though Constantinople's largest orphanage, an imperial foundation, was directed by an *Orphanotrophus*, generally a priest, responsible only to the emperor.

The Byzantines were well aware of the need for psychological care in addition to the physical and provided treatments of a type which were not available for centuries to come in the Western world and which still, today, are not fully appreciated even in certain countries which enjoy a high living standard. Of what may be described as valuable psychological amenities the right of each

56 Part of Constantinople's Cistern of 1001 Columns

private householder, at any rate in Constantinople, to a view of the sea or of a local historical monument was one that was fully recognised, though anyone claiming that the sight of a monument, such, for example, as a statue of Apollo, had been denied to him was obliged, in order to have it restored to him, to prove that he was sufficiently well informed to be able fully to appreciate it. The Byzantine concern for a plentiful supply of water was based on more than either psychological needs or those of convenience, for adequate supplies were essential to their cities' teeming populations if these were to withstand a long siege—and from the eighth century the threat to Constantinople's security was so great that the inhabitants were instructed to keep three years' supplies of basic foods in their store rooms. It was thus a primary duty of the nation's engineers to provide all towns with a lavish supply of water. In the case of Constantinople this was at first done by means of a series of aqueducts, one of which, that built by Valens (364–78), still survives in the centre of old Istanbul. The supply was based on a system of waterworks which started far beyond the town's boundaries, carrying water from sources in the Forest of Belgrade to the north of the Golden Horn to the city. However, the Byzantines soon realised that a supply such as this could easily be cut by a daring enemy and they therefore devised a system as spectacular architecturally as it was practical. They set about building vast subterranean cisterns in which immense quantities of water could be stored safely for long periods, establishing them at various central positions. More than 30 of these have been surveyed. Some of the largest and finest are situated near the cathedral of Haghia Sophia, not far from the Great Palace's main entrance. Two are veritable architectural masterpieces, comparable in size and excellence of proportion to a great, many-columned church. Large enough to boat in, their domed ceilings are supported by a veritable forest of columns; indeed, the Turks have aptly named the more spectacular of the two 'The Cistern of A Thousand And One Columns' (56).

With their liking for water, the Byzantines were almost as fond of taking baths as were the Romans; though three baths a day were considered excessive by the Church, two baths were not regarded as unusual; nevertheless, in the eighth century clerics who bathed twice a day were severely rebuked by their superiors. Only the very rich could afford to have bath-houses of their own. That in which Romanus III (1028–34) died—he was probably murdered—was near the palace in which he was then living. It was his practice on entering the bath to start by washing his head and then his body, and to finish with a swim—a method which clearly indicates that Byzantine baths were similar to those used by the Romans. When Michael IV (1034–41) built the church dedicated to the two *Anargyroi* or healers, SS Cosmas and Damian, he provided a fine bath-house with fountains as an adjunct to the church. The same practice was probably followed by other emperors. There was no scarcity of public baths in any town, for the notables followed the examples set by their emperors, often building such establishments in the poorer districts of their cities. As in Rome, so in Byzantium, the public baths were generally impressive and well built; their façades were often ornate and their interior decoration and equipment luxurious. By Justinian's day, and probably from long before, cubicles and lavatories had come to be regarded as essential; these generally encircled a round bathing-pool, the water for which was heated in a bronze boiler and fed to the bath by pipes terminating in an ornamental spout. A cold and a hot swimming-pool and a hot steam bath were all placed in the same building as the hot bath. The establishment was open to men throughout the day, but in the evenings it was reserved for women.

Apart from the great religious festivals and processions, events organised in the Hippodrome and meetings with friends in public squares, gardens and bath-houses, organised diversions were rare. They were largely limited to a series of seasonal functions of a semi-religious, semi-official nature which were eagerly awaited by the poorer people. The processions accompanying a venerated icon's annual parade through a town always attracted a vast crowd; annual pilgrimages to monasteries or shrines were occasions for much rejoicing. A pilgrimage to the Holy Land was a unique emotional experience and a test of physical endurance, but many people, from Byzantium and abroad, managed to undertake it, and towns on the pilgrim route, such as Ephesus, prospered. Inns serving wine and food were numerous, though on Sundays and feast days they could not open before eight in the morning and had to extinguish their fires and close their doors at eight in the evening.

The festivities associated with pagan festivals were more care-free in character and were so much enjoyed that, even when university students were forbidden to take part in them, the majority continued to rank as holidays at least until the eighth century, and some for much longer. Later they were treated much like Hallowe'en parties in present-day Scotland. Thus, at the Brumelia feast held in honour of Dionysius, masked men paraded

57   One of the ivory plaques from the Veroli casket

the streets. At a new moon, fires were lit in the streets, as they still are in remote villages in Sicily on the day of the Virgin's Assumption, and young men in the district were expected to jump over the flames. There were in addition the local seasonal fairs at which sages, astrologers and healers, in spite of intense disapproval by the Church, attracted large crowds, and did a good trade in charms, amulets and potions. There were also unexpected diversions, such as the arrival of foreigners dressed in unusual costumes or the appearance in the city's streets of outlandish animals such as elephants accompanied by their mahouts, camels led by Negro grooms or giraffes. Less kindly and innocent excitement was aroused by the passage of condemned criminals being led to their place of execution or torture, seated back to front on a mule with their hands tied behind their backs. If the sentences were carried out in public crowds flocked to watch.

But even incidents such as these were rare and life in Byzantium revolved round the family which, in its turn, centred almost entirely on family religious ceremonies—baptisms, engagements, marriages, deaths and burials. Periods of fasting and penitence, rituals associated with the cooking of the paschal lamb—still today an important part of the Greek Easter celebrations—excursions to shrines and monasteries, pilgrimages followed by periods of retreat, or even the entry of a relation into a monastery or his taking of Holy Orders, punctuated the family's lives.

At birth the newly born child was washed by the midwife and swaddled in woollen bandages—scenes which are often illustrated in Byzantine paintings of the Nativity. The infant was kept in that condition for two or three months. Richer families often employed wet nurses to rear their babies. From the sixth century it was considered essential for a child to be baptised within a week of its birth; during the ceremony the baby was immersed in holy water three times and was then carried home accompanied by its parents and their friends who carried lighted candles and sang hymns. Until about the sixth century it was usual for a child to have only one name and, in order to distinguish it from others bearing the same name, the Greek custom was followed of adding its father's name in the genitive case, so that the child became known as, for example, Nicholas Theodorou, meaning Nicholas, son of Theodore. However, at the time it was also feasible to follow Roman practice and to add to a child's first name or *praenomen* its *nomen gentilianum* and *cognomen*. Surnames started coming into use in the sixth century and were soon widely applied. Little is known about the food given to babies, but a young widower living in the tenth century reared his infant on barley gruel, honey and water. Cereals, small quantities of white wine and vegetables were considered suitable for toddlers, but meat was not given until a child had reached its teens.

Christianity did a great deal to raise the status of women by investing marriage with new meaning and importance. The country's civil law continued to recognise divorce in cases where both parties desired it regardless of the Church's opposition to it. Although divorce never ceased to be legal it fell into abeyance in all but the eleventh century, when it became quite common and was often arranged by contract. The Church also disapproved of second marriages, but these were never forbidden, though a third marriage incurred a severe punishment, and a fourth, when not contracted by an emperor, led to excommunication. These measures did much to strengthen the unity of a family and largely as a result family life remained all-important. Although women played a secondary part in public life they often ruled in the family circle. The legendary hero Digenis Akritas always waited for his mother before starting a meal, placing her in the seat of honour.

58 The marriage of David, detail from a silver dish

Psellus' mother certainly ruled her family, and although her concern for her son's education may have been unusual among women of her class her hold over her family was in no way so. Yet, apart from reigning empresses, women, even if they dominated their husbands and households, were not their social equals, though Psellus loved his sister as though she were. All women, including empresses, had to cover their faces with a veil whenever they went out;

they were not allowed to appear in processions and few entered the reception rooms in their homes when their husbands were entertaining male guests. No men other than members of their family and the eunuchs attached to their households were allowed to enter their apartments. Both at court and among the rich, eunuchs, many of them Caucasians, were employed to wait upon the ladies of the household. But although women were expected to live a secluded life they were not segregated even if, in the richer families, they had to be accompanied by an attendant whenever they went out, and even if such outings were permitted only to enable them to go to church (where they had to occupy the gallery), to visit a close relation, or to go to the baths. Many women thought it right to wear bathing dresses when in the bath.

The hereditary principle was in force in the middle class, yet it was possible to rise in the social scale by accomplishment or marriage. Engagements were treated as very important commitments of almost religious significance. A broken engagement was strongly condemned by the Church and was punishable by fines. This attitude resulted in the engagement of very young children, even though it was quickly made illegal for girls to marry under the age of 12 and boys under 14. Parents decided upon the union, the engagement being ratified by a written contract. When the date of the wedding was settled invitations were sent out to relatives and friends. The day before the wedding the walls of the bridal chamber were hung with precious stuffs and the family's most valued possessions and pieces of furniture were placed in the room to the accompaniment of singing. On the wedding day the visitors assembled dressed in white. The groom came, accompanied by musicians, to fetch his bride. She awaited him elaborately dressed in a brocaded gown and a finely embroidered blouse; her face would have been covered by a veil. As her bridegroom approached her she would raise the veil for him to see her, supposedly for the first time. He would find her face heavily made up. Surrounded by her parents, attendants, friends, torchbearers, singers and musicians the bride and her groom would walk together to the church, passing along streets where people standing on balconies showered them with violets and rose petals. In church their respective godparents stood behind them, holding marriage crowns above their heads throughout the ceremony, in their cases the crowns replacing the lengths of precious stuffs placed above the heads of imperial brides and their grooms. Rings would be exchanged and, from the eleventh century, a marriage contract, which had been drawn up prior to the marriage, was produced for signature before witnesses. After the ceremony all returned to the bride's house by the same route as they had come by, to sit down to a banquet. Men and women were placed at separate tables, all of which were elaborately laid, the family's best vessels, dishes and cutlery being used for the occasion. At nightfall all the guests accompanied the newly wedded as far as the bridal chamber; they re-assembled there on the following morning to wake them with their songs.

Certainly from the seventh century it appears to have been the custom for the bridegroom to present his bride with a bridal ring and belt. The ring does not seem to have been the one used at their wedding and it is thought that the husband gave them to his wife when they entered their bridal chamber together for the first time. More bridal rings have survived than belts, and it may well be that only the very rich could afford to give their wives a belt. Though the rings that are now to be found in museums are made of gold it seems probable that less expensive ones of silver or bronze were also used. The gold examples consist of a plain hoop or an octagonal-shaped one; in the latter case seven of its faces were generally decorated with biblical scenes, often executed in niello, whilst the central octagon was adorned with a bezel of varying shape displaying a marriage scene, more usually one showing Christ standing between the bride and bridegroom in the act of joining their hands. A rather more symbolic rendering of the same scene was, however, equally popular: it showed the bridal pair standing on either side of a cross, with their marriage crowns poised above their heads. At times the word *Homonoia* (Concord) was written above. It has been suggested (by Dr Marvyn Ross) that the marriage rings evolved from the custom introduced by the

59   Gold marriage ring

early emperors of issuing special coins on their wedding days—as, for instance, the coin showing Theodosius II standing between Eudoxia and Valentinian III, who were married in Constantinople in the year 437, and those showing Christ standing between Marcian and Pulcheria, and Anastasius and Ariadne.

60 Honorius and Maria, with hair-styles fashionable
at the end of the fourth century

The marriage belts which have survived are far more elaborate
and costly affairs than the rings. The majority are made of a series
either of rather small, round discs or coins or of gold medallions,
with two much larger gold medallions serving as buckles and clasps.
Often the small disks or plaques were decorated with pagan,
generally mythological motifs and therefore contrasted sharply
with the two central ones which generally displayed Christ
standing between the bridal pair, with the bridegroom to His right,
in the act of joining their hands. The designs were generally
stamped on the disks and then chased. Often an inscription was
engraved above each scene. On an example preserved in the
Dumbarton Oaks collection in Washington it reads: '*EΞ ΘEOY
OMON[O]IA XAPIΣ YΓ[E]IA*' (from God concord, grace, health).

A wife's dowry was carefully safeguarded for her. Legally
drawn-up wills were usual in Byzantium, but verbal ones, stated
in the presence of two witnesses, were treated as valid. As in
Roman law, a husband had to leave his wife's dowry to their
children, but at the same time he had to bequeath her enough
to live on should she survive him, by endowing her with money,
furniture, slaves and even, if he possessed them, his rights to issues
of free bread. If widowed, unless she re-married, the wife became
the legal guardian of their children, controlling her late husband's
property in her capacity of head of the family and household. If
the husband were offered a bishopric during their joint lives he

161

could only accept the post if the wife willingly agreed to leave him to enter a convent.

Even relatively humble families owned slaves or employed servants to help with the housework. Though Psellus' father was far from rich the family employed two servants. In rich families the large number of free and slave retainers employed was greatly increased by that of their poor relations and hangers-on. In the sixth century slaves under ten years old were being sold for 10 *nomismata*; the price of older, but untrained men was double that, but a scribe fetched as much as 50 *nomismata*, whilst doctors and other educated men were worth over 60. However, the price kept dropping through the centuries. Naturally enough the Church disapproved of slavery. Theodore of Studius went to the length of forbidding monasteries to own slaves, yet the system endured till the end. Although the number of owners who thought it right to abolish slavery steadily increased, paradoxically, relatively few granted theirs their freedom.

The Byzantines changed very considerably in their outward appearance with the passing centuries, with fashion dictating different styles in costume, hairdressing and beards. Women's fashions seem to have changed less than those affected by men, but this impression may be a mistaken one and the result of lack of information. Basically, from the time of Theodora onwards, empresses and their ladies followed the example of emperors and their courtiers and wore a close-fitting silk tunic over which they placed a dalmatic embroidered at the shoulders and hem; above this they wore a pallium, that is to say a long piece of embroidery with a circular opening for the head at its centre; the back panel extended to form a train which could be pulled forward and carried over the left arm. The costumes of middle-class women were also inspired by those of their menfolk, and consisted of a tunic and a robe with a side panel of sufficient length to enable it to be draped round the shoulder and pulled over the wearer's head. Sometimes they covered their heads instead with a veil, with fabric and colour of their choice. Some of the robes were made of linen, some of silk, some of transparent fabrics, the use of which angered the Church. All wore cloaks similar to those worn by Justinian and Theodora in the Ravenna mosaics. The clothes of the rich were lavishly trimmed with embroidery. On the plaques forming the eleventh-century crown of Constantine IX Monomachus, Empresses Zoe and Theodora wear what are known

61   Central motif from a purple Eagle textile, *c.* AD 1000

62 Silver sauce-boat, fourth century

63 Gold cup and cover,
seventh to ninth centuries

64 Filigree gold and glass
rouge pot, sixth century

amongst dressmakers as robes of the 'princess shape'; these are almost identical. The tunics worn by the dancing girls shown on the other plaques differ slightly in detail; though all are of hip length and embroidered at the neck, round the bottom and along the front opening, some have their skirts cut on the cross whilst others have triangular insertions to give them a flared effect; some have round necklines, others V-shaped ones; all are accompanied by belts of differing widths. The girls wear heel-less shoes; some wear jewelled gloves and all have circlets on their heads. Though wigs were worn at certain periods, on the whole women parted their hair at the centre and coiled it up on either side of their heads, where it was held in place by strings of gold, silver or pearls. Sometimes linen bands were used instead. Occasionally ivory or tortoiseshell combs were worn as additional adornments. Eyebrows were plucked to form a long, straight and narrow line, and this was emphasised by having them underlined by a black line whilst the pupils were contracted by means of belladonna to become black dots. Lips were heavily rouged. In Palaeologue times women were even more heavily made up than before, and the richer ones acquired so many clothes that the Grand Logothete Theodore Metochites complained about his wife's bulging wardrobes.

During the fifth and sixth centuries working-class men went barefoot. They wore short woollen tunics held in place by a belt inserted into a strap passing over the left shoulder. Those who were better-off wore longer tunics, the best of which were made of silk; the cheaper ones were sleeveless, but the finest had long sleeves gathered into tight-fitting, elaborately embroidered cuffs. Those worn by courtiers were very lavishly trimmed with embroidery, much of it worked in gold thread. In cold weather men wore over these long coats which some scholars think took their shape from the coats worn by Chinese mandarins. Most of these coats were plain, but those belonging to men of wealth were lavishly embroidered, and if their owners could afford it they were also lined with fur—much of it a luxury import from Russia.

Byzantine men were very interested in fashion. In the seventh century they were attracted by oriental styles and took to wearing shoes of eastern shape in summer and soft leather boots in winter in preference to Roman sandals; at the same time they substituted a short, close-fitting tunic for the longer, more flowing one. The skirt of the short tunic was slit at the back where a triangular strip of fabric was inserted to give it width; at the neck this garment was finished off by a small collar. Its origin is perhaps to be sought in the tunics worn in northern Persia, where extremely elegant, though longer tunics were liked. In the eleventh century a very short version trimmed with gold was used by the emperors as their riding costume; then too hose reaching to the knees was popular. The Comnenes introduced an era of great luxury in dress. Manuel Comnenus (1143–80), ambassador to Louis VII of France, appeared at the king's court at Ratisbon dressed in a tight-sleeved, knee-length tunic made in a magnificent silk. The freedom of movement it afforded was so new that Western envoys compared the ambassador's appearance to that of an athlete. Andronicus II (1282–1328) tried to curb the fondness for expensive clothes but failed, and under his successors the passion for them encouraged every eccentricity. Foreign trends, whether Syrian, Italian, Bulgarian or Servian, became the rage; Syrian influence introduced the fashion for black cloaks. Even the economic crisis which persisted from the return of the emperors to Constantinople in 1261 to Byzantium's fall in 1453 did not put an end to the fondness for magnificent and extremely elaborate clothes. Particular admiration was felt for both Italian and Turkish styles. The tunic once again became heavier and straighter till it regained the appearance of a robe. The Great Logothete Theodore Metochites obtained special permission to wear the extraordinary hat in which he is shown in the mosaics of the Church of the Chora, when at the height of his power in about the year 1305. His costume, like that painted in 1346 of the High Admiral Apocauchus or that of much the same date of John VI Cantacuzenus (1347–55), does not suggest that lack of money had forced silk manufacturers to produce plainer and cheaper stuffs (*29, 55*).

Though Justinian wore a sort of tiara or *toupha*, in early times hats were generally used only by travellers. By the end of the tenth century, however, a sort of bonnet held in place by a ribbon was being worn so often by men that Michael VI (1056–7) turned it virtually into a uniform by ordering the wearing of a red one; nevertheless by the end of the century a white bonnet was often preferred. Its introduction was followed by a variety of hats, but their shapes quickly became standardised and linked with specific social classes, clerics wearing the *skiandion*. The *kalyphta* which was favoured by civilians was a pyramid-shaped affair which may well have had a Turkish origin. A later form of civilian headgear is illustrated in a mural painting in the Church of the Pantanassa at Mistra; it takes the form of a brimmed hat. John VIII Palaeologus (1425–48) appears on a medal designed by Pisanello wearing a hat with a brim at the back and a button at the top of the crown known as a *kamelakion(65)*.

65 Pisanello's medal of John VIII Palaeologus

To begin with, men followed the Roman custom of wearing their hair short and appearing clean-shaven, only philosophers having a small beard. However, under Justinian, members of the Blue Faction wore beards and moustaches, and grew their hair long at the back, but cut short on the forehead in the Hunnic style. Constantine IV (668–85) was the first emperor to wear a beard; by doing so he set a fashion which was carried to extremes, and men wore their hair in plaits or curled it by sleeping in curlers; the long plaits, which sometimes reached to the waist, aroused the protests of the Church. Constantine V (741–75) passed a law obliging everyone to shave. Theophilus, who was bald, went a step further and ordered the army to shave their heads, but the practice was not retained after his death, perhaps because it was customary for criminals to be shaved and to have their beards removed. Then, from the latter part of the tenth century, even the Church declared itself in favour of beards and long hair, maintaining that these helped to distinguish their wearers from eunuchs. Priests and monks had made a habit of growing their hair and beards from a far earlier date, as they still do today in the Orthodox world.

The sophisticated taste of the Byzantines enabled them to inspire the creation of lovely jewellery. There was nothing ostentatious about it, the designs of each piece being light, the dimensions restrained, the workmanship exquisite. Even later crowns took the form of gold circlets with gilt and jewelled pendants of real elegance and grace. Christian symbols such as fish were among the most popular designs, though crosses (8) worn as pendants were in universal use. In addition people wore rings of copper, bronze, silver or gold. Some had gems set in them which

were engraved with monograms, Christian symbols or inscriptions. In early times, under Roman influence, cameos were popular, but they were soon to be

66 Silver belt buckle monogrammed in the roundel

replaced by brooches set with jewels. Earrings (47), bracelets, necklaces and pendants were widely worn; some of the finest were made of gold filigree and are of remarkable delicacy. Many included gold cloisonné enamels or paste inlays. Jewellers often drew their inspiration from the East. Thus Persian taste to a great extent dictated the style of the crown worn by Theodora (to be seen in the glass mosaic in the church of San Vitale at Ravenna) and was also responsible for such details as the lion-headed terminals which appear on many of the finest bangles, and for the periodic fashion for confronted animals flanking a central motif. Egypt may have inspired many smaller animal designs, such as ducks and fish fashioned in gold and strung together to form necklaces. The Byzantines' demand for jewels was only controlled by the size of their purses. The wealthy were particularly fond of pearls, amethysts and emeralds, most of which were obtained from India. They used them for the pins which held their *chlamydes* (cloaks) in place—a garment which was discarded for the robe late in the twelfth century. They also used them for setting in brooches, pendants, belt buckles, rings, crosses, in jewelled headdresses and saddles, and as adornments for other horse trappings. By modern standards the quality of these stones was seldom high, but the workmanship of the settings was always superb. Jewellery or clothes were discarded when they looked shoddy or tawdry, for unlike European society which, even as late as the eighteenth century, often ignored the most elementary rules of personal cleanliness, the Greeks were as fastidious as the Romans, not only spending a great deal of time in the baths, but making sure that their clothes were fresh and in good condition.

Byzantine ideas about food were closer to the ones we hold today than to those which prevailed in Europe in medieval times. Three meals were considered normal; breakfast, a midday meal and supper. Periods of fasting were rigorously observed, but at

67 A fourteenth-century Byzantine family at dinner (detail)

other times three courses were generally served in well-to-do households both at midday and for the evening meal. At these hors d'œuvres were served first; they were often followed by a fish dish accompanied by a sauce, popular in pre-Christian times, called *gakos*; some form of roasted meat provided an alternative, and the last course consisted of a sweet. Food was so varied that personal preferences dictated the choice of meals. Constantine VIII is known to have been particularly fond of tasty sauces; Zoe had a passion for Indian herbs, especially if they had not been dried, as well as for dwarf olives and bleached bay leaves. A housewife could select her meal from a wide variety of game, poultry and meat; as in present-day Greece, so in Byzantium, pork and ham were favourite dishes; birds were as often boiled as they were roasted or grilled; ducks and much fish were eaten. Soups, many of them elaborate and requiring long hours of cooking, were customary; tripe and stews were often on the menu, and so were salads of many sorts. Cheese was much liked and so was fruit, whether fresh or stewed. Apples, melons, figs, dates, raisins and pistachios were stable items of diet; asparagus and mushrooms were in smaller supply. Oil was used for cooking and much wine—

mostly from Chios—was drunk: Michael VI was not the only drunkard in the Empire. A meal represented on a mosaic discovered at Antioch is seen to have included artichokes, a white sauce, grilled pig's trotters, fish, ham, ducks, biscuits, fruit and wine, as well as hard-boiled eggs served in blue enamel egg cups with small long-handled spoons to eat them with. Gourmets were numerous and took delight in serving regional specialities such as Vlach cheese; indeed, the importance attached to food was such that, when a daughter of Constantine VII was told after his death that she was to be exiled to a convent, she insisted on being accorded a dispensation to allow her to eat meat there.

The trouble which the Byzantines took to serve their food as attractively as possible is in keeping with present-day habits. In Byzantium tables were generally carefully laid. At a time when such care was unusual in western Europe, they were generally covered with clean, often beautifully embroidered cloths. People were expected to change out of their outdoor shoes before entering a dining room. When giving a banquet members of the imperial family and those in court circles ate from couches drawn round a table till as late as the tenth century, even though they appear to have used chairs at the time for everyday purposes. Grace was said at the start of a meal, and probably also at its end. Quite often people ate with their hands, yet a variety not only of spoons and knives but also forks were provided (68). The latter were probably invented in the Eastern world and introduced to Europe by Italians who had learnt their use in Byzantium. They were so much a part of everyday life in Byzantium that when a young princess was given in marriage to a doge of Venice she took some two-pronged ones to Italy with her; their appearance startled and shocked the Venetians. Dishes of many different shapes, varieties and sizes were

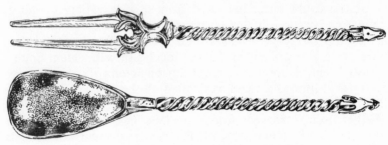

68   A fourth-century silver spoon and fork

made in a number of materials, as were glasses, flagons
and other vessels. What must
have been a customary sight
is recorded in an illumination
painted by Manuel Tzycan-
dilis in 1362 for a codex
belonging to John Cantacuzenus of Mistra. Though it
sets out to illustrate an incident in the *Book of Job* the
scene is treated more as a
genre painting than an icono-
graphic rendering(*67*). It
shows Job dining with his

69   Oil lamp of a foot in a sandal

wife, six sons and three daughters at a table laid with knives,
bowls, jugs and glasses. The youngest girl is bringing in a dish with
a roast sucking pig on it; the family dog is begging for a morsel. The
faces of all are strongly individualised; the diners sit on shaped
stools, wearing their hats; these are of three shapes.

Singularly few of the vast number and variety of objects produced by Byzantine craftsmen during the centuries have survived
to our day. Most of those which have been preserved are precious
objects, whose intrinsic value, quite as much as the quality of their
workmanship and design, induced people to treat them with the
care which less costly examples failed to receive. Because of this,
most of the objects which survive take the form of jewellery, of
particularly spectacular pieces of silver tableware or of fine pottery.
To these must be added quite a number of articles in ivory. The
most important of these were caskets or jewel-boxes. The majority
are rectangular and carved either with geometric patterns or with
mythological scenes, as is the case of the lovely tenth-century Veroli
casket preserved in the Victoria and Albert Museum in London(*57*).

Another large group of objects is made up of oil-burning lamps
and candlesticks. Though many of these were intended for church
use, the domestic ones were probably very similar, though the
Christian symbols decorating the religious objects may well have
been replaced by classical or geometric designs; the cheapest
examples of all may even have been left undecorated. Table lamps
were made in various shapes and materials; in the earlier centuries
simple Roman lamps were produced, fashioned in pottery as well

171

70 Romano-Byzantine balance and weight

as in elaborate metal versions resembling those made in eighteenth- or nineteenth-century Europe by designers who, perhaps as a result of discoveries made at Pompeii, also turned to ancient Rome for inspiration. The self-fuelling lamp invented for Emperor Justinian may well have been an elaborate version of the latter type. In addition there were candlesticks of many different sizes; the majority, if not furnished with a plain round base, had a tripod-shaped one or, when something more elaborate was desired, a lion's paw.

Bronze and iron weights, often with their balance pans, have also come down to us in considerable numbers (70). These were constantly examined by inspectors to ensure that customers were not being defrauded. Even when making such essentially utilitarian objects as these, Byzantium's craftsmen endowed them with distinction. In preference to cutting metal into slabs of the correct weights they gave them the form of a woman's head and shoulders. Lead seals used on documents and by customs officials resembled coins in size and, in addition to an inscription, often displayed a religious symbol or scene.

Chance finds have provided a wide range of objects, which include such everyday articles as buttons and needles, and less usual ones such as a pocket compass of great precision. These suffice to show that life in Byzantium, at least in well-to-do households, was so highly developed that it stimulated the production and use of objects which can stand comparison with those known to western Europe, often a couple of centuries later. The main gap was the failure to devise a method of book printing; its omission is the more surprising since wooden stamps were used for transferring designs to textiles as well as to bread. Nevertheless the Byzantine inventory of goods was extremely long, making it all the more frustrating that so few objects survive. Not a single piece of domestic furniture has been preserved. To form an idea of what it looked like, one has to turn to the pictorial records of the Byzantines, whether in the form of mural paintings, book illuminations, carvings or sculptures. Records speak of the ivory and gold tables used for banquets in the Great Palace. We are told that one was round in shape. Illustrations of the Last Supper suggest that, if not T-shaped, it is most likely to have been D-shaped, but paintings of the Marriage of Cana indicate that rectangular ones were popular in humbler homes. Though couches and chairs were used in the Palace, the average household made use of benches and stools similar to those shown in religious paintings of post-iconoclast date. The grander chairs are thought to have been of the *curule* form used in Rome and to have had, in addition, terminals shaped as lions, winged victories or dolphins combined with lyre-shaped backs. The *curule* was the Roman chair of office used by a *curule* or

71 Roman type clothes of fourth century

senior magistrate, or even by an emperor; its carved supports were often made of ivory, but it was backless, to enable it to fold flat like a stool. However, the ivory throne made for Bishop Maximian of Ravenna has a tub-shaped base and rounded back of Greek origin. Some chairs doubtless resembled thrones and all were probably piled high with cushions resembling those shown in religious paintings of Christ and the Virgin.

Built-in cupboards similar to those that still exist in many monasteries were doubtless known to the Byzantines from early times, but then they were probably something of a luxury and seldom very high. Though it was more usual to store goods and household linen in chests, some were probably arranged on shelves in these cupboards; hanging cupboards seem to have been unknown there. Nor do chests-of-drawers appear to have existed, though a piece of furniture representing a cross between a lectern and a desk (so far as can be judged from the paintings showing the apostles engaged in writing their gospels) was customary. Such pieces to some extent resemble a Regency davenport, for they contained a side cupboard fitted with shelves; they appear to have varied in size, design and decoration, though not in their basic shape; some were provided with book rests, but the paintings also show that free-standing lecterns existed.

To see what beds were like we must once again turn to religious paintings, and more particularly to those illustrating the miracle of the sick man who picked up his bed and walked away with it on his back. These vary from a cheap and simple one consisting of boards equipped at the four outer corners with square legs, and only occasionally having a plain headpiece, to others with their legs turned as elaborately as in mid-Victorian times and with a high head-piece and lower end. Bedding varied according to people's wealth, the rich using sheets, blankets, quilts and coverlets made either of precious fabrics or beautifully embroidered, while the very poor had to make do with rags and sacking. Hangings and draperies were as essential a part of a house's furnishings as were cushions and carpets.

Nor were children overlooked. Toys consisting of clay carts and horses, earth or stone models of houses, knuckle bones, balls, whistles, flutes, tops and hoops were made for boys whilst girls were given wax, clay or plaster dolls. But in Byzantium children grew up young and these simple toys, however passionately cherished, had generally to be laid aside when a child's age reached double figures.

8

COUNTRY LIFE

During early Byzantine history the emperors, and more particularly Arcadius (395–408), appeared to favour the townsman rather than the countryman. He, indeed, even introduced a system of taxation which was quite definitely to the advantage of the former, for it lifted the tax from trade and industry and imposed it instead on the peasants. He made matters more difficult for the countrymen by compelling them to pay dues in gold rather than in kind, even though the price fixed by the government for the sale of their produce was intended firmly to control their profits. Throughout the whole of Byzantium's history the taxes imposed on the agricultural community were such as to undermine their well-being. This is an especially curious situation to find in a country which, after the Muslim conquest of Egypt, depended very much on home-grown supplies, and which expected its agriculturalists to produce much of the simpler foods wanted in the towns, as well as all the commodities which they themselves needed. It was only rarely that the government felt concerned over the hardships which its economic policy inflicted on the men who produced most of the country's basic necessities.

The poverty to which they were often reduced led the peasantry to loathe the tax collector and their landlord. Especially in later times they rightly ascribed their numerous, acute misfortunes to the heavy burden of taxation, and it was this that largely caused the hunger which so often induced them to riot. Risings occurred with particular frequency between, roughly speaking, the ninth and the eleventh centuries—the very time when Byzantium was at the height of its glory. When disorders such as these broke out political and religious dissensions often helped to fan them into veritable revolts. One of the worst of these outbreaks occurred in 820 and lasted for three years. It was led by one Thomas the Slav, who won the support of most of the Slavs whom the government

had moved to Anatolia from their Balkan homelands. The distur-
bance spread to neighbouring districts, where minority groups
consisting of other Slavs as well as of Armenians and Georgians
rallied round Thomas, as did many Greek lovers of icons, who
naturally hated the iconoclast government. Scarcely 20 years later
a Slav rising of considerable proportions disrupted the peace of the
Peloponnese. Soon after, Paulicians, preaching their doctrine in
Anatolia, gained numerous supporters among the peasantry and
the revolt which followed spread across Asia Minor. Rioters scored
so many victories that the army had to be called out to deal with
them, and it was not until 872 that peace was restored. This was
the second Paulician rising in 50 years; both outbreaks owed much
of their success to the support which the free peasants had given the
sectarians when they realised that a new, extremely severe tax was
likely to reduce them to virtual serfdom. The revolt which took
place between the years 920 and 944 coincided with rises in
taxation imposed by Romanus Lecapenus, and with the introduction of a law making the neighbours of a man who absconded
without paying his taxes responsible for them. Similar grievances
sparked off numerous riots in the frontier zones, where rises in
taxation aggravated the nationalist aspirations of the local minority
groups.

Apart from the soldier-farmer or *theme*-holders working the
land in the border areas, and those of their sons who kept themselves by cultivating land which they had come to own by making
it productive, there were singularly few peasants in the Byzantine
world (using the word 'peasant' in the sense of a self-employed
smallholder). Most people engaged in food production were either
labourers, with scarcely more liberty than serfs, or slaves. Though
villages were numerous many formed part of a large estate and
their inhabitants came under the landlord's jurisdiction instead of
the state's. Until the seventh century (and possibly even later) life in
the eastern districts revolved round the large estates. These
belonged either to members of the old Roman aristocracy or the
new Byzantine nobility and had grown up at the end of the third
century when the economic crisis led people to invest their money
in land.

Because of the survival of documents (written on papyrus)
relating to one such family, the Apions, we possess more information about landowners in Egypt prior to the Arab conquests of the
seventh century than about those living at other periods in other

parts of the Empire. The Apion records cover the years 488 to 625. The founder of the estates, Theodore John, was almost certainly a Greek, not an Egyptian. He was a distinguished Byzantine official, a member of the Sacred Consistorium, who was appointed governor of the Egyptian province of Arcadia. His son Strategius also became a distinguished civil servant and was rewarded by Justinian with the title of *gloriosissimus patricius*. Those who succeeded him as head of the family spent their lives in Egypt, often serving as senior administrators in the district in which they lived. The family was at its most prosperous during Justinian's reign. Its estates were administered on lines very similar to those followed by Justinian in governing Byzantium. Strategius employed some 20 men, each with power of attorney, for the purpose. Each was expected to send Strategius detailed reports at regular intervals. Some of these agents acted as accountants, others as legal advisers, others as estate managers. The Apions had what amounted to a private bank where money and goods due to them were paid in, loans to peasants handled and charity dispensed. They had their own fleet of boats, their own service of mounted messengers and couriers, even their private soldiers to protect the accountants transporting the taxes due by the Apions to the government tax inspector in Alexandria. Though Justinian attempted to ban private armies such as this one, a number survived on the larger estates both in Egypt and in Cappadocia. It is, however, even more astonishing to find that (from about the end of the fourth century) some landowners such as the Apions maintained their own private prisons. They contained runaway slaves who had been recaptured, and villagers whom they decided to punish, who served sentences which the landlords themselves imposed. A record for the year 538 reveals that 139 men imprisoned in one such institution were allowed the same issue of wine on Easter Day, Epiphany and St Michael's Day as were the men serving sentences in the state prisons.

Wine and oil were very important products. On the Apions' estate deliveries of both were made direct to the head cellarer, who decided how much was to be stored in his masters' cellars and how much sold. However, cereals formed the main crop, with animal husbandry filling an equally essential role. When the Arabs conquered Syria and Egypt these estates were destroyed and many Christian landowners were forced to abandon their homelands and migrate into Byzantine-held territory. Many settled there on land

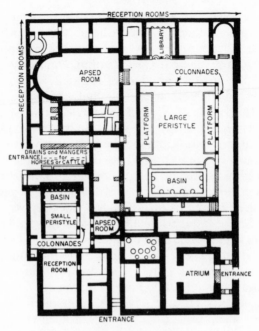

72 Ground-plan of the Romano-Byzantine
palace at Stobi in Yugoslavia

which had never been cultivated, to eke out a living as small, independent farmers. However, others were able to acquire large estates in a relatively short period of time. Though many landowners had come to consider life in the country the equivalent of exile and to cling to the capital and its court, others delighted in living far removed from governmental supervision. Some became very powerful. Like the turbulent barons of medieval Europe they were bold and strong-willed; many conducted themselves in the manner of petty chieftains. Certain of them even minted their own coins, and they built villas which were often superb. In these the rooms were placed round a central courtyard which was often adorned with a mosaic floor. Their interiors were divided into two by a corridor, the reception rooms being on one side and the private apartments on the other (72). Others preferred to live in old houses of architectural merit.

The family of the future Patriarch Philaretus, whose daughter was to marry Emperor Constantine VI, were among those who preferred old architecture to new. In the eighth century, when

Philaretus was still a youth, they were living on their estates in the district of Sinop in a magnificent old house. Its sumptuous furniture included a round ivory table inlaid with gold, large enough to hold 36 diners, and chests filled with precious gold and silver articles and fine clothes. The family numbered 30 people, for, in addition to Philaretus and his parents, his two married sisters, their husbands and children, were all living in the house. They employed numerous slaves and servants to attend to their needs. Their estate included 48 villages each so well supplied with springs that an elaborate system of irrigation was developed. Their stock numbered 100 oxen, 600 head of cattle, 800 mares, 80 mules and riding horses, 12,000 sheep and numerous hives—at that time an essential on every farm.

It was during the fifth century that two categories of farm workers, in addition to that of the smallholders, had become established. One consisted of men who, though technically freemen and as such obliged to pay taxes were in fact tied to a particular piece of land and were thus virtually serfs; when the land they worked was sold they were automatically transferred with it to its new owner. The other, rather larger group, was made up of slaves. Some landowners owned so many of them that when they were called upon to provide soldiers for the army they did not hesitate to send their slave agricultural workers. Numerous though the slaves were there were never sufficient people to cultivate all the available land. By the seventh century the shortage of farm labourers was so acute that the emperor sent the Slavs he had taken prisoner in western Europe to Asia Minor to provide sorely needed peasant labour.

The shortage eventually induced the government to afford a measure of protection to the peasants. Regulations were drawn up during the seventh century and embodied in a code known as the 'Farmer's Law'. It set out to ensure that the men who were lucky enough to be independent smallholders should become the owners of the land they worked. Nevertheless, many of these seemingly fortunate people were in fact often deprived of this advantage by the system of taxation in force in the rural areas. Known as the *annona*, it stipulated that a village, with its orchards, fields and common grazing lands, was to be assessed as a single unit instead of individually. Since slaves were not taxed even though many helped to swell the population of a village, yet since the total number of inhabitants were taken into account in the assessment, it fell to the smallholders and serfs, even though they often constituted a minority of the inhabitants, to raise the taxes for which the village as a whole was liable. Taxable land was re-assessed every 15 years, and so were the farm animals; these were treated as a similar source of revenue as harbours, markets and saleable goods. When an assessor had completed his calculations he informed the village elders of the result; the latter had to notify each taxpayer of the amount he was expected to contribute. It was customary for this tax to be paid largely in kind and to be handed to the government's tax collector, but in later times the villagers frequently found themselves obliged to deliver it to the local landowner who, as often as not, kept it for himself.

When it was first introduced the *annona* took the form, as we have already seen, of a combined land and poll tax. As such it had the effect of making the neighbour of a defaulter responsible for the fugitive's share, and this in turn tied the taxpayer to the land. By depriving him of the liberty to move from the village the *annona* gradually reduced the taxpayer to the status of a serf. The 'Farmer's Law' attempted to avert this by separating the poll tax from the land tax. With their liberty of movement restored, the freemen among the peasantry quickly realised that there was no longer anything to prevent them from leaving the village in search of better land or easier working conditions. Until the eleventh century, when the Seljukid advance into Anatolia made farming there both dangerous and often unprofitable, there was always a good deal of uncultivated though productive land to be found in Asia Minor. Indeed, to begin with there was so much of it and the country's need for food was so great that the emperors attempted to solve their economic difficulties by giving large tracts of land to private individuals who then had to cultivate it and, as property owners, pay taxes on it.

Though many small freemen farmers generally owned a couple of slaves or employed a servant to assist them in the house and on the land, they were so poor that few who did so owned more than a single horse, a donkey, a cow with its calf and a couple of oxen; yet, in the eighth century, the great landowner who owned 100 yokes of oxen, 500 head of grazing cattle, 80 horses and 12,000 sheep was equally typical. In addition to working their own plots of land the small farmers often therefore had to hire themselves out to a neighbouring rich landowner. Even then many fell into debt and built up tax arrears. If it came to the worst they were left with no alternative but to sell their fields to their rich employers and to continue working them in the capacity of serfs, helping thereby to

73 Goatherd
From a silver dish, sixth century

74 Harvesting
An ivory plaque showing Adam and Eve, tenth century

75 Shepherd loosing his dog in pursuit of game

76 Ploughing with oxen
*Both from illuminations in an eleventh-century ms of
the Homilies of St. Gregory Nazianzus*

increase the possessions, wealth and powers of the large land-owners. By the tenth century estates comparable in size to the earlier ones in the east had grown up in the Empire's western regions such as Boeotia. One very rich landowner in the Patras region, the widow Danielis, owned 80 estates and a number of towns where women working together in workshops wove considerable quantities of linen and silk. Her treasure chests were reputed to be filled with valuables and sumptuous clothes. Whenever she set out in a litter she was accompanied by 300 slaves. At her death she bequeathed her possessions to the emperor, who promptly freed 3,000 slaves and sent them to Italy as colonists.

Romanus Lecapenus was particularly anxious to protect the small agriculturalist and in 934 he passed a law which aimed at limiting the size of large estates by forbidding their owners to purchase agricultural land. Since most peasants had by then become so poor that the taxes were a burden they could no longer endure, they did their utmost to evade the regulation in order to dispose of the land on which they were taxed. Their anxiety to get rid of it was such that they were even ready to exchange their status of freemen for that of serfs. Furthermore, since land was then the only existing form of investment, its sale and purchase continued to take place as often as in earlier times, even though the law contained a loophole which enabled a dishonest purchaser to avoid paying the seller. Ill-feeling between rich and poor was further aggravated by the failure of many wealthy landowners to make good the damage they might have done to the property of a smallholder.

Throughout the years it was always the poorer countrymen who bore the brunt of the rural system of taxation. Both the rich landowners and the monasteries continually benefited from special privileges and exemptions. Yet it was precisely when they had secured so many advantages that the *pronoia* was re-introduced: it had been in existence during the opening phase of Byzantine history, but had since lapsed in so far as civilians were concerned, though not the Church. It was designed in its revived form as a reward for those who had rendered signal service to the state. The beneficiary was to receive an estate for use during his lifetime. In return for cultivating and developing it he could retain all its revenue without paying any taxes on it. Many *pronoia* holders used the wealth they obtained in this manner to buy up land owned by tax-paying peasants or smallholders; by adding these fields to the *pronoia* estates the once taxable strips ceased to be so. As a result, from the eleventh century, government revenue from the countryside steadily decreased whilst the exemptions accorded to privately and Church-owned lands increased, even though the *pronoia* estates were not at the time heritable. The Comnenes made *pronoia* holders serve in the army if needed, but by removing them from their estates the output obtained from the latter diminished. The state's supply of food was accordingly reduced at the very time when more funds and supplies were needed by the army fighting the Turks. Whilst the emperor's coffers remained unfilled, private families benefiting from the *pronoia* increased their wealth, and monasteries owning vast estates grew steadily richer. To control the growing economic crisis Constantine IX Monomachus had to take a step which all his predecessors had so far avoided: he was forced to debase the value of the *nomisma*, a step which deprived it of the position it had enjoyed for centuries as an internationally recognised currency.

Many landowners who made fortunes between the years 1025 and 1071, when the Seljukid victory at Manzikert ended their prosperity, had to abandon their estates to live in the capital. There their aggressive temperament enabled them to oust the military from their privileged position at court and in the administration. In the countryside the small farmers and agricultural workers became more dependent on the remaining landowners. Many peasants were drafted into the army; the land suffered as a result, nor did the army benefit from the intake. Following the defeat at Manzikert, fighting against the Seljuks continued intermittently throughout the next century and a half, and wherever either army passed the peasantry suffered; crops were ravaged, fields laid waste and cattle and poultry slaughtered. Yet following his return to his capital in 1261 Michael VIII thought it essential to propitiate the landed gentry. To do so he decided to let sons of *pronoia* holders inherit their fathers' estates, thus perpetuating the family's right to the property, and the latter's continued exemption from taxation. It was a high price to pay for their loyalty, for the change inevitably worsened the country's already acute economic crisis.

Until the Seljukid conquest of Anatolia disrupted the region's agriculture, Asia Minor was an important cattle-breeding area and a granary. The cattle breeders were not nomads in the true sense of the word; like many present-day Turkish shepherds, they spent the winter months in their villages, and at the approach of summer moved to pasture their beasts in the fertile uplands. In this

77   A smith and his wife at work

way they reared large numbers of horses, donkeys, mules, cattle, sheep, goats and pigs. This was assuredly a freer, happier form of life, and perhaps also an easier one, than that which fell to the lot of labourers employed in cultivating the soil. Though both ran the risk of being robbed by brigands or attacked by wolves, the shepherd had his dog to defend him and could seek refuge in the surrounding hills.

The villagers were always in danger of being despoiled by their own soldiery or being stripped bare by foreign troops, whether coming as invaders or, as in the case of the Crusaders, as supposed friends. To work the soil they had tools as primitive as those that had been used in early Christian times. These consisted mainly of a simple wooden plough pulled by oxen (76) or mules, a double-pointed hoe, two-pronged forks, spades, sickles, scythes, mattocks, double-headed mallets, a planting stick and sometimes also a sharp, heavy, pointed stone or prod fitted into a handle. Mules were used to transport loads, oxen to drag all heavily loaded carts since, in the fifth century, even post-horses could not pull a load exceeding 492 kilos in weight, for if they did so their collars choked them. Oxen were also used for pumping water and for threshing; as in many countries in the Middle East today, they

185

were lashed to a pole and walked round and round the hard threshing-floor, trampling the grain with their unshod feet. Even riding horses were not shod with iron shoes till the ninth century and were ridden with no more than a saddle cloth, halter or snaffle. However, from the ninth century a saddle and stirrups were widely used as well as iron shoes, and the village blacksmith, who had until then been employed in making and mending the simple tools and implements needed by the villagers, now shod horses as well. A woman(77) or small boy kept his fire going by working the bellows. Land was measured by means of ropes of prescribed length, being dragged by oxen in the presence of an official called an *apographeus*.

The peasants wore long tunics which were sometimes sleeveless but always worn pulled in at the waist, with the fullness gathered in the front. Their breeches reached to their ankles and they either went barefoot or wore heel-less shoes. Often they tied a cape round their shoulders, but they seldom appear to have worn hats. Their houses were generally little better than square cabins, at best divided into two rooms and roofed with tiles, but the more successful farmers lived in two-storeyed houses. In these the ground floors served as hen houses, stables and store rooms, and the upper ones, with access by an external staircase, contained the family's rooms. In mountainous areas these cottages were built of stone; elsewhere they were constructed of brick. The village potter and brickmaker was often one and the same person, but in the larger villages these occupations were distinct. In either case these craftsmen were fully employed providing both the local landowners and the peasants with building materials, storage vessels and table utensils. They were as essential to the rural inhabitants as the carpenters who, with the blacksmith, were the only other artisans to be found in the villages.

78   A typical village well

186

Great importance was attached to the village water supply. Wells (78), often built to serve also as embellishments, were placed at convenient points, forming pleasant meeting places for the women. Irrigation channels and open drains, often very unhealthy, ran through the village streets. Mills, whether worked by water, wind or animals such as oxen,

79 A water mill of the sixth century

mules or donkeys, stood at convenient points, often attached to the local church or monastery. The use of the water mill (79) led to the establishment of the miller's trade as separate from the baker's, as the need for wind or a large flow of water often made it necessary for the mill to be built at some distance from the village and its bakery.

Those who could afford the luxury maintained gardens. Digenis Akritas' love of gardens was by no means unusual, though it is otherwise rarely recorded in literature. Most people had no space for flowers and grew them in pots. From the eighth century villages in prosperous districts were generally encircled by a belt of orchards, fig groves or vineyards, which in their turn gave way to arable fields. In the latter the peasants grew cereals, vegetables and salads. These fields were privately owned, but the pasture which enclosed them belonged to the village as a whole and was common land. A competent police force was entrusted with the duty of protecting the peasants' property. To aid them in this difficult task travel in the countryside was strenuously discouraged, and all those who were obliged to undertake long journeys to the frontier areas had to carry travel documents.

The peasants' lives revolved round their family and church. The village priest played a very important part in their existence, not only performing the rites of the Church for their benefit, but

80   Labourers at work in a vineyard

comforting and guiding them, often teaching their children to read, write and count. Nor was the peasant's life devoid of seasonal pleasures. In addition to the great Church festivals, which were celebrated with all pomp and solemnity, and the homage paid to local saints commemorated in neighbouring monasteries, there were family events such as weddings to enjoy. There were annual markets to attend in the regional capitals and smaller, equally lively markets in the local towns. Unfortunately the ailing, old and needy often had to take advantage of being in a town to borrow from the local money-lender; few could escape recourse to his services at some time or other. Nevertheless, the countryside provided the hale with robust and carefree pleasures. Thus, the wine harvest was accompanied by drunken but very enjoyable feasts. The gathering of the last of the harvest was boisterously celebrated with food and drink, wandering acrobats, jugglers and mimers. Even the end of a long day's work was a cause for satisfaction. A fifteenth-century book illumination successfully captures the relaxed atmosphere in which men and beasts make ready for food and rest. It shows two labourers unloading a corn cart and another unharnessing the oxen under the watchful eye of their master, whilst a huntsman takes from his dog a hare which it has just retrieved. Judging from the peaceful, enchanting scenes decorating the mosaic floor of the Great Palace it was realised in the sixth century that country life had something to commend it. In the mosaic a shepherd's life seems full of idyllic attractions of a Virgilian sort. In the eleventh century, when Romanus Lecapenus'

81 Agricultural workers receiving their pay

efforts to abolish the large estates had come to naught, people were flocking back to the country. At the start of the twelfth century life there was being fully appreciated. Kekaumenos, once an eminent official living in Constantinople, was revelling in country life and asserting that the best way of ensuring happiness lay 'in working the land, growing corn, making wine, raising animals'. Even members of the imperial family and officials such as Theodore Metochites were acquiring estates in many parts of the country and monasteries on Mount Athos were buying vineyards as far away as Serres and paying anything, between 1296 to 1333, from one to 24 *nomismata* for each. In 1341, when Guy de Lusignan captured John Cantacuzenus' estates in Thessaly, allowing his men to loot them, in a matter of hours the latter had made away with 500 oxen, 2,500 mares, 200 camels, 300 mules, 5,000 donkeys, 50,000 pigs, 70,000 sheep as well as great quantities of corn which had been stored in barns, and coffers filled with gold and silver.

Fishing was not only profitable but also delightful. Though seafaring fishermen often had to fish by night by artificial light or, by day, to drag heavy nets, the countryman could sit placidly, rod in hand, over a quiet pool or fresh running stream in apparent ease and safety. Yet many of the fast-flowing streams were as treacherous and dangerous as the open sea, and both inland and seafaring fishermen followed the example of sailors in commending themselves to St George and St Phocas.

In the country there was always game to snare or a swift hare to

82   Hunting scene from a mosaic in the Great Palace

be caught by a dog, or by a boy deftly throwing a basket over it. Peasants were adept at netting and snaring and often used wooden decoys. Hunting was enjoyed by all classes (82). Rich landowners kept large retinues of both free and enslaved huntsmen, kennel boys, trackers and falconers. They used cheetahs as well as hounds when hunting big game, calling them together with ivory hunting horns and killing their quarry with spears, arrows, or the help of eagles, hawks, gerfalcons and peregrines, all of which had bells tied to their legs. Falconers carried their birds on their left hand and wore elbow-length leather gloves as protection. Hares were often pursued by hawks but also hunted on horseback. Other animals hunted in those ways were foxes, stags, does, gazelles and bears. Partridges were raised by dogs and shot with arrows. Cretan hounds were particularly valued on account of their keen scent, but the large Indian breeds were preferred for hunting big game. A professional huntsman wore a short tunic and pointed hat, and carried a bow and arrow as well as a whip, an axe and a net; he also attached a knife to his belt. Peasants were not so well equipped, but many were astonishingly skilled at catching singing birds for which there was always a ready market.

9

SCHOOLS, SCHOLARS
AND MUSICIANS

The Byzantines inherited from the classical world a profound
respect for learning and a particular delight in the culture of
ancient Greece. Time and again Greece served as an inspiration
and had a revivifying effect upon their imagination. In the tenth
and eleventh centuries, and to a lesser extent again in the thirteenth,
it was responsible for revivals of an ancient imagery in art and of
basic principles of reasoning in philosophy. However, from about
the middle of the seventh century, Arab scientists and mathematicians stimulated the work of many eminent Byzantine
scientists, doctors and inventors.

Although much that had been created by Byzantine scholarship
perished in the fifteenth century, and even though some written
works may still lie undetected in some remote monastic library,
the harvest sown by the Byzantines made a vital contribution to
European culture. Perhaps the greatest service which the Byzantines rendered was to preserve most of the Greek classics which are
known to us. But for Byzantine transcriptions many of these
would have perished with the destruction of the great library at
Alexandria; but for the devastations wrought by the Latins and
the Ottomans the number of surviving works would assuredly be
much larger than it is. In addition to their achievements as
preservers of the past the Byzantines have provided our civilisation
with a large number of works which deserve to be recognised as
cornerstones of European thought. Most consist of theological
works which have greatly influenced the cultures of the various
Slavic nations belonging to the Orthodox Church. Almost as
important is the rich store of information contained in the
chronicles, though it was the genius of Constantine Porphyrogenitus which, perhaps finding inspiration in Procopius' *Life of*

Justinian and Eusebius of Caesarea's *Life of Constantine I* rather than in the works of Greek and Roman historians, finally transformed history into a discipline which, from the eleventh century, often possessed literary merit.

The destruction of practically every object relating to secular life in Byzantium has unfortunately tended to turn the attention of scholars to the religious aspects of Byzantine history and art at the expense of social and everyday matters, with the result that we now have a somewhat one-sided view of daily conditions there. A glance at the educational facilities available in Byzantium and at the standard achieved in advanced studies helps to bring the picture into truer perspective by focusing attention on the layman as well as on the priest.

Although religion was the mainspring and controller of life in Byzantium, even in the tenth century, when monasticism was at its height and half the population is believed to have withdrawn from worldly affairs, secular learning survived. Despite the Church's disapproval it maintained its hold. Though it had first been intended to keep the two disciplines apart secular studies became deeply rooted in the Christian doctrine. St Basil had been in favour of admitting all children to the Church schools, whether or not they were intended for a religious life, but the Church Council of 451 had forbidden this. However, it seems unlikely that the prohibition was ever rigorously enforced either in country districts or in wealthy families, for throughout Byzantium's history priests and monks were often engaged to tutor children, and especially to teach them the Scriptures. They were given full permission to beat idle and unwilling pupils.

The emperors founded quite a number of schools for orphans. These used the same syllabus as the one followed in the country's primary schools, but children from upper- and middle-class families were often educated by private tutors who preferred well-tried Graeco-Roman methods. By the sixth century education was provided for a considerable proportion of children of freemen and the number increased steadily thereafter, though it continued to vary between regions. In the eleventh century, under Alexius Comnenus, free schools were open to all children regardless of nationality or class. A child generally received its first lessons in the women's quarter of its home; in educated families these were usually given by its mother. This was the case with Michael Psellus, whose mother taught him to speak fluently and clearly as well as to write a good hand; both were considered important assets. Every child was expected to know the Bible by heart. Servants in the Psellus household were forbidden to tell the children horror tales for fear of frightening them. Psellus was sent to school at the age of five, but he was an unusually intelligent child and by the age of 14, when the average pupil was expected to be well-versed only in Aesop's *Fables*, he was already able to recite the *Iliad* by heart.

As in present-day Greece, three forms of Greek were in simultaneous use from about the eighth century: the vernacular Romaic was used by the uneducated, Attic Greek was used by educated people when writing, and a more elaborate version for conversation. The last was closer to classical Greek than to Romaic and was used for orations, thus widening the gap between the written and spoken forms. On entering school children were first instructed in grammar—a term which included reading and writing. This was followed by more advanced grammar, syntax and introduction to the classics; each pupil was expected to learn 50 lines of Homer by heart every day and to have read the commentaries on them. Sons of the very rich were taught by tutors, who sometimes stayed on to prepare their pupils for entry to the university. However, at the age of 14 most boys joined their contemporaries in the school classroom. There their time was spent in studying rhetoric: this included pronunciation and enunciation as well as the study of great prose writers such as Demosthenes. In their last year at school boys were taught philosophy, the sciences and the 'four arts'—arithmetic, geometry, music and astronomy.

Each bishopric had its own religious school; and in addition many monasteries, following the precepts of St Basil, not only established their own libraries and *scriptoria*, but also included some scholar monks who studied the texts preserved in the monastic libraries and taught other monks. Younger monks were directed to teach novices and children destined to become monks. The closing of all public libraries in 476 struck a blow at secular learning for it obliged scholars to rely on the monastic libraries which, naturally enough, contained mostly theological books.

Scriptoria, that is to say rooms where scribes worked at copying every type of book available, from grammars and dictionaries to novels and religious works, were attached to all libraries, whether public or private, secular or religious. As early as the fourth century Emperor Valens regularly employed four Greek and three

Latin scribes in his library at Constantinople. Calligraphy was considered an art at which all educated people should excel. Many eminent people including Emperor Theodore II Lascaris (1254–8) delighted in transcribing books. In the *scriptoria* the scribes (84) devoted as much care to the beauty of their script as to the accuracy of the text. It was in these centres that the script known as the minuscule was evolved. Many impoverished scholars increased their earnings by acting as scribes. Books were far from cheap; in the eleventh century the cost of a copy of Euclid was the equivalent of about £12. As a general rule it is unlikely that the illuminations in the form of figural scenes which adorn so many Byzantine books were produced by scribes; though the marginal devices, chapter heads and tail-pieces may well have been executed by highly skilled calligraphers, the full-page illustrations were generally the work of illuminators who filled in the spaces left blank for the purpose by the scribes.

The first books produced in Byzantium were written on papyrus and were shaped as scrolls. This form was retained for official documents and imperial diplomas even after the fall of Egypt to the Arabs; it passed into general use in medieval Europe and survives to our own time in the case of certain ceremonial documents. The pieces of papyrus which were used for documents carried an imperial stamp, but those intended for literary purposes did not need one and so escaped the tax levied on the former. From the fourth century parchment began to be preferred to papyrus and Constantine I is said to have ordered 50 copies of the Gospels written on parchment for the 50 churches he is supposed to have founded. The change-over was hastened when papyrus became hard to obtain after the Muslim conquest of Egypt. The term 'parchment' is said to derive from Pergamon in Asia Minor and it may be that it was first produced there. The bulk of it was made from calf hide and as a result it became known in the West as vellum—the same word as veal. But much of it was actually produced from the skin of oxen, antelope, gazelle and sheep. The famous *Codex Sinaiticus* in the British Museum is one of the earliest examples that we know of a book written on parchment. Cotton and linen paper was imported from China in the eleventh century, but it remained scarce until the thirteenth, when the Byzantines were able to produce all they needed for themselves.

Scrolls were of two types; the one was read from top to bottom, the other was more like a roll. It was intended for literary purposes and was horizontal in shape, the text being written in sections, which began at the left and ended at the right. These ceased to be exclusively used with the invention of the *biblion* (originally the Greek name for the Bible). The latter was made up of sheets folded very like a modern book, the bound volume formed in this way being called a *codex*. When the number of folded sheets formed either three or six double pages they were known as a

83 Gospel cover showing Christ and the
Apostles, twelfth century

tetradia. To begin with no more than 45 *tetradia* could be bound together, but later the number was increased. Books made up in this manner varied greatly in size. Their names were related to their subject matter. Books in which the lives of saints were arranged in the form of a calendar were known as *Menologia*; the four Gospels were called *Tetra Evangelia*; when the Gospels were arranged in the form of daily lessons the volume was called an

Evangelistrion, whilst the first eight books of the New Testament formed an *Octateuch*. In addition there were psalters, volumes of homilies, and so on. The majority were bound in wooden boards, generally oak. When a volume was intended for ceremonial use in a church or designed for a dignitary, the outside cover was often made of some precious material such as ivory, silver or gold. It was always elaborately worked, being carved, chased or embossed, and sometimes enhanced by the addition of precious jewels, cloisonné enamels, paste inlays, niello work or gems (*83*). When made for an emperor the pages were dyed purple and the text often written in letters of gold; the binding was also generally stained purple, though the top cover might well be of gold and adorned with cloisonné enamels. Gospels of this type are called Purple Codices.

Byzantine scholarship was at its peak roughly between 842 and the start of the twelfth century. During that period the learned and energetic prelate Photius was moulding the minds of a new generation of intellectuals; the saintly brothers Cyril and Methodius were devising the Cyrillic alphabet for the use of the converted Slavs; Bardas Caesar, a keen admirer of Photius, was founding the Magnaura University; Leo VI, himself a pupil of Photius, was spending his leisure composing theological works—some of which remain in use in the Orthodox world of today; Constantine VII Porphyrogenitus was writing works of permanent value; whilst Michael VII, a pupil and friend of Psellus, had been so immersed in learning and the arts that, try as he could, he was unable to reorganise the army, shattered by the nation's defeat at Manzikert, thereby further imperilling his kingdom. Only a few years later Anna Comnena, the daughter of Alexius Comnenus, was exiled to a convent by her brother. She occupied her time there writing a life of her father which is surely one of the world's great biographies.

The boyhood experiences of St Cyril were not unusual for the ninth century. The son of a worthy if far from prosperous notable living in Salonica, the boy was born in about the year 822 and was named Constantine. His father died when he was about 14 years old. When this became known in Constantinople the imperial chancellor, who had heard Constantine well spoken of, wrote to the boy's mother offering her son a vacancy in the imperial school where the future Michael III (842–67) was a pupil. The school was the best of its day. The offer was accepted and in due course Constantine set off alone for Constantinople. He was 16 when he entered the school; within three months he had qualified as a grammarian and was able to pass to more advanced work, studying geometry with the great mathematician Leo and dialectics and philosophy with the equally famous and distinguished Photius, twice patriarch of Constantinople. In addition he studied rhetoric, astronomy, arithmetic, music and, in the words of a contemporary, 'other Hellenistic arts'. It is curious to find no mention made of theology. Constantine was 22 years old when, having completed his education, he left the school to become patriarchal librarian at Haghia Sophia. It is interesting to compare him with Psellus who, some two centuries later, pursued his education till he was 25, devoting his last few years of study to becoming a good public speaker and to mastering deductive and inductive philosophy, the natural sciences and mathematics. In addition to his duties as librarian Constantine was also expected to act as secretary or personal assistant to his former teacher, Patriarch Photius. At this period in his life he took Holy Orders, entering the church under the name of Cyril. On completing a thesis he was appointed deacon and offered the post of professor of philosophy in his old school. This was a high honour, for in addition to teaching in the school, its professors were expected to act as cultural advisers to the emperor. Nevertheless, Cyril refused the offer and it was not until about the year 850 that he finally accepted a professorial chair. Some ten years later he gave up teaching in order to undertake missionary work with his brother Methodius, first in the kingdom of the Volga Khazars and later among the Slavs of central Europe, for whom he devised the alphabet which still bears his name.

As a general rule girls were not as well educated as their brothers, but so long as the boys were taught at home they were generally able to share their lessons. Even so, girls could not enter a university and if they wished to pursue their studies they had to do so with the help of a tutor. Nevertheless, quite a number of them were very learned. The daughters of Constantine VII Porphyrogenitus were noted for their scholarship. The talented Anna Comnena begged to be forgiven her temerity in writing her father's life since she lacked 'the science of Isocrates, the eloquence of Pindar, the impetuosity of Polimon and of Homer's Calliope as well as Sappho's lyre'—yet she produced a work of equally enduring quality. She married Nicephorus Briennius, himself respected as an historian. Irene, daughter of the Grand Logothete Theodore Metochites, was a distinguished scholar and so were many other women; more still qualified as doctors and worked in the women's wards of hospitals, where they were the equals of their male colleagues.

By the ninth century the Patriarchal School in Constantinople ranked as the best of the religious educational establishments. All its teachers were deacons at the cathedral of Haghia Sophia and its director was an ecumenical professor. The younger children who were admitted to the school received the same general education as that provided for children in secular schools; that is to say they were taught the subjects included in grammar by one set of specialists, those in rhetoric by another, and those in philosophy by a third. Any of their teachers could be called upon on such occasions as the emperor's birthday or similar events to carry out the duties of Crown orator. However, pupils in that school also followed a full course of religious instruction. Once again the subjects covered were divided between three groups of teachers; the school's director personally taught all pupils the Gospels; other specialists studied the Epistles with them and others the Psalms; these scholars could also be asked to act as court orators. Before long specialists in the Old Testament were attached to the staff, and the school soon came to rank as a university or teachers' training college. At that level churchmen and laymen were taught separately, with a view to providing educated men for the upper clergy or teachers. From about the tenth century men of all ages took to meeting in the school's courtyard to discuss methods of education. By that date the school had become attached to the church of The Holy Apostles. That magnificent building stood on the summit of Constantinople's highest hill; it was largely because of its prominent position that it was pulled down and its treasures destroyed by Sultan Mehmet and that it was replaced by a mosque some years after the conquest of Constantinople. Its loss is one of the saddest in Byzantine history. Under the Byzantines, grammarians, rhetoricians and dialecticians would meet in the church's *narthex* to propound their opinions, whilst physicians, doctors, mathematicians and those concerned with geometry and music would take possession of the *atrium*. When their arguments became too violent the patriarch would be asked to intervene.

From the start the Byzantine emperors were determined that Constantinople, as the New Rome, should become the world's cultural, quite as much as its political centre. The ancient pagan

198

universities of Athens, Alexandria, Beirut and Antioch had been renowned for centuries before the founding of Constantinople. A Christian centre of advanced studies had been established in Alexandria in the course of the third century, and soon after that a Christian academy had been founded in Caesarea; other centres of Christian learning came into being shortly afterwards in most of the larger towns in the East. Constantine I attached great importance to education and, to encourage learning as well as to ensure a supply of enlightened administrators, he soon founded an academy in his new capital. The interest which he took in this institution was shared by many of his successors, but it was Theodosius II who, in 425, transformed Constantine's academy into a fully fledged university, controlled and supported by the emperors. In doing so he had the wholehearted approval of his grandson and even more of his wife Athenaïs-Eudoxia. She was by birth a pagan, the daughter of a professor of rhetoric at Athens University—so ardent a stronghold of paganism that Justinian was to put an end to its existence in 529. On marrying, Eudoxia became a devout Christian but she did not lose any of the ardent love for the Greek classics which her father had instilled into her during her childhood. It may well have been due to her influence that even at that early date Greek was made as prominent as Latin in the syllabus of Constantinople's first university. The new foundation was allotted ten chairs of Latin and ten of Greek with, in each case, three additional chairs of rhetoric. The holders of the Latin appointments were given the names of orators and those of the Greek of sophists. Since the emperors appointed and dismissed the university's teachers they sometimes attended their classes even though it was the duty of the senate to submit the names of candidates for these chairs (at any rate until the fifteenth century, when it fell to the Great Logothete to do so). Laymen and priests were chosen for these positions in preference to monks. Many a holder of a chair was at some time in his career called to abandon teaching to serve his emperor às an ambassador.

Secular education at Constantinople followed Christian lines whilst looking back to the ancients for its major disciplines (namely, those which they grouped under the headings of grammar and rhetoric), so that, at any rate till the sixth century, even classical studies were made to accord with the Christian doctrine. Thus philosophy, though closely associated with mathematics, found itself linked to theology, and as a result subordinated to Christianity.

Nevertheless, until Justinian closed the university at Athens many young Constantinopolitans had been sent there to complete their education. Yet within a century of its foundation Constantinople's university had already become too small for the needs of a steadily growing population. With the fall of Alexandria, Beirut and Antioch to the Muslims, it became the only one available to Christians. Students from all walks of life flocked to it; by the ninth century they included many foreigners; some were orientals, others Slavs, Georgians, Armenians and, later still, Italians. In 856 Caesar Bardas, an uncle and first minister of Michael VIII, decided that a second university was needed in the capital. He established it in the Magnaura Palace and, perhaps because an ecclesiastical college was already in existence there, he gave his foundation an essentially secular syllabus. Many students attended its courses till it was closed down at the end of the tenth century, probably at the wish of Basil II. When at the height of his scholastic career Photius, who was to become renowned as patriarch of Constantinople, taught grammar, rhetoric, divinity and philosophy in the capital. Adopting the aims of Caesar Bardas, he founded secular libraries in which the works of Plato and the Greek dramatists were made easily available. Photius also undertook the exacting task of compiling the *Myriobiblion*, which, even though the entries were not arranged in alphabetical order yet, like a modern encyclopaedia, contained all the basic information concerning grammar, history and literature to be found in works written from ancient times to his own day. Learning continued to flourish after Photius' death and within another two centuries the school which was attached to the Great Palace had grown into an Institute of Historical Studies.

In 1045 a third university was established in Constantinople for the sole purpose of training men for the civil service and judiciary, no lawyers being henceforth allowed to practise until they had graduated from it. Within a few more years Constantine IX Monomachus enriched it with a chair of philosophy. As a result, both theology and the classics were now taught there, and although particular stress continued to be laid on philosophy and Roman law, the culture of ancient Greece now had a part. It became customary for students to start their training by studying grammar, rhetoric and dialectics; they passed on to arithmetic, geometry, music and astrology, and ended with philosophy and advanced studies. Their final courses were conducted by Michael Psellus. He

84 Scribes, whether Byzantine or German were very similar
in appearance
From an ivory, ninth to tenth centuries

85 Muse playing her lyre
Detail from an Alexandrian ivory,
c. AD 50

86 Manuscript page with
illuminations
From a Byzantine herbal

87 Priestess of Bacchus at altar to Jupiter
*From a diptych celebrating the marriage between
members of two important families, c.* AD 392

was the most outstanding scholar of the age, the man who, more than anyone else, gave effect to the aspirations both of Caesar Bardas and of Constantine IX. He became the guardian of ancient traditions and at the same time the prime sponsor of active, original thought. He thus became chiefly responsible for the new outlook, that which can best be described as the humanistic; it was to express itself most eloquently in the arts of the twelfth century.

As early as the ninth century teachers had begun to favour a more humanistic scholarship, based on a philosophic attitude founded on the learning of ancient Greece. In the eleventh century Michael Psellus directed their attention to the works of Plato. These had been almost forgotten since the death of Photius. By bringing them to light Psellus created a new atmosphere and an outlook on life which differed radically from that which Christian theologians had instilled into philosophy. The Neo- or New Platonists, as those who thought along the same lines as Psellus were called, refused to accept without question the theories held by theologians, but showed a searching curiosity and more adventurous approach. One result of this was a revival of the sciences, with particular interest being taken in the works of contemporary Arabic and Persian mathematicians and astronomers. As in the days of Theophilus and Leo VI, the Wise, this contact with the East, tempered by the new humanism of the Byzantines, produced men of a more flexible stamp.

Although interest in the works of Plato fostered the development of this humanistic outlook it caused a strong divergence of views between the clerical and lay scholars. Fearing that a return to Hellenism might lead to a revival of idolatry, or rather of paganism, the clergy strove to encourage mysticism in place of the realistic, enquiring approach advocated by laymen. Nevertheless, members of the upper clergy continued to study grammar, philosophy and poetry alongside the lives of saints and commentaries on religious texts. Monastic libraries were now expected not only to contain religious and medical books, grammars and dictionaries, but also the works of Aristotle.

When in 1204 the court was transferred to Nicaea the centre of studies moved there with it, but continued to look to ancient Athens for inspiration and, on the emperor's return to Constantinople in 1261, the classics were studied with even greater enthusiasm than before the Latin occupation. At the same time Eastern (Persian and Mongol) influences, transmitted to the capital by Trapezuntine scholars, and Western ideas bequeathed by the Latins, produced a new intellectual vitality and a creativeness in art as great as that during Byzantium's most prosperous days. Typical of the period was Theodore Metochites (1260–1332), Great Logothete to Emperor Andronicus III. He was both a distinguished humanist philosopher and a notable scientist; he set much store on mathematics and strove to dissociate the study of astronomy from that of astrology. From ancient times, the latter had been linked both in popular imagination and by astronomers with magic and, as a result, alchemists had enjoyed the same regard as scientific thinkers. An admirer of Plato and Aristotle, even though he did not share the latter's metaphysical beliefs, Metochites possessed a truly encyclopaedic fund of knowledge, and he combined it with a keen artistic perceptiveness. He built at his own expense one of the finest monuments of later Byzantine art, the exquisitely proportioned, superbly decorated Church of the Chora in Constantinople.

The respect in which magic was held in a society as profoundly religious and as intellectually developed as the Byzantine is difficult to explain. Neither deep religious feeling nor the many trained and qualified doctors could shake the faith which even the highest in the land displayed in spells, incantations and the advice of itinerant healers. Nevertheless much serious work continued to be done in the spheres of medicine, botany and zoology. The study of medicine was based on the teaching of Hippocrates, but it was combined with methods advocated by largely self-taught practitioners (for example, Alexander of Tralles in the sixth century) who based many of their conclusions on experience, observation and common sense. Sufficient doctors were trained annually to ensure the staffing not only of the state hospitals, but also of those attached to monasteries, convents and orphanages. However, no advances were achieved in Byzantium comparable in importance to those attained in the West in the medical schools of Bologna or Paris.

The best Byzantine doctors generally resorted to purging and bleeding as their most reliable remedies. Eminent physicians frequently disagreed on how best to treat a patient. Anna Comnena wrote with bitterness of the ineffectiveness of the doctors gathered round her father's death-bed. Even fewer

88 Bronze
dividers

significant advances were made in the related fields of botany and zoology, for although a great many botanical books and bestiaries were written and accompanied by numerous illustrations, these volumes were more in the nature of records of known information than accounts of new discoveries. Nor did Byzantine geographers greatly add to the existing store of knowledge. On the other hand cartography was well advanced; maps were widely used and many valuable discoveries were recorded in books which took the form of itineraries, collections of travellers' tales and scenic descriptions.

Though the Byzantines took more delight in existing disciplines than in investigating new fields of knowledge their admiration for learning was both genuine and profound. It is reflected in the attitude of Theodore II of Nicaea who, during the bitter time of the Latin occupation of Constantinople, nevertheless insisted that 'whatever the needs of war and defence it remains essential to find time to cultivate the garden of learning'. Even though the Byzantines did not succeed in leaving us a great secular literature with masterpieces comparable to those of ancient Greece and Rome, they were as a result able to provide Europe with a legacy which contains much to be grateful for.

Little secular poetry has survived, and most of that which does exist seems rather dull to us today. It was seldom written with a view to being read; rather was it meant to be heard, being sung or recited, since the poet and musician were often one and the same person. As in medieval Europe, so in Byzantium, he depended for his living on the patron for whom he produced the greater part of his compositions. But he also had a special part to play on public occasions such as the Spring and Brumelia festivals, during carnivals, in the circus and in certain processions when madrigals were often sung and serious poems listened to with enjoyment. The poems which Pisidias composed on the subject of Heraclius' great campaign against the Persians in 622 and on the Arabian attack on Constantinople in 626 were enthusiastically received and compared by his listeners to the masterpieces of Euripides.

The ancient Greeks used the flute and zither to accompany their secular songs and dances; to these the Byzantines had added the organ, cymbals and lyre (85). It has been suggested that Theophilus, who delighted in Arabic culture and the dances of Arab girls, introduced the lyre into the country, but in fact the instrument must have been known there from far earlier times. Musicians

89   A piper

composed works for all these instruments, adopting the 16-tone scale for secular purposes in preference to the 8-tone one used for religious music. Until the ninth century music was transmitted from one person to another, but in that century a form of notation was devised. It differs so much from western notation that scholars have only recently begun to master it. Both for this reason and because very little written music has survived our knowledge even of Byzantine religious music is still very limited.

The finest hymns were written in what can best be described as rhythmical rather than rhymed verse. Many remain in use today as canticles of the Orthodox Church. They were written by both laymen and clerics who often also composed their own music; it was always vocal and never instrumental, but distinctions were made between renderings in coloratura and recitative. Largely because the earliest-known hymn book happens to have come from Syria, it has been suggested that the sung portions in Orthodox services (that is to say the Liturgy) are of eastern origin, but this theory still awaits confirmation. That hymnal dates from the sixth century and was the work of a certain Romanus, a Jew from Nisiana in Syria, who became converted to Christianity, moved to Constantinople and became a deacon there. Emperor Justinian wrote some magnificent hymns in addition to some fine theological works in prose. By the eighth century Greek hymns were so much admired in western Europe that Charlemagne arranged for a selection to be translated into Latin.

Important though these hymns proved to the West, the greatest contribution which the Byzantines made to European church music resulted from the re-introduction of the organ into Europe in 757, when Emperor Constantine V sent one as a gift to King Pépin of France. Although it was the first wind organ to reach Europe it was by no means the first of its kind, not even the first to be heard in the Western world. Hydraulic organs had probably been made from as far back as the third century BC. Their invention is ascribed to Steribius of Alexandria. The instrument became known in Rome during the first century AD. It was much admired there and remained in favour as late as the time of Augustine. Then it fell out of use and was soon forgotten in Rome, though not in the East, where the Byzantines replaced the earlier hydraulic type by one in which wind was blown through pipes of differing lengths. By the eighth century, when the more up-to-date version was re-introduced into Europe, the Byzantines were producing organs of several types. Most were very large, but some must have been easy to transport, for Emperor Constantine VI (780–97) and his mother Irene were able to take one with them when they visited the army stationed in Thrace. In Byzantium the instrument was probably reserved for secular purposes, but in the West it must have been considered as better suited to church requirements for it was widely used in the monastery of St Gall, where other forms of Byzantine music were also adapted to western tastes. In 873 the pope did much to establish its popularity by commissioning an organ, as well as a man able to play it, from Bishop Anno of Freisig.

Martyrdoms, or Lives of Saints, were widely read in Byzantium. The first collection to appear in book form was compiled in the sixth century by Cyril of Skythopolis and was written in Syriac. Its appearance may well be linked with Palladius' *Book of the Paradise*, as his enquiry into the truth of the miracles and experiences ascribed to the hermits and holy men of the Egyptian desert is called (see page 77). By the end of the sixth century another volume of lives, written this time by John Moschus, had also appeared. From then onwards the number multiplied and included stories written in the form of edifying romances. Both the real and the fictional accounts became extremely popular among all classes of society, the fictional accounts quickly coming to stand in the same relationship to the true ones as does the Apocrypha to the Gospels.

The Byzantines had the same

90   A sixth-century bard

satirical turn of mind and lively interest in politics as the Greeks of today, but fewer outlets for these tastes. Nevertheless, political pamphlets were written, and they enjoyed a wide circulation. In the drawing-rooms of the great, epigrams were extremely popular and a young man who was able to produce a neatly turned phrase was much admired. Though many of these epigrams were based on classical themes, the majority were very pertinent. Theodore II Lascaris was the author of many a barbed witticism. Successful verses were collected into anthologies which also included anagrams and word games. Professional writers spent much of their time composing imperial panegyrics, funeral orations, homilies based on the principles laid down by rhetoricians, all of which abounded in mythological references, for the Greek classics were a source of universal delight. Much pleasure was also derived from memoirs. Letters were not only written to entertain friends but also as literary exercises; these were therefore addressed to imaginary people. Readers who delighted in letters as a literary form also took pleasure in novels and romances. The novel, to use the word in its original sense (meaning a tale), became known to the Byzantines when John of Damascus translated into Greek the story of Baarlam and Josephus, which was very popular at the court of the Omayyad Caliphs. The story's title is somewhat misleading for in its original form it consisted of the Indian version of the life of Buddha, Buddha appearing as Josephus in the Greek version. Many romances followed the appearance of this first novel. A particularly popular one told of the love of Theagene and Chariclea. Stories such as these were so numerous and so much enjoyed in Constantinople that they travelled westward, and diverted Racine among others.

91　Musician playing a stringed instrument

Even though the bulk of the country people were less well educated than most of the town dwellers, it is thought that many of the men were literate. However, few books came within their reach and their intellectual activities were largely confined to reading tracts on magic and oracular pronouncements, to watching an occasional Passion play performed in their local church with, from the ninth century, clerics acting all the parts, or to listening to the songs and tales told by singers and wandering storytellers.

The working class, whether living in towns or villages, took particular delight in burlesques and rough satires. These played much the same part in their lives as did epigrams in those of their

92 Digenis Akritas and his dragon

masters. Some drolleries had come down to them from classical sources, but some were the outcome of Eastern influence. By the ninth century the more popular of these skits had been collected into anthologies; they appeared under such titles as *The Industrious and Clever Advocate, The Miser, The Swindlers, Dunces*, and so on. Epics were, however, the best-loved type of song. One that gave unfailing delight to all classes of people and which has survived because it remained so popular is the *Epic of Basil Digenis Akritas* (meaning: a frontier guardsman of twin birth). It was largely inspired by Byzantium's fight against Islam in the ninth and tenth centuries, a fight which was mainly waged by members of the *themes* or frontier guards. The hero personifies Byzantium's resistance to the Saracens, but the epic reveals that the contestants felt considerable respect and liking for each other. This attitude is also reflected in history, for the mutual regard which Saladin and his Christian opponents experienced for each other enabled prisoners to be regularly exchanged and other humanitarian measures to be carried out. It has been suggested that the epic is based on the life of a real character, Panterius, a man of mixed parentage, his mother a member of the renowned Byzantine family of Ducas, his father an Arabian Emir who accepted Christianity for love of her. Panterius became a civil servant under Romanus Lecapenus and in 941 helped to repel the dangerous attack launched on Byzantium by the Kievan Russians. In the epic Digenis Akritas(92) is described as the son of no less a person than the Muslim Emir of

Edessa, who either kidnapped or eloped with and then married the daughter of the Greek *strategos* Andronicus Ducas. The first section of the epic deals with that incident; the second and older part of the story is concerned with Digenis' early life. With various digressions, it tells of his childhood and education, of the deeds of chivalry which he performed in his youth, of his valour, and of his love for the beautiful Eudoxia, the daughter of a Christian chieftain who killed anyone who attempted to woo her. Digenis contrived to elope with her, but the lovers were pursued by the angry father and his retainers. They escaped from many perilous situations and, finally, their courage won her father's respect. He agreed to their marriage, which was celebrated with great pomp and gaiety. Digenis then had many more adventures, all of which are recorded in a racy and picturesque style. They include Eudoxia's encounter with a dragon, which follows a course similar to that of St George's princess, and Digenis' contest with Maximo, an Indian descendant of Alexander the Great. This section of the epic reflects the love of adventure and delight in daring feats of arms, glitter and courage associated with European chivalry, together with something of Roland's gallantry and the dash of Robin Hood, all expressed with Chaucerian pungency. In the last section of the epic Digenis and his wife are found living in luxury in a splendid palace situated on the banks of the Euphrates. Their life had become more peaceful, but Digenis, who was fond of bathing in the river, died after swimming in its icy water.

In the eleventh century many great landowners abandoned their estates and moved to Constantinople. Accustomed as they were to the type of life lived in Asia Minor, they found themselves so much out of sympathy with the Neo-Platonist tendencies gaining ground in the capital that they took little part in its intellectual life. They formed a community of their own where, withdrawn from the main stream, they diverted themselves with the tales, burlesques and satires with which wandering actors had amused them when they lived in the country, and listened with undiminished delight to the tale of Basil Digenis Akritas.

10

ARTISTS AND ARCHITECTS

A nation's tastes and mentality are nowhere more clearly preserved than in its arts. These embody its loftiest ambitions and most telling achievements. Byzantium's arts clearly reflect the national genius, for the sharp division between religious and secular art did not hamper Byzantine artists; since both flourished side by side, artists had ample opportunity for self-expression. Though there was no place for humour or fantasy in the religious arts, the mosaic floor of the Great Palace proves that both elements found expression in the secular. The scene showing a recalcitrant mule throwing its rider and administering a sharp kick on his posterior as he does so records the incident with delightful malice, whilst the architectural features which appear in the same floor, whether in the form of *tempiettas* or fountains, reveal an architectural imagination as keen as that which existed at Pompeii. That sumptuous secular arts abounded cannot be doubted. Written records contain many references that testify to the luxury of the imperial apartments in the Great Palace, but these do not deal with isolated cases, for the description of Digenis Akritas' house and garden proves that private individuals devoted as much thought and care to the settings in which they spent their days as did the emperors.

According to surviving records the empress's winter apartments in the Great Palace at Constantinople were built of Carian marble, the floors were of white Proconesus marble and the walls adorned with mural paintings of a religious character. In contrast the Pearl Pavilion, designed for use in summer, had a marble mosaic floor which, in the words of a contemporary, resembled 'a field carpeted with flowers'; its bedroom walls were faced with slabs of porphyry, green marble from Thessaly and Carian white, while those in the other rooms displayed hunting scenes executed in glass mosaic. The result was so successful that the room came to be called the Chamber of *Mousikos*, meaning harmony.

93 A typical rural scene. Note the boy's falcon

The mosaic floor of the Great Palace is the finest known to us, but future excavations may well reveal further examples of comparable beauty and serenity. Serenity is surely the key which unlocks the door to the magic world of Byzantine art. Byzantine art is not dramatic—even the immense dome of Constantinople's Haghia Sophia is not at first sight overpowering yet it overwhelms gradually because the art is majestic. Even on the minute scale required for book illuminations, portative mosaics—where each cube is often scarcely larger than a pin's head—or cloisonné enamel plaques, many of them little more than an inch in size, it retains a monumental quality. Nor is the art when seen at its purest (that is to say, with least Syrian or Eastern influence) emotional. Instead it is transfused with profound yet restrained feeling. In addition Byzantine art is seldom pretty, yet it is with but few exceptions truly beautiful and admirably suited to its main purpose. Furthermore, it is astonishingly distinctive and could never be mistaken for anything other than itself.

Not the least achievement of Byzantine artists was their ability to develop tentative innovations or minor forms of art into something wholly new and so significant that they became not only major forms of art, but styles which profoundly affected European art of the future. Thus, in architecture, they were responsible for the acceptance of the domed church(*94*); in religious painting for the creation of a style, more particularly in icons, which not only greatly influenced the work of the Italian Primitives but also formed the basis of the religious art which came to characterise the Orthodox world; finally, in interior decoration they established the glass mosaic panel as the finest, most opulent form of wall decoration and the *opus sectile*, or coarser stone or marble geometric mosaic as the most enchanting floor.

The Byzantines built their first churches according to the forms and techniques which they had inherited, first from the classical world, and second, from their Eastern neighbours. They roofed the Greek temple in the basilical form in which the Romans had transmitted it to them, with wooden beams, and they retained the apse which the Romans had added at one end to hold the throne of their *judex* or judge in order to set up their altar there. They also made use of the circular buildings which the Romans had evolved to serve as mausolea for their dignitaries and which, like the Pantheon, they had roofed with a dome made of masonry. Till about the sixth century, even though neither of these forms was wholly suited to the Christian ritual, the need for churches was so great that it was simpler and cheaper to build them on these lines. Of the two the basilical type proved the easier to adapt to Christian needs, for the altar could be placed in the central apse and the interior could easily be divided into aisles, the piers or columns which formed the divisions serving also to support the galleries designed for women worshippers. Three aisles quickly became customary, though in exceptional cases five were used; with the sixth century the central aisle became wider than the others. A magnificent example of the style is the cathedral of St Demetrius in Salonica, built in the fifth century and restored in the seventh. It was extensively damaged by fire in 1917, but although it lost most of the sumptuous decorations of its original interior it has now been faithfully rebuilt.

By the sixth century architects were placing impost blocks on the column capitals to support the galleries, but before long sculptors devised a capital which combined the two functions in a single block of stone. It was also in the sixth century that the habit of adding a transverse chamber at the west end was adopted; it was known as an *exo-narthex*. However, it was not until the thirteenth century that churches were provided with porches or detached bell towers; this was largely a result of Western influence, for church bells were not originally used in the Byzantine world. Instead, as is still the case in a number of monasteries in Greece and the Balkans, the faithful were summoned to prayer by a *simantron*, a wooden bar beaten with a wooden mallet.

Though the basilical plan suited the needs of the early Christian Church, the Byzantine conception of the universe made a domed church particularly desirable. The Byzantines visualised the universe as a sort of inverted cone which was divided into clearly defined sections, like their own society. Thus, soaring at the top of the celestial sphere were God the Father, Christ His Son, the Holy Ghost and the Virgin; St John accompanied by the archangels, seraphs, cherubim and angels came next; beneath them were assembled the evangelists, the prophets, the fathers of the Church and the ranks of saintly and holy men and women. Separated from these by the ether, the emperor stood at the summit of the terrestrial sphere, accompanied by the patriarch, his family and courtiers, and so down the social scale. However, buildings circular in plan, though roofed by the dome which, to the Byzantines, seemed best to symbolise heaven, were ill-suited to the Christian ritual which required a focal point, such as an apse, for the altar. On the other hand the transition from a square to a rectangular ground plan and a circular roof was difficult to accomplish. Experiments were made using columns to create a central, octagonal core within a square building, enabling at any rate the central portion to be roofed with a dome, but the result was inclined to seem crowded. The solution appears simple today, but when it was reached it represented a revolution in architecture, enabling even the less skilled architects to erect domed buildings.

One answer lay in inserting in the corners of a square building a triangular shaped section of masonry with curved sides, which is called a pendentive, its broad ends being placed at the top of the wall and slightly inclined inwards so as to transform the roof opening into a circle; a similar result could be obtained by building out over the square corners of the building a small overhanging arch known as a squinch. It is unlikely that the Byzantines invented either of these devices for, by their day, the pendentive was already being used in Syria and the squinch in Persia, but the Byzantines were the first to realise the full potentialities of both forms and to exploit them by extending the walls of a square or rectangular structure to achieve a cruciform plan. The resulting building was superbly suited for use as a church, for its plan helped to remind the faithful of Christ's suffering on the cross whilst the dome at its centre symbolised the heavenly sphere.

Excavations which are at present being carried out in Constantinople suggest that a domed church of the new type existed there before Justinian built the four splendid churches associated with his name. The destruction wrought in Constantinople during the Nika riots spurred Justinian to experiment in this new style. For St Irene, begun in 532, immediately after the riots had been quelled, he chose a three-aisled basilical plan, with a dome over the main square, supported in this instance by brick piers. Indeed, in the hands of all future architects the use of marble columns or of piers built either of brick or stone and covered with plaster served not only to support the galleries but also to help the squinches or pendentives to carry the weight of the heavier domes. When columns were used to support these arches, imposts were introduced above the capitals, but where piers were substituted the arches sprang directly from these, this form of support probably being the earlier of the two.

The destruction of Constantine I's church of Haghia Sophia during the Nika riots was regarded as a national disaster. Not only was the church the first to be built in Constantinople, but it had from the start been intended to serve as the official fountainhead of Christianity. The church had played so important a part in the lives of the Byzantines that Justinian announced his intention of replacing the destroyed cathedral with another of the same name, but one which would vie in beauty with any church in Christendom. He employed as his architects a mathematician, believed to be an Armenian, called Anthemius of Tralles, and one Isidore of Miletus. Working in close collaboration with Justinian they made use of all the known architectural devices to construct in the course of only five years one of the largest, most complex and most impressive buildings in the world; they erected it with such skill and care that it has withstood earthquakes, bombardments and numerous other vicissitudes for nearly 1,500 years and has never ceased to arouse the wonder and admiration of all who see it (23).

Begun in 532, Haghia Sophia is virtually a three-aisled basilica, the central aisle being much wider than the others. It measures 241 feet long and 224 feet wide; but its outstanding features are its height, its walls towering 179 feet above floor level, and the diameter, 100 feet, of its immensely broad but surprisingly low, flat dome. Piers and columns combined to support the galleries, where the empress's pew occupied the whole of the west end, thus facing the altar. Four great piers carried the weight of the large central dome and the two semi-domes set at either end of it. It is, however, the central dome which is the marvel of the cathedral. It is set so low that it is difficult to think of its base as a drum; its gentle curve seems to reflect that of the sky when seen over the sea. Though by no means the tallest dome in the world it was, until present-day methods of building in concrete were evolved, the largest in circumference and the lightest in appearance. Indeed, the first dome was too shallow and too wide and collapsed in 558 as the result of an earthquake. It was rebuilt without loss of time, with but slight alterations and with complete success. Architects of all ages have been dazzled by its quality; so much so that Sir Christopher Wren, commissioned to replace St Paul's Cathedral after the Great Fire of London, sent for the measurements of the dome of Haghia Sophia.

The dome was accepted as unique and even Justinian and his architects never tried to re-create it. Instead, when building the scarcely less famous church of the Holy Apostles in Constantinople, to serve as the imperial mausoleum, Justinian gave it a cruciform plan and roofed each of the arms as well as the central area with smaller domes. This decision led to the introduction of a new style in architecture and a new shape in the skyline for, whereas Haghia Sophia's dome was almost impossible to reproduce, the five- or multi-domed roof-line was capable of endless repetition and variation, and it was the multiple-domed type of church that came to characterise the Orthodox world and to serve as a model for St Mark's Cathedral at Venice and for other domed churches elsewhere. In the ninth century, after the iconoclasts had been overthrown, church plans became increasingly complicated; double churches like that of Mary Panachrantus, or triple ones like that of Christ the Pantocrator—both of which may still be visited in Istanbul—became popular, at any rate in the capital. As time went on the drums supporting the domes of such churches became higher, the domes themselves smaller and the windows cut in the drums taller. After 1261, when the Byzantines regained control of Constantinople, the churches built there became smaller still and far more intimate, but their style and ground plans did not change and at any rate the Church of the Chora (Karieh Camii) retained the sumptuous interior decorations associated with a more prosperous age.

94   The Monastery of the Brontocheion, Mistra

The Romans had generally used brick or stone for their buildings, setting both in cement and constructing their vaults on a wooden centring. Until about the seventh century it was quite usual in Constantinople to use large blocks of dressed stone for buildings of importance, but the technique which was to become customary in Byzantium was already employed at Haghia Sophia; it consisted of using several, generally five, courses of brick to alternate with several courses of stone. Indeed, the method had been used by Theodosius II (408–50) when building the walls of Constantinople. Byzantine bricks were stamped with a mark or monogram from very early times. Builders appear to have worked by eye rather than rule so that, when drawn out, their buildings are seen to be strangely asymmetrical. However, this was never evident to the eye. Masons went to great pains either to point the outside walls as neatly as possible or else to cover them with plaster and colour wash. External sculptures were never used to decorate the façades of the earlier churches, though from about the thirteenth century bricks were often set in the external walls to form decorative patterns; in such cases the walls were left unplastered. Glazed pottery dishes were sometimes set high up in

217

them to add a touch of colour. From the thirteenth century, as in the church of Haghia Sophia at Trebizond, external sculptures were occasionally introduced, but in Byzantium their role was never so important, nor their number so great as in the Caucasus or in Western Europe.

It is not only the professional builder who evokes our admiration; Byzantium's monks were time and again responsible for the construction of some of the most astonishing and picturesque buildings that exist. They invariably chose to construct their monasteries on sites of great natural beauty, usually on crags extremely difficult of access. Hacking away great ledges they erected formidable structures which seem to cling to the rock face like splayed-out sponges (24). The monasteries which survive on Mount Athos are superb examples of the form, and though mostly of comparatively recent date, they reflect the style of the Byzantine age. They are built either of stone or of wooden beams forming a sort of framework which is filled in with clay. Because of their remote situations monasteries were always enclosed within stout defensive walls and were generally provided with no more than one entrance gate. It led into a courtyard where the monastery's main church occupied a central position, and its subsidiary chapels less important ones. The galleries containing the abbot's lodging, the monks' cells and the guest rooms, without which no monastery was complete, encircled the courtyard. The refectory was generally situated at ground level; it was fitted out with D-shaped tables similar to those shown in Byzantine paintings of the Last Supper; these were built of stone and were fitted with either marble or scrubbed wooden tops. The kitchens, store rooms, workshops and distilleries, all of them essential features of a monastery, were also situated at ground level but, as a precaution against fire, the library was generally to be found in a free-standing tower.

The architectural skill of the monks was shared by artisans. If wells in the poorest villages were simple constructions formed of wooden beams, in the richer towns they were far more decorative for they often followed classical models. Here, as in so much of their art, the Byzantines do not seem to have felt any great desire for novelty, for comparison between the wells and fountains illustrated in the sixth-century mosaic pavement of the Great Palace and those which appear in the mural mosaics of the fourteenth-century church of the Chora shows that no marked change of style had developed during the intervening years.

95   Reliquary for a fragment of the True Cross. At the top
Christ appears between two angels; Helena, Constantine and
Longinus are shown at the bottom
Ivory, with a silver cross, c. AD 963–9

96   The Annunciation to St Anne
A glass wall mosaic from Kahrie Camii, fourteenth century

The Byzantine love of severe forms, especially in the architectural exteriors of the earlier churches, was matched only by their delight in splendid interiors. Their ingenuity and wealth made the latter magnificent. This was especially true of their churches and palaces, both of which were considered to mirror different aspects of the celestial sphere. It was for this reason that even in the poorest parishes attempts were made to adorn the interior of the churches from floor level to dome. Whenever funds permitted, the earlier floors were made of carefully selected marble slabs similar to those used in Constantinople's Haghia Sophia. In later times geometric effects were preferred. In the (probably twelfth-century) marble floor of the monastery of Studius in Constantinople, round stones were set at the corners of the floor; these were hollowed out into animal and other shapes and the incisions filled in with either inlay or carved stone or marble of contrasting colour. Inlaid decorations of this type had become extremely popular as early as the tenth century. Somewhat earlier, floors formed of stone and marble mosaic sections (generally triangular in shape) and of coarser appearance than Roman floor mosaics started to be laid. The technique is known as *opus sectile* and is thought to have been used for the first time by Basil I (867–86) in the church of the Nea in the Great Palace. In due course the incised and *opus sectile* techniques were combined to produce such astonishing icons as the one of St Eudoxia which was discovered during excavations of the church of Mary Panachrantus in 1928 in Istanbul(97). On it the saint's figure is hollowed out of a marble slab, her face is made of a carved piece of ivory whilst her garments are formed of inlaid stones, the border being executed in *opus sectile*.

At the height of their prosperity the Byzantines relied to a great extent on wall mosaics for the splendour of their church interiors. Immense skill was required for comparable effects to be achieved by means of small glass cubes as by brushwork but they proved superlative masters of this difficult technique. The art of wall mosaic was not invented by the Byzantines. It had already been tried out in Pompeii and in early Christian Rome where the first mosaics to be set up in churches were placed in the apse. By the sixth century, when the magnificent mural decorations at Ravenna were produced, the art had fully evolved. The techniques consisted in setting glass cubes of appropriate shades and sizes into plaster which was sufficiently damp to hold them in position.

97 Tenth-century icon of St Eudoxia

The glass reached the mosaicist in the form of slabs; these were divided into rods which were then cut to the desired sizes, the smallest cubes being used for such sections as eye sockets and the larger ones for draperies or backgrounds. The cubes were made in a vast range of delicate as well as deep colours, together with others where a glass base was covered with gold leaf secured on top by a thin layer of glass; the gold cubes produced a vibrating, shimmering effect admirably suited for backgrounds symbolising paradise. They were so skilfully set by Byzantine artists that the most subtle and delicate compositions were created, the material serving not only to catch and hold the eye, but also to reflect light.

In their religious paintings and mosaics the Byzantines, once again combining those elements which appealed to them from Hellenistic, Roman and Eastern art with their own strongly mystical yet basically earthly conception of the physical appearance of the holy hierarchy, succeeded in transforming the existing idioms into something wholly new. The personages depicted in Byzantine art differ from ordinary human beings both in their physical appearance and in their style of dress. They are clothed in draperies (variants of the classical costume) of the glorious colours which we associate with the sky, whether seen in rainbows or sunsets, because the sky—the abode of these privileged few—is but the floor of heaven. To emphasise the celestial nature of the colours and

the ascetic character-
istics of the personages
the human figures repre-
sented in the paintings
are considerably elong-
ated. Their faces are not
abstracted, yet they are
not strictly naturalistic.
Their eyes, the mirrors
of man's soul, are
greatly enlarged, owing
their shape to Egyptian
funerary portraits of the
opening centuries of
our era. The mouth, the
vehicle of pain and de-
light, assumes a form

98 Sixth-century mosaic of a water mill

devised by the Byzantines to express these sentiments. The thin,
slightly pinched nose is lengthened whilst the faces (furrowed
by the suffering endured by those who have mastered the flesh),
though initially based on prevailing Greek features, are given a
triangular shape in order to express the Byzantine conception of
pain. On the other hand the frontal manner in which most of the
figures are presented derived from the East. The use of draperies,
both as robes and as hangings suspended from two buildings to
indicate that the scene is taking place indoors (for no interiors
appear in Byzantine art), stem from classical Greece; so too do
certain venerable figures, such as Joseph, whose appearance
frequently recalls that of an ancient Greek philosopher. On the
other hand much of the realism of the art came from Rome, whilst
where emotion intrudes into the solemnity of a biblical scene
Syrian influence was at work, the dramatic element being absent
from the art of Constantinople and Salonica.

Decorative motifs other than those consisting of Christian
symbols may in the first instance have been inspired by designs
common to Hellenistic Greece, Rome and Pompeii, but in later
times Byzantium's Eastern neighbours also often acted as
prompters, the marvellously inventive decorations produced at
one time or another by the artists of Persia, India, even of Central
Asia and China being greatly appreciated in Byzantium. These
numerous trends acted as stimulants, spurring the Byzantines to

create designs so varied, so ingenious, so elegant and, in some cases, so in advance of their time that, if seen out of their context, they are liable to be mistaken for Renaissance discoveries.

From wall to panel painting was only a short step. The Byzantines lost no time in taking it, adapting the funerary painted portraits in use in Egypt to create the icon. Of the few that survive many deserve to be numbered with the great religious paintings of Christendom. On two occasions Byzantine art excelled itself; both periods rank as golden ages in its history and are seen at their most splendid in painting and sculpture. The first Golden Age derived its impetus from Justinian, the second flourished during the years when the gifted members of the Macedonian dynasty ruled the Empire. The book illuminations which were produced during these periods are among the loveliest in existence. The interlaced designs devised for the chapter headings and tail-pieces are remarkably inventive and elaborate. Decorative capital letters add variety to the script, and marginal adornments, whether in the form of a flower, an animal or a minute *genre* scene, enliven the pages of many volumes. However, it is the full-page illustrations that constitute their chief glory. Once the ban on figural art had been lifted, the religious illuminations evolved along the same lines as the mural and icon paintings, but interest in portraiture was given freer outlet in the illuminations than in the larger works. A rich gallery of imperial portraits, eminent public men and wealthy donors survive; though extremely severe and formalised they yet succeed in revealing character. Furthermore they reflect the image which Byzantine dignitaries strove to project when acting in an official capacity.

Many of the emperors delighted in sculpture. As late as the eleventh century, when sculptures were being produced at the wish of Romanus III (1028–34), Psellus noted that 'of the stones quarried, some were split, others polished, others turned for sculptures: and the workers of these stones were reckoned the like of Phidias, Polygnotus and Zeuxis'. Nevertheless, the nation as a whole appears to have been less drawn to that art than to any of the others. This is rather surprising when we remember the legacy left to the Byzantines in this field by ancient Greece and Rome, but the lack of interest is surely to be explained by the fear that statues in the round might lead to a revival of idol worship—a practice which required combating if not within Byzantium's borders, then at any rate in areas visited by Greek missionaries.

In early times at least the Byzantines had been keen followers of the Roman tradition, not hesitating to erect statues to their emperors and to encourage sculptors to record their features. A number of heads of Constantine I survive. These, like the statue of Valentinian I at Barletta, the head of Arcadius at Istanbul, of Theodora at Milan and of Flacilla, the wife of Theodosius, in the Metropolitan Museum show that they were accomplished portraitists. The earliest of these heads are strongly Roman in style, but though more vital and strongly individualised they are not as perceptive as the later ones. In early times carved sarcophagi were produced. Like the contemporary busts they adhered to classical conventions. The series of fourth-century Sidamara sarcophagi are decorated with scenes of a Hellenistic origin combined with a background of Eastern scrolls (99). However, by that date the Byzantines had started to prefer plain sarcophagi decorated at most with a monogram.

Until about the sixth century the capitals which they used in their churches were executed in an under-cut technique designed to give the abstract, stylised or geometric patterns a lace-like quality which made the design stand out against a dark ground (100). Especially characteristic of the art as a whole are the slabs on which symbolic or abstract designs of marked distinction appear in low relief. It is, however, to their ivory carvings that we must turn to appreciate to the full the genius of Byzantine sculptors for, although these works are small in size, most are monumental in character.

The carved ivory plaques constituted a most important branch of Byzantine art. Not only Constantinople but, during the early Byzantine period, Milan and Rome in the West, and Antioch and Alexandria in the East were leading centres of the

99 Detail from a Sidamara sarcophagus

225

100 Capital in Haghia Sophia

industry. Ivory plaques were not only used by the consuls to announce their appointment but also by those wishing to record their marriage. A fine panel (now in the Victoria and Albert Museum in London) was made to mark the marriage of a member of the Symmachi family to a Nicomachi. Even more ornate plaques were carved to record coronations. In the fifth and sixth centuries plaques displaying religious designs were fitted together to form *pyxes*—round or octagonal vessels for holding the Host. At the same time other artists, reacting to the same influences as those which led metal-workers to create designs personifying nations, cities or rivers, adorned their plaques with personifications of Rome or Constantinople(*101*). Others preferred to seek inspiration in classical literature, others in *genre* scenes. The plaques were mounted to form doors, furniture, such as the sixth-century throne of Bishop Maximian (now preserved at Ravenna), jewel boxes, such as the magnificent tenth-century Veroli casket (in the Victoria and Albert Museum), book covers and so on.

Many of the earlier silver dishes, produced in the imperial workshops and stamped with the imperial silver marks, display the same gift for sculpture and the same delight in classical themes as the early ivories(*102*). After the fall of the iconoclasts, that is to say, during the middle period of Byzantine art, ornate, lavishly ornamented vessels of a different, typically Byzantine type became fashionable. The decorations on gold, silver or copper gilt ones, and more especially on the Gospel covers, were often executed in the repoussé and filigree techniques and enhanced with precious or semi-precious stones, enamel inlays and cloisonné enamels. The latter demanded the utmost skill in their execution. Generally they were made of a gold base, often no more than half an inch across. The technique consisted in attaching wire-like partitions to the base and filling in the spaces with paste, which was then fired to give a translucent effect. The designs chosen for these enamels generally consisted of busts or figures of Christ, the Virgin or some particular saint, though sometimes a floral motif or bird was chosen instead. No less popular than vessels of metal were those in which the body was made of some semi-precious stone such as onyx, rock crystal, alabaster or the like, set on elaborately worked gold stems. Splendid examples of these, in some cases enhanced by the addition of inset stones or enamel, are to be seen in the treasury of St Mark's at Venice; some of them were probably taken there by returning Crusaders.

The earliest Byzantine textiles probably resembled those from Coptic Egypt. During the fifth and sixth

101 Gold cup depicting the spirit of Constantinople

centuries the decorations acquired a more markedly Byzantine character. Floral compositions or baskets of fruit, corresponding in style to the decorative sections of the mosaics of Haghia Sophia and of the floor of the Great Palace at Constantinople, were produced in brighter colours than in the earlier stuffs. These designs were often used in conjunction with the Chi Rho and other Christian symbols. More varied techniques and more elaborate weaves had also been evolved by then, the designs being sometimes made by the use of a 'resist' substance employed prior to being dyed.

The first silks produced in Byzantium were experimental. They were largely intended as trimmings and the designs chosen were therefore kept small whilst the colours were generally restricted to two shades. But by the middle of the sixth century many more colours and infinitely more ambitious designs were being created. Much of the inspiration came from Persia and Egypt. There were scenes of animals and birds, sometimes with lion heads, which were shown either singly or confronted, frequently with a stylised tree of life between them. Such creatures were often enclosed in a circle. Other designs, such as Samson wrestling with a lion, or that of an archer, though Byzantine inventions, follow Persian traditions. Perhaps the most famous of surviving Byzantine stuffs are the fragments of the Quadriga textile(*43*), a magnificent lion silk inscribed with the names of Romanus and Christopher (921–31), a ninth-century piece with a great eagle as its central design(*61*) in the church of St Eusebius at Auxerre, which is believed to have come from the same workshop as the lion silk,

102   Samson wrestling with a lion, from a sixth-century silver dish

and the elephant stuff which Emperor Otto placed in the tomb of Charlemagne which he opened in the year 1000.

Very little glass has survived from the Byzantine period. Some of the finest is also some of the earliest; it has come down to us mostly in the form of broad bases for stemless vessels in the *fondo d'oro* technique, that is to say of a figural, animal or geometric design executed in gold leaf set between two thicknesses of glass.

It is probably due to this double thickness that the bases of glasses whose sides were made of a thinner layer owe their survival. Many must have been made in Egypt, but by the sixth century Jewish glass-blowers had workshops in Constantinople and may well have made the glass lamps with which the cathedral of Haghia Sophia was lit in 563. These lamps are thought to have resembled some found at Jerash which are shaped like small inverted bells. By the ninth century, and probably well before, flat-bottomed vessels with bulbous sides and long, narrow necks, candlesticks with flat bases and stems not unlike tall, narrow tumblers and glass lamps were being made. The latter were often set in elaborate mounts made of silver or gold. However, certainly during both Golden Ages, much of the glass-maker's output must have been devoted to producing the slabs from which the small square, rectangular or octagonal window panes were made and the coloured sticks which were cut into mosaic cubes, the gold ones being made on the same principle as the *fondo d'oro* vessels. The ability to make the coloured glass sticks bears out the literary references to the existence of coloured glass vessels but, so far, the only example known to us is the tenth-century red glass bowl preserved in the treasury of St Mark's in Venice. Other vessels of comparable quality are thick, moulded ones in uncoloured glass and decorated with animal designs executed in rather high relief.

Recent discoveries in Constantinople suggest that, by the eleventh century, the Byzantines may have begun fitting the windows of their churches with stained glass set in lead and decorated with paint to form pictorial compositions similar to those produced for the same purpose at only a slightly later date in the West. If this theory is confirmed it would indicate that the Byzantines, and not Western Europeans, invented and first practised this glorious form of church decoration.

CHRONOLOGY OF EMPERORS
OF BYZANTIUM

Note: where dates overlap, the emperors in question were co-rulers

Dynasty of Constantine
Constantine I, the Great, 306–37
Constantius, 337–61
Julian, 361–3

Intermediary dynasty
Jovian, 363–4
Valens, 364–78
Valentinian II (371–92)

Dynasty of Theodosius
Theodosius I, the Great, 379–95
Arcadius, 395–408
Theodosius II, 408–50
Marcian, 450–7

Dynasty of Leo
Leo I, 457–74
Leo II, 474
Zeno, 474–91
Anastasius, 491–518

Dynasty of Justinian
Justin I, 518–27
Justinian I, the Great, 527–65
Justin II, 565–78
Tiberius II, 578–82
Maurice, 582–602

Phocas, the Usurper, 602–10

Dynasty of Heraclius
Heraclius, 610–41

Constantine II and Heraclonas, 641
Constantine III or Constans II, 641–68
Constantine IV Pogonatus, 668–85
Justinian II Rhinotmetus, 685–95

Leontius (usurper), 695–8
Tiberius (usurper), 698–705

Dynasty of Heraclius restored
Justinian II Rhinotmetus (second reign), 705–11
Philippicus Bardanes (non-dynastic), 711–13
Anastasius II (non-dynastic), 713–15
Theodosius III (non-dynastic), 715–17

Dynasty of Isaurians
Leo III, 717–41
Constantine V Copronymus, 741–75
Leo IV (husband of Empress Irene), 775–80
Constantine VI (son of Empress Irene), 780–97
Irene, 797–802

Nicephorus I (usurper), 802–11
Stauracius (usurper), 811
Michael I Rhangabe (married to Empress Procopia), 811–13
Leo V, the Armenian (usurper), 813–20

230

Dynasty of the Amorians or Phrygians
Michael II, the Stammerer, 820–9
Theophilus, 829–42
Michael III, the Drunkard, 842–67

Dynasty of Macedonians
Basil I, 867–86
Leo VI, the Wise, 886–912
  (Alexander, co-ruler, 886–913)
Constantine VII Porphyrogenitus,
  913–59
  (co-ruler with his father-in-law, Romanus Lecapenus, 920–44)
    Romanus II, 959–63

Nicephorus II Phocas (usurper),
  963–9
John I Tzimisces (usurper), 969–76

Dynasty of Macedonians restored
Basil II Bulgaroctonos (or Bulgarslayer), 976–1025
Constantine VIII, 1025–8
Romanus II Argyrus (husband of Empress Zoe), 1028–34
Michael IV, the Paphlagonian (second husband of Empress Zoe), 1034–41
Michael V Kalaphates, 1041–2
Zoe and Theodora, 1042
Constantine IX Monomachus, 1042–55
Theodora, 1055–6

Michael VI Stratioticus (non-dynastic), 1056–7

Ducas and Comnene dynasty
Isaac I Comnenus, 1057–9
Constantine X Ducas, 1059–67
Romanus IV Diogenes, 1067–71
Michael VII Parapinakes, 1071–8

Nicephorus III Botaniates (usurper), 1078–81

Dynasty of the Comnenes
Alexius I Comnenus, 1081–1118
John II, 1118–43
Manuel I Comnenus, 1143–80
Alexius II Comnenus, 1180–3
Andronicus I Comnenus, 1183–5

Dynasty of the Angeli
Isaac II Angelus, 1185–95 (and again, 1203–4)
Alexius III, 1195–1203
Alexius IV, 1203–4

Alexius V Ducas Mourtzouphlus (usurper), 1204

Latin rulers of Constantinople
Baldwin of Flanders, 1204–5
Henry of Flanders, 1206–16
Peter of Courtenay, 1217
Yolande, 1217–19
Robert II of Courtenay, 1221–8
Baldwin II, 1228–61

Greek emperors of Nicaea
Theodore I Lascaris, 1204–22
John III Ducas Vatatzes, 1222–54
Theodore II, 1254–8
John IV, 1258–61
Michael VIII Palaeologus, 1259–82

Dynasty of the Palaeologi
Michael VIII, 1261–82
Andronicus II, 1282–1328
Andronicus III, 1328–41
Michael IX, 1294–1320
John V, 1341–91

John VI Cantacuzenus (usurper), 1347–55
Andronicus IV, 1376–9
John VII, 1390
Manuel II, 1391–1425
John VIII, 1425–48
Constantine XI Dragases, 1449–53

BOOKS FOR FURTHER READING

ANNA COMNENA, *The Alexiade* (transl. by E. A. S. Dukes) (London, 1928)

BAYNES and MOSS, H. St L. B., *Byzantium: an Introduction to East Roman Civilisation* (O.U.P., 1948)

BREHIER, L., *Les Institutions de l'Empire Byzantin* (Albin-Michel, Paris, 1948); *Vie et Mort de Byzance* (Albin-Michel, Paris, 1949); *La Civilisation Byzantine* (Albin-Michel, Paris, 1950)

BROWNING, R. *Justinian and Theodora* (Weidenfeld & Nicolson, 1971)

BYRON, R., *The Byzantine Achievement* (Routledge, 1928)

CONSTANTINE VII PORPHYROGENITUS, *Le Livre des Ceremonies* (transl. by A. V. Vogt) (Les Belles Lettres, Paris, 1935); *De Administrando Imperio* (transl. by R. J. H. Jenkins) (Budapest, 1949)

DALTON, O. M., *Byzantine Art and Archaeology* (Constable & Co., 1961)

DIEHL, G., *Byzantine Portraits* (transl. by H. Bell) (Alfred A. Knopf., 1927)

GRABAR, A., *Byzantine Painting* (Skira, 1952)

HAMILTON, J. A., *Byzantine Architecture and Decoration* (B. T. Batsford Ltd, 1956)

HUSSEY, J., *The Byzantine World* (Hutchinson, 1957)

HAUSSIG, H. W., *Kultur Geschichte von Byzanz* (Alfred Kröner, Stuttgart, 1959)

MACLAGAN, M. *The City of Constantinople* (Thames & Hudson, 1968)

OSTROGORSKY, G., *History of the Byzantine State* (O.U.P., 1956)

PSELLUS, M., *Fourteen Byzantine Rulers* (Penguin Books Ltd, 1966)

RUNCIMAN, S., *Byzantine Civilisation* (Edward Arnold, 1933)

——— *Mistra, Byzantine Capital of the Peloponese* (Thames & Hudson, 1980)

TALBOT RICE, D., *The Byzantines* (Thames & Hudson, 1962); *The Art of the Byzantine Era* (Thames & Hudson, 1963)

INDEX

The numerals in **heavy type** refer to the figure numbers of the illustrations.

233